I0394566

SEX CHANGES

ALSO BY CHRISTINE BENVENUTO

Shiksa: The Gentile Woman in the Jewish World

SEX CHANGES

*A Memoir of
Marriage, Gender,
and Moving On*

CHRISTINE BENVENUTO

St. Martin's Press   New York

www.stmartins.com

Design by Anna Gorovoy

ISBN 978-0-312-64950-0 (hardcover)
ISBN 978-1-250-01861-8 (e-book)

eISBN 9781250018618

First Edition: November 2012

10 9 8 7 6 5 4 3 2 1

For the kids' team

SEX CHANGES

"Oh, hey," a friend says conversationally. We are sitting at my kitchen table. "I was at the checkout counter in the supermarket and there was this ugly woman who looked vaguely familiar on line behind me. Then I realized that's no ugly woman—that's your husband!"

The two other friends drinking coffee with us look up expectantly. One of them jumps up to run interference with our four preschoolers playing nearby.

"I'll tell you what was really creepy," my friend continues. What was *really* creepy? I wouldn't want to miss that. "What was really creepy was that he was dressed in clothes identical to yours. It was like he was trying to be you."

Picture two photographs. In the first, a happy family of five snuggle close: a man and woman who love each other and the three children they adore, a family who smile like they'll last forever. In the second, a blur of fragments: that same family blown to smithereens because the man's decided that he's a woman.

Welcome to my family.

For six years my life has been about change. To say I didn't welcome the changes that came my way, particularly when they began flying at me, is a laughable understatement. To say that they caused me engulfing grief and rage is a laughable understatement. What I can say is that I clung to stasis like a fraying lifeline, kicking and screaming as it slipped through my fingers. But against my will and finally because of it, my life changed, and changed me with it.

At the time my youngest child celebrated her first birthday, my husband always wore the skullcap that is a symbol of religious Jewish manhood. Ritual fringes, another such symbol, brushed the bottoms of his shirts. Otherwise his look was secular: hair, beard, and mustache kept trim; jeans with T-shirts whenever he could get away with it. When his hazel eyes sparkled he was almost as boyish as when we met in late adolescence and unquestionably more handsome.

Two years later, he didn't look like that anymore. His eyes hadn't changed color, but they no longer sparkled, at least not in my presence. The skullcap and fringes were gone. The beard and mustache were gone, and the sessions to laser-burn them off left him looking raw, pink, and greasy. His hair had grown into a long gray-brown hank of scrub brush. As for his clothes, the old ones no longer fit since he'd lost thirty pounds. At home he still wore jeans, smaller ones, with piles of sweaters that didn't seem to warm his perpetual chill so much as contain it. When temperatures climbed into summer, the sweaters peeled away and his baggy polo shirt revealed hairless forearms, a V of shaven chest, the outline of a sports bra. Away from home, he told me, he preferred conservative suits, jackets, and skirts. Apparently his greatest ambition was to be taken for a nondescript middle-aged businesswoman. Or maybe it was to not attract any notice at all.

For two years I watched my husband die. I listened to the fading echoes of his voice as he reached up up and away from his natural register, adopting a faint, high-pitched singsong that suggested he was continually on the verge of fainting. I watched him wither from a deeply ethical man with wide interests and a brilliant sense of humor into someone sickly and self-absorbed, incapable of pleasure, seemingly devoid of moral bearings. A person he called Who I Really Am. A person he called a woman.

His explanations for this transformation varied from the dire to the trivial. "Either I live as woman," he threatened regularly, "or I die."

On other days he said, "I need to expand my clothing choices." Once he got even more specific: "The narrow palette of colors available in a male wardrobe is just too unfair!"

Stunned, I could only manage, "Our children are going to suffer for this wider palette."

To which he responded, "Many children suffer."

We were so young when we embarked on our lives together that even in the milieu of an Orthodox neighborhood, where early marriage isn't rare, we stood out. In the close, crowded pocket of a Washington Heights kosher butcher shop, we bought dinner, me with a blue wool seaman's cap pulled down over my head, my long hair tucked inside. The men on both sides of the counter were charmed. "Are you brother and sister?" they wanted to know. "Or husband and wife?" We were twenty, twenty-one. I thought we were forever. Once he'd embarked on his transformation, he told me we were never. He told our then twelve-year-old son that for him, divorce was always an option. He said the person I had loved for so many years was not him. In fact, he never existed at all. Erasing his own past, he rewrote the whole of my adult life as a love affair with a phantom.

In the triumphant coming-out tales told by transgendered people, I've missed the story of the bereft spouse who loses her marriage and her husband, the present she enjoyed, and the future she imagined. Who loses her past. These losses— that last one in particular—threw everything I thought I knew about myself into question.

In earlier, happier days, my family once spent half a year in Israel. I picked up the minutiae critical to functioning in my daily life, the bus routes, the words I needed at the elementary school and at the corner grocery, the customs associated with celebrating on a national scale holidays I'd known only within the confines of our American Jewish community. When babysitter Asaf greeted us ashen-faced because he'd feared we'd been killed, I learned that in the thick of *ha'matsav*, the situation, you always call to say you'll be late. When the bus doors closed on an elderly woman trying to reach the street, I heard myself shouting to the driver along with the other passengers in Hebrew I hadn't known I knew. And when the time came to leave the country, I had accumulated this store of knowledge and skills I could not take with me—that were now useless. I lost a place and the reason for knowing the things I knew about how to live in that place.

It was like this when my marriage ended. Everything I knew about my husband and our relationship: useless. Everything I knew about myself: equally so. I had lived in this marriage not for half a year, but for the whole of my adult life. Then that life, that me, was *over*. It is cliché to speak of the segments of a life as chapters. The disjunction I've experienced seems to require a whole new book.

"I'm thinking constantly about my gender."

That's what he said. Seconds after making love. The instant our bodies broke apart. "I'm thinking constantly about my gender." The hinge between before and after. Everything to come spins out from it. So much pain, so much destruction. And in the end, astoundingly, so much joy. As postcoital murmurs go, this one was a doozy. Sex, among other things, would never be the same.

Throughout my marriage I was shy, intensely private, even secretive. Our relationship, for reasons I didn't really understand, intensified an inherited inclination. I grew up in a family and a culture in which, if something bad happened, you didn't advertise (shame made certain of that), and if something good happened, you didn't advertise (for fear of shamelessness or its appearance, a dread of calling attention to oneself, of drawing down *malocchio*, the evil eye, the spirit of revenge reputed to hover over every source of happiness). The things that happened during the last two years of my marriage drove me into an even deeper furtiveness. There were days—they happened often, increasingly over time— when I took my children to school, talked with professional contacts, went through the motions of social occasions, in a state of shock. I felt like a woman whose husband had died the night before and no one knew. I was obliged to keep my sudden widowhood to myself. My husband had died, but even to say it aloud, "My husband died last night," would have been the grossest impropriety. It was like a nightmare, a recurring one throughout my life, that something was terribly amiss and I had to act as if everything were fine. The pressure to *say nothing* grew and grew as our home life became more surreal.

Even if I could have lived with that pressure indefinitely,

my husband wasn't about to let me. Slowly and painfully, I began to talk with people I called friends, people whom I thought I knew and who thought they knew me but with whom I might actually have remained lifelong strangers if the circumstances of my life had not compelled me out of myself. One awkward little lurch forward at a time, I made my way from a place of self-containment so extreme that it amounted to withdrawal to a place of exhilarating, terrifying openness.

Becoming a person capable of sharing her most intimate secrets with others meant also becoming a person with whom others shared their secrets. I now regularly hear stories of private—often marital—heartache. I've discovered that many marriages, like Impressionist paintings, resemble what they are supposed to be only from a distance; up close they are inchoate muddles. Sure, my relative openness has inspired a similar opening up in friends. But let's face it, people who might once have shied away from sharing painful confidences with the woman who seemed to have it all no longer have that qualm. More than once I've been told, by friends in truly awful circumstances themselves, "I wouldn't trade places with *you* for anything." This isn't a hurtful thing to say. On the contrary. I've heard it as positive confirmation that I was going through my own little hell and was allowed to feel stressed by it. And I've never wanted to trade places with them, either.

When I began to let friends in on what was happening in my life, many, eager to encourage, would tell me, "At least you're going to get a book out of everything you're going through!" I wasn't cheered. People imagined that I would voluntarily relive this? Make it even more public than it was? Were they nuts? The thought of writing about my experiences left me cold at best, at worst horrified. But when I began to listen to other people's sorrows, I realized that along with their stories, I heard resignation. I heard despair. I saw friends so afraid of change that they preferred to sit tight in known, degenerating situations, no matter how bad, rather than hazard the risks and possibilities of movement. All this made me begin to think about telling my story. I've despaired, too. I've been through enough emotional ups and downs to know, even on a good day, that hopelessness might catch up with me tomorrow, maybe even later on today. Mine is a story that is still very much in progress, my life's myriad messes far from tidied up. I write without the happy ending, by which I mean: My life hasn't ended. Until it does, I now know well that anything might happen.

Once, in the early stages of writing this book, I lay in the dark, phone cradled between the pillow and my ear, enjoying one of the long and intimate conversations in which, magically and mundanely, life and friendship truly happen. For my dear friend Michael on the West Coast, it was late. For me in the East, three hours *later*. The night between two frenetic days of work and single motherhood was vanishing, but I needed to hear his opinion of what I was taking on.

"Write from the most honest place," he advised. "The place where you don't have the answers. Share your ability to look at the contradictions and find the humor. After it's done, we tell ourselves things that are not quite true. Have the courage to tell it while it's happening."

So I'll say this: For a long time I was trapped in a place from which I couldn't act, believing that things could only get worse, that any action I dared take could only make them worse. I don't live in that place anymore. Now I live on a roller coaster. Life regularly shakes, terrifies, and puts me in danger of losing my cookies. It sends me gifts of love, joy, and what I'm going to call by the lovely, old-fashioned word *fellowship* that leave me breathless. I feel more alive than I could ever have imagined.

Even after I began to consider writing about my experiences, the task looked dauntingly grim. That changed during a visit to my friends Sid and Oriole. Every now and then I stop by their home, often on a Sunday morning, to shock and amaze them with tales from my trenches. As Oriole has told me, they've become sophisticated—what a person of another generation might call cool—just by knowing me. Sid and Oriole and I live in a cluster of small New England towns that I will hereafter refer to as the Valley of the Politically Correct. One Sunday morning I sat in their beautiful dining room, surrounded by sunlight-spilling windows, regaling them with some choice anecdote about my politically incorrect anguish in the Valley, where, as I will chronicle, not all pain is equal. Sid and Oriole reacted quite appropriately to my absurd and agonized saga: they laughed. They laughed and they told me, "You have to write about this! You have to write about this because it's *funny*!" And for the first time in my then three-plus years of turmoil I thought, Maybe I can write about it—it's funny.

Yes, funny. Also sexy. Much to my surprise, my story turns out to be, among other things, a tale of erotic awakening that, as they say on National Public Radio, may not be appropriate for all listeners. For the first two and a half years of my six-year odyssey, my life was awash in anguish, loss, terrible fear for my children's well-being and our future. How do we survive such periods? Actually, I know how I survived:

through the deepening connections I was even then making with friends, not only the love and support I received from those friends, but the good times and the laughter we shared no matter what we were seeing one another through. For the next three and a half years, my story continued to contain all that but something else as well: a passionate relationship of a kind that I had never known and thought had passed me by. It contained relationships with God and with community so powerful, the me I once was could never have believed they'd be mine.

At times the particulars of my story may startle or dismay, titillate or alienate, provoke outrage or shocked laughter— hey, they've done all that for me—but in the end it's a story about a woman who believed she knew someone deeply, trusted him absolutely, and found herself confronted with a stranger. A woman who thought she had become all that she was going to become and found herself confronted with the demand that she be someone different. And finding herself so confronted, tried all the coping skills in her arsenal: denial, refusal, despair, rage. And when all those failed, a new one. Change.

Many people suffer midlife crises. Men in particular seem to be known for them, known for having them out loud and in color, for making decisions that entail the ending of marriages, career metamorphoses, large expenditures of cash, the acquisition of new toys. Women, according to my entirely informal survey, seem to expect themselves to grapple with midlife turmoil by planting a garden, taking up a textile art, or otherwise finding a corner in which to quietly implode. By any measure, Tracey's crisis was impressive. (I am going to refer to my former husband as Tracey, not because it is his name—it isn't—but because it is a gender-neutral name that works before and after and either way.) Tracey never called his midlife crisis a midlife crisis. He represented it as a kind of gender sneeze, an involuntary explosion in reaction to the mounting irritation of inhabiting an identity that didn't feel like his. In other words, a midlife crisis. It erupted in the middle of our lives. It was a crisis. And like some midlife crises and unlike others, Tracey's changed everything.

On one level, there really isn't anything quite like having your husband of twenty-odd years decide to live as a woman, and relatively few people find themselves in that precise situation. But many of us have our lives upended. Illness, death, divorce, other family upheavals. Job loss, geographic dislocation. Life happens. Sooner or later, most of us experience change that is not of our choosing. We fear that we will never regain our equilibrium. We soldier on, racked inside by doubts about whether we are up to the challenges thrown our way. Often, we have no idea how strong we really are. We can't begin to imagine how happy we may become.

Inevitably, the material of my life gives rise to questions, questions about the nature of transsexuality, about the nature of gender itself. Fears, misconceptions, and prejudices about those who cross gender lines once made serious, compassionate discussion of those issues impossible. In some places, political correctness now threatens to do the same. ("He's a transsexual," I've been told. "Anything he does is justified.") My story is not an attack on or defense of transsexuality. It is not *about* transsexuality. Transsexuals tell their own stories, and rightly so. This story is mine. It is a story about the reconfiguration of a family and the remaking of a woman. It is a love story, a story of love lost and love found. To tell it, I must sidestep both the stereotyping and the political grandstanding. The process of my transformation from a person who didn't believe she could survive this story, much less tell it, into the person telling it *is* my story.

But the story isn't only mine. As an acquaintance who knew whereof he spoke put it: Divorce is a very private and very public failure; it creates communal as well as personal chaos. So while the story I tell is my own, it is also a community's. It belongs in a sense to the circle of friends who have lived it by my side and seen me through. It belongs in every sense to my children.

Shepherding any children through any divorce is rough. Shepherding my three children through divorce *and* their father's decision to live as a woman has presented parenting challenges for which the *What to Expect* book has yet to be written. (My youngest child will be the one to write it. She'll call it *What to Expect When Your Dad's a Girl*.) Again, literature about the transsexual experience plays down or altogether omits the loss experienced by a child whose parent changes gender. Mine is a story of telling three young children that their childhoods are at an end, then holding them while their hearts break, not once but over and over. My children's grief and trauma are the most painful aspects of my family's experience. Our legal and emotional battles over the children, and the failure of the community they've grown up in to support them, are surely the ugliest. In the Valley of the Politically Correct, my children and I have sometimes been blindsided by the unexpected ways our private sorrow has played out in public. A religious community we thought we could rely on fell away; once peripheral friends drew close. Community lost and community gained have provided some of the bitterest disillusion and sweetest joy I have known.

Despite the images of before and after photographs I have

just described, what happened to my family wasn't an explosion that took place in an instant. It was more like a crash in which the fall to earth occurs in agonizingly slow motion. Like a vessel that with great pain and extreme reluctance is finally permitted to fall and to shatter.

A Talmudic passage describes a rabbi dying a protracted and excruciatingly painful death. His students, unwilling to part from their beloved teacher, keep him alive by means of a continual stream of prayer. To end the rabbi's suffering, a servant girl deliberately drops a clay vessel, prayers are momentarily disrupted, and the rabbi's spirit is released.

When I encountered this story a few years ago, I was in the midst of the deep crisis that was tearing my family, my life, and my sense of self to shreds. At the time, I identified easily with the rabbi in pain, with the students who couldn't live without him, with the sacrificed clay pot. But I understood that it was the servant I needed to become: a woman who recognizes a vessel that must shatter, and lets it go.

Part One

THE VESSEL CRACKS

I'm thinking constantly about my gender. It's on my mind all the time, constantly. I've tried to deal with this on my own and I can't. I need to talk about it.

It was a mild June night the week before Father's Day.

The weekend before, I went away with a group of women I've been friends with for some sixteen years and counting. On my way out the door, apropos of nothing, I turned to Tracey and with prophetically bad timing told him, "I want us to use the coming year to create the really good life I know we can have. I want to cherish our family and not lose sight of what matters most. Let's not let the daily grind or worrying about money or careers get in our way. Let's not let anything stop us from being happy."

Tracey looked mildly surprised. He said little in the way of response. That didn't trouble me. There wasn't time for a conversation.

Overrun by motherhood and domestic details, I hadn't been feeling like a person lately, much less a wife. My words must have sounded like a bolt out of the blue. But I meant them. When, during the course of the weekend away, one friend shared details about the messy state of her marriage, I felt more determined than ever to reclaim mine.

"I'm thinking constantly about my gender."

What happened that night was that we made love, and immediately after, he told me. "I can't stop thinking about it," he said. "It's on my mind all the time, constantly. I've tried to deal with this on my own and I can't. I need to talk about it. I keep feeling like I'm the wrong gender, a lot, all the time, constantly. It's like a continual pain. I want to talk with you about it and I want to talk with a therapist. Maybe find a support group."

That was the gist of it, more or less the words. I don't remember mine, the very first ones with which I responded. I know that I stayed relatively calm. Surprisingly calm, for me. I heard the urgency in his voice—the conversation took place in semidarkness, in bed—and I tried to be open and supportive, as I would often fail to be in the many conversations that would follow.

I didn't say, *Whoa. Can we please hold up a minute here?* But in retrospect I think I began to do automatically what I would do frantically and intentionally in the months and years to come: I tried to slow it down. I asked questions, conveyed compassion. I didn't pretend that I wasn't terribly upset, but I also didn't say, *Can we please not talk about this now? Or ever?* I didn't say, *Talking about this won't work for me. I can't be married to someone who wants to talk about this.* I spoke to my husband as if he had revealed himself to be in an extreme and precarious state of mind, which he had. As if he had revealed a bomb he might detonate.

He wanted to talk. To me. To a therapist. To a support group.

"I just want to talk," he assured me. "I'm not going to *do* anything." By which he meant, it went without saying, anything to his appearance. To his life. Our lives.

So we lay in bed and talked. For hours, like two people inside a marriage, two people who loved each other, facing a mutual problem.

I was stunned. Our marriage, our family, and everything that up until that moment had constituted my story was over. That much I understood at once.

The years leading up to that night in June had been full and hectic, challenging, sometimes traumatic. Tracey and I had met and fallen in love during our freshman year in college. After graduation we left the East Coast for Europe, followed by California, where we had no particular reason to be and where we married. We worked at various jobs, pursued creative endeavors, traveled. We lived in a way that was in many respects very pleasant and that felt to me, even at the time and certainly in retrospect, disconnected, somewhat pointless. During those years, my twenties, I was dogged by the sense that real, adult life eluded me. I wanted to feel connected to a community, to find greater fulfillment in my work. I danced hesitant steps around a spiritual identity that I was afraid to embrace. I passionately longed to have children. I came to believe that all of these things would happen if we moved back east. Oddly, I was right.

Tracey decided to go to graduate school, and we moved to New England. Once there, I began to build community connections and found a spiritual home. My work as a writer deepened and expanded. A lifelong city girl, I discovered a sense of belonging in small-town and rural life that amazes me to this day. We had a first child, then a second, then a third. We moved around a bit, spending a couple of semesters and an academic year in various places, and many semesters together only part-time, while Tracey went to school or worked in one state and the children and I lived in another. I worked continually as a freelance writer with weekly deadlines I met even in weeks that included childbirth. I worked on several longer projects and published my first book.

The two years just prior to that June night were particularly packed. We moved from Oregon back to New England late in my third pregnancy and spent a grueling summer teaching every day, he in the morning and I in the afternoon, passing two children back and forth between us. Near the end of summer, I gave birth to a baby who spent a week in neonatal intensive care. A week after we brought her home, Tracey began commuting to a new job that took him away half of each week, leaving me with the sole care of a medically fragile newborn and her two attention-starved siblings. When my first book was published in the spring, I took a four-day lecture trip, leaving my children for the first time in their lives for more than a single night. My older children suffered my absence extravagantly, complaining to Tracey that they couldn't even concentrate at school knowing I was away. My baby became listless and apparently depressed. While she took in just enough fluids to keep herself alive, I sat on the floor of a friend's guest bedroom continually pumping and tossing out milk to relieve my absurdly aching breasts—and decided not to promote the book if it meant leaving her again overnight.

A few months later, at the end of summer, we bought our

first house. Again, a week after moving in, surrounded by
unpacked boxes and with the interior painting of the house
not finished (it still isn't), Tracey resumed commuting to his
job. Largely on my own, I juggled all the elements of life in a
rural home through a long and particularly difficult winter.
By June—the June when this story begins—I felt ready for a
change, though not the one I didn't know was coming. Tracey
had been awarded a fellowship and granted a year's leave of
absence from his job. I was coming to realize that the two
years we'd lived through, in particular my baby's birth and
the ongoing health concerns surrounding her, had kept me in
a kind of low-level post-traumatic stress. The year with him
at home, I believed, was my chance to heal. To get a grip on
the career that had languished during two frantic years of
mothering. To repair the disjunctions that had—inevitably,
I thought—jangled our marriage.

Wrong.

I understood at once. Okay. In one sense, that's true. Everything was about to change. It *had* changed the moment his
words were spoken. But did I really understand this? I think I
did, in a bottom-dropping-out, plunging-elevator kind of way.
But I tried to believe that our life together was going to continue, because, quite simply, I couldn't believe that it would
not. Tracey had a psychological problem, a big one. We would
find a way out of it. We had to. What other choice was there?

What is unquestionably true is that from that evening on,
there would never be another easy moment between us.

The next afternoon we took a walk on our winding country road, Lilly, not yet two, in the stroller, Adam and Bibi on
bicycles. (Adam, Bibi, and Lilly are not my children's names.)

It was a bright June leafy-green day, there were the shouts of happy children, all made distant by shock. I felt numb.

But Tracey was in turmoil. He was having some kind of breakdown; I had to be the stable one. When the older kids were out of earshot, I nervously asked him, "How are you feeling? Do you want to talk some more?"

"I'm not feeling so good." He shrugged. He repeated the salient points of the previous night's conversation. He felt wrong in his body. Increasingly so. That is, the sense of wrongness was on the rise. Also the time he spent feeling wrong, thinking about feeling wrong. It had gone from being an occasional thought to a frequent one to a constant state of mind. An obsession. "I can't stop thinking about it," he told me. "I think about it all the time at work. Sometimes I feel like I'm not going to be able to function."

Tracey mentioned again that he wanted to find a therapist, possibly a group of people struggling with similar feelings.

"Could you give me a little time to get used to all this before you contact therapists and groups?" I asked him. It was selfish, since I could see that he needed professional help. Irrational, since there was zero chance that I was going to "get used to" the feelings Tracey described. It was my way of trying to hang on to a sense of *us*. I wanted to catch my breath. If he needed to "deal with these feelings," didn't that mean we needed to somehow deal with them together? Before new players were introduced into our intimate lives?

"I can wait a while," Tracey said. "But not long."

As a surprise, I had made plans for our family to spend the coming weekend in Maine. I had made those plans just a week or two earlier, spontaneously, when it occurred to me

that the perfect Father's Day gift would be a weekend away.
We loved spending time together, and a celebration at the
beach would give us all pleasure. Our family was something
to celebrate. My husband was a wonderful father, and *that*
was something to celebrate.

We went away for Father's Day weekend as planned. Well,
sort of as planned. We went to the beach, soaked in a hot
tub, sipped white wine at a patio table beside the swimming
pool while the kids swam. We ate at family-friendly restau-
rants. We were nice to each other. But I doubt that either of
us relaxed or enjoyed ourselves for an instant. The photographs we took hint at the story. There are the shots of an
exuberant trio of children laughing and clowning in bril-
liantly colored swimsuits. Then there's a shot of the children
and me on a rocky path above the ocean in which I stare at
the camera as solemnly as if the cliff behind us is the one we
are about to tumble over. There's one of Tracey staring
down, away, palpably miserable. His head hangs as if his
neck can't bear the weight.

We went home. Family life went on, as it will with three
children. If it was abruptly drained of color and joy, it was
still our family, our life. Tracey was depressed but calm. Still
Tracey. Still the man I loved. He told me that he was glad
that he could confide in me, grateful that we could talk about
his feelings. What Tracey didn't say was that I wasn't the
first person he was confiding in. I discovered that accidentally, the week after Father's Day, Thursday. Yet another
walk with the children, this time on a quiet tree-lined street
in town that ended on a local college's track. The big kids
raced ahead to get to the track. Tracey's cell phone buzzed.
The caller was a friend and colleague who lived abroad and
who I had never met. For several years they had carried on an

e-mail correspondence, but recently they had been talking on the phone. Daily, or nearly so. Suddenly I understood why.

"You've told her!" I exclaimed when Tracey ended the brief call.

Tracey declined to answer. Which, of course, said it all.

If Tracey was talking to this woman, he must be talking to others. He was. He had been confiding in women friends, some he didn't even know all that well, for months. This wasn't something he just needed to share with me, a therapist, a support group. Something he wasn't going to *do* anything about. For the first time since his announcement (but not the last!), I was distraught. Betrayed. In his response—angry, cold, dismissive—I caught my first glimpse of the new Tracey. "Of course I'm talking to my friends!" he snapped. "I have to talk to someone and I can't talk to you!"

It would be hard to overemphasize the impact of this moment on all that was to come. The revelation that he had been talking to other women. That he had misrepresented the situation to me. Above all, his utter lack of concern for my distress. I had been working very hard to think about what Tracey needed, to be compassionate. To believe that our family was stronger than Tracey's problem and might survive it. But Tracey and his problem had already stepped outside the realm of our marriage. His family was no longer his first priority. I just hadn't known it.

Tracey, who sees his life as an epic tale of liberation akin to the Passover story, might possibly liken the period that began then to the days of intensified suffering leading up to the Jewish people's deliverance from bondage in Egypt, the darkness before the dawn. For me it was just darkness. By which I mean both that it was horrible and that I couldn't see. I didn't know what was coming next. I couldn't visualize it even when, technically, I had a pretty good idea what was to happen. The result was that I was paralyzed. Paralyzed with fear.

I still sometimes dream of this period and its immediate aftermath now, years later. In one dream I arrive at an apartment that is supposed to be our home in great reluctance to see him, only to find that he's gone. I see empty hangers and a note that reads, "After so-and-so-many years I have finally decided to leave." The figure named is meant to represent the duration of our marriage, but it strikes me as wrong. He is ending our post-marriage, not our marriage, which he's already ended. His message goes on to offer some "fun pages" scattered throughout the apartment, photocopies of little puzzles, pointless bits of practical advice, the sort of stuff used to fill out the columns of small-town newspapers. I don't ask myself why, when he was obviously planning to leave, he would do so while I was out, without the decency of a warning or good-bye. Instead I feel a version of bereft, not quite the real thing, which would require a loss that at this point has already occurred long in the past. It is more a profound experience of aloneness. Also, thanks to his cheerful, offensively useless pages, I feel the stirrings of anger. Walking through rooms of empty hangers and photocopies, my bereft dream-self doesn't know it yet, but when all else fails that anger will see me through.

What I'd like to do now is move forward from that June, telling my story, my new story, the one that began then. It's a painful story, difficult to tell for many reasons, yet preferable to revisiting everything that came before it—that is, my marriage. It is excruciating to revisit my marriage. It requires me to call up the face, the voice, the smile, of a person from whom I thought I would never part but who purposely took himself—along with his face, his voice, his smile—out of existence. Out of my existence. It requires creating a cognitive link between all that was and the present, a task I seem unable to accomplish. But I have to say something about my marriage, don't I? Screwing myself up to it, I feel certain that people don't write about themselves because it gives them pleasure. Anyone who does it must have other reasons, as do I.

What did she know and when did she know it? That's the question that everyone would eventually ask: Did Tracey's revelation come as a total surprise, or did I realize that he had "issues" about his gender? It's a question that the thumbnail sketch of my marriage I've just provided doesn't begin to answer.

During the months when he was blowing our world apart, Tracey often accused me of responsibility for his crisis. Precisely what I was responsible for varied from day to day. Some days it was:

"It's your own fault! You knew how I felt!"

Other times it was:

"It's your own fault! You didn't know how I felt! I've suffered from gender dysphoria for years and you were oblivious!"

From some of his sympathizers I would eventually hear, "He says you *knew* he was a transsexual." Left unspoken: *Why complain now?*

From people who sympathized with me I would hear, "Of course you never *knew* he felt this way."

To accusers and sympathizers alike, I had one answer: I knew and I didn't. To the extent that I knew, I didn't understand. In our twenty-plus years together, there had been times when I was aware that something was slightly, or on occasion more than slightly, off-kilter about Tracey, that as good and close as I believed our relationship to be, there was a distance that could never be bridged, a connection that couldn't be made. I operated, without examining my motives, as if this thing weren't there. As if I knew that to face it head-on would destroy our marriage.

"I hate myself."

We sat side by side on the wide stairs in the bright, open stairwell of the modern dorm that housed us both, the boys' floor where he lived above, the girls' floor where I lived below, building-high windows in front and back of us. We were eighteen, freshmen. It was May. We'd been lovers since February. Tracey was getting ready to go home for the summer, and the thought of returning to his family provoked an outpouring of anguished self-loathing.

"I hate myself. I'm never good enough. Nothing I ever do is right." He sat hunched over, clutching at himself and sobbing. He'd always felt scrutinized and belittled by his parents, inadequate no matter how hard he tried to please. They didn't love him. That was his fault. He was unlovable. "I can't remember a time when I didn't hate myself. Even when I was small I would think about killing myself. Sometimes I would wish I was a girl."

I'd never seen Tracey upset before, and I'd never heard anyone express this kind of self-loathing. The Tracey I knew was sharp, funny, and irreverent, tenacious in a political argument but easygoing in other ways. The depth of pain he revealed now was shocking. At eighteen I might have been scared off by it. I might have slunk away from our fledgling relationship. Instead I consciously chose to jump in. Leaning over, I put my arms around him and held him. I told him his parents were dead wrong. I told him he was exactly right just the way he was. I told him he was wonderful. Point for point I outargued every negative thing Tracey said about himself. I threw every rope I had down his awful black well and urged him to climb up out of it. And he did.

Tracey had been brought up with the explicit obligation to model himself on his father. That he would therefore have trouble embracing manhood didn't strike me as odd: I'd met his father. In those months of getting to know each other, Tracey had already told me a lot about himself and his family. A spring break visit with his family had told me more. No one was very happy in Tracey's home, but everyone was intensely dedicated to maintaining a veneer of sunny suburban satisfaction. Appearing normal was at a premium. In this family, that included an adherence to gender roles that struck me, among educated Democrats in the 1980s, as slightly surprising. "Don't tell them you can type," Tracey's father advised him about job hunting. "If they find out, they're going to look at you funny." Funny meant gay. Typing meant gay. It went without saying that Tracey would never get a job if people thought he was gay.

Tracey's father was an uncharismatic man, his face affectless behind the thick lenses of his black plastic-rimmed glasses. He had a mediocre career he didn't enjoy and spent nights and weekends engaged in solitary hobbies in his basement workroom. He had no friends of his own, and when he spoke at social occasions organized by his wife, it was with a slightly sneering condescension, as if no one present were really worthy of hearing what he might say. If he didn't want Tracey to be gay, he also wasn't pleased by his son's heterosexual high school exploits. Disapproving of the string of girlfriends with whom he (accurately) guessed Tracey was sexually active, his father stopped speaking to him—for several years. When Tracey graduated from college and we married, his father decided to cut him off completely, never stating his reasons. He went to his grave more than two decades later still refusing all contact with his son. Though she kept in touch with us, Tracey's mother complied with her husband's wishes by never inviting Tracey, me, or our children to her home.

Because he was the man of the house, Tracey's father was its uncontested ruler. Because he wasn't much of a man, it was everyone else's job to be very careful not to upstage him, something it was exceedingly easy to do. For Tracey, the implications were intricate and complex. As a talented student and the only boy in a middle-class Jewish family, he was supposed to succeed; as his father's son, he was not. Wasting no time on his escape, Tracey graduated from high school and left home at the age of sixteen—carrying all the family baggage with him. The tensions surfaced in many ways. One small example, insignificant in itself but emblematic of the rest: Tracey's father couldn't find his way out of a paper bag and would get lost for hours even during drives (he always had to be behind the wheel) the family took regularly. When we traveled together, I noticed that Tracey would smoothly negotiate our route while repeating the mantra that he himself had a terrible sense of direction, just like Dad. Finally I pointed out the discrepancy. "You can stop saying you have no sense of direction," I told him. "Your father's limitations didn't have to be yours." Boy howdy, did that turn out to be true.

Who would want to be a man if being just like Tracey's dad was what it meant? Yet Tracey didn't come across as feminine. His signals were heterosexual and male. In college he was deeply into martial arts, he was belligerently passionate about politics, and he spoke often of his plans to move to Israel after graduation and enter the Israeli army. He initiated our intimate relationship and responded to me in the ways I expected within it. We would often meet in the city. I can still see his look of stark sexual appreciation when he spotted me walking toward him on a platform in Grand Central Station or where he waited under the arch in Washington Square Park, his smug pride climbing down from the cab of a big rig whose driver had given him a ride to meet me and told him he thought I was sexy.

Given the normal college-boy indicators, and the fact that I knew absolutely nothing about transsexuality, the only explanation I could imagine for his wish to be a girl was psychological—a radical rejection of self if ever there was one, particularly in the context of the suicidal impulses Tracey confessed to. Neither suicide nor girlhood was presented or struck me as a viable career plan. But that was where I came in. What I could do for Tracey's sense of direction, I could do for the rest of him. I saw his strengths; I would mirror them back to him, as his parents had failed to do. I loved him, and being loved would free him from his past. In short, I wasn't the first woman to think she could heal a damaged man, and I won't be the last.

Tracey *was* damaged. Blaming his feelings about manhood on his upbringing was an easy fit. I now know that happy families also produce transsexuals. I didn't know it then. I understand a little more about gender identity and transsexuality than I did in those days. But Tracey is the man I was married to for over two decades. My response to his transformation is not my response to other transsexuals. It's embedded in my personal, entirely subjective experience, an experience knotty with different strands: religious, moral, emotional, sexual, cultural. I was brought up with deep-seated Mediterranean convictions about male and female: not opposite ends on a spectrum of lovely rainbow colors bleeding into one another, but entirely separate, if not to say opposing, categories. These convictions have proven remarkably tenacious, and in the Valley of the Politically Correct, where I live, not to mention the transuniverse, this marks me as hopelessly retrograde. But while some transpeople see themselves as challenging gender norms, what I've witnessed up close and personal—obsession with a certain body type, pride in "feminine" emotionalism and shrinking muscles, a taste for bodice-hugging clothes—would seem to reinforce them. Tracey never wanted to topple the gender wall. He just wanted to hurl himself over it to the other side.

During our marriage, Tracey would laugh at my over-charged mind-body connection. When I'm worried or upset about something, these feelings express themselves physically. Being in good physical shape is closely linked to feeling emotionally upbeat; being sick depresses me. In the past this seemed like a liability, a way in which my body was at the mercy of my moods and vice versa. In recent years I've become far more conscious of the sense of inhabiting my own skin, of the physical and emotional being in tune, as sources of strength and pleasure. It also makes me rather squeamish (*squeamish* doesn't seem like a strong enough term, but it will have to do) about surgical and chemical alterations of the body. I'm okay with pierced ears but not much else. The ingestion of mind- and body-changing medication troubles me. The thought of flesh being sliced into is deeply disturbing. These are gut reactions, but I'd be lying if I claimed that they are devoid of an ethical element. My sense of the integrity of the body and the respect with which it is to be treated, deep-seated personal values that are echoed in Jewish thought, has a tough time reconciling with major surgical alterations performed on healthy breasts and genitals. But I've also come to realize that, being present in my body, I never grasped the extent of Tracey's absence from his. *I didn't get it.* The man I loved was indivisible from the face and body I loved. How could his experience of himself be otherwise?

When Tracey sat in that stairwell and for the first time spoke of wishing that he'd been born a girl, it was a given— that is, in my mind it was a given—that at his lowest moments he had wished to be something *that he knew he was not.* That in his fantasies the love and acceptance he craved had become tangled up with something *that he knew he could never be.* He couldn't be a person who had been born and grown up female. He couldn't be a girl because he was not one. It was inconceivable to me that he could choose the life of a transsexual. So my initial response was horrified sympathy that he felt so ill at ease with himself.

When Tracey told me a few years later, early in our marriage, that he was struggling with these feelings again, my response was just horror. I still thought Tracey had a psychological problem, and I still thought he was investing gender with a power to resolve his childhood anguish that it didn't have. But this time it hit me that he wasn't just expressing regrets for a life that he accepted would never be his. I realized that he had at least contemplated cross-dressing. This understanding was so powerfully, viscerally disturbing that it nauseated me and made me dizzy. For me there was no wiggle room: I couldn't engage in an intimate relationship with a man who dressed in women's clothes. Not even occasionally. Not even in secret. I couldn't have sexual or romantic feelings toward a man who actually wanted to be—or, beyond that, felt that in some obscure way he was—a woman. This was not simply a reflection of the limits of heterosexuality. I had never desired a woman, but I could imagine such desire. It seemed to me that Tracey's gender dis-ease represented something else again, a violent self-destruction that I couldn't enter into. It would be catastrophic even to think of Tracey rejecting his masculinity. I told him if he wanted to go deeper into this rejection of self, he had to go it alone. I couldn't go with him. He had to choose.

Given the strength of my reaction, it may sound strange and inexplicable that I thought I could continue in a relationship with a man who had disclosed these feelings—in hindsight, it does to me. I offer a parable, a metaphor: A twenty-something couple, very much in love, reach an impasse. The young man says, I love you and our relationship is the center of my life. However, I don't think it is in my nature to be monogamous. Let's have other lovers. The woman, deeply unhappy, refuses. She tells him that what he describes would be intolerable for her. If you want to be with me, these are the only terms I can live with, she tells him. That he has even raised the issue casts a pall. But she imagines that if he really wants to be with her, he will relinquish an impulse that is destructive not only of their relationship, but of himself. If he gives up this fantasy, it must be something he doesn't want very badly, doesn't need. Not something he *is*.

Tracey chose me. He put aside these feelings. That's what I believed. I didn't think he had suppressed the feelings; I thought that he had let them go.

I loved Tracey. I *knew* Tracey. I trusted him absolutely. He was the man whose feet I liked to stand on so that we could dance around the room as one crazy, careening body. The person I was closer to than I had ever been to anyone. My husband. It isn't possible to be completely wrong about everything you think you know.

Over the years that followed, there were moments when Tracey seemed distant and preoccupied. There were no more expressions of self-loathing or suicidal impulses; he'd just withdraw. Then he'd return. We'd go on with our lives. No doubt if I had been older, more experienced with men, sure of myself and what I wanted, I would have wondered more about what was going on inside Tracey. As it was, we'd met as teenagers. We were busy growing up together, and I accepted that we each had our demons to wrestle. And for the most part, we were in harmony. We worked consciously and conscientiously to build a strong relationship, to develop and hone our communication. Everywhere we lived or traveled we took long walks, frequented cafés and bookstores, spent hours at home reading aloud, cooking, and drinking wine. Tracey was an avid football fan, and he taught me the game so that I could enjoy it with him, albeit without his zeal. He tried, and largely failed, to get me to share his love of science fiction. I introduced him to photography and European cinema; he lived with my preference for what he called relationship films, and I lived with his for films involving aliens and violent death. Judaism grew increasingly important over the years, as a set of ideas to explore, argue over, agree upon, and ultimately express as life practice. We supported each other's work and career aspirations. Against my own economic interests, my desire to start a family, I pushed Tracey to get off a steady, relatively lucrative, but dull path through the

business world and go to graduate school. As a writer, Tracey
was the reader I wrote to, for, against; usually the first, always the most important, responder to anything I'd written.
Not that I necessarily took his editorial advice. We often
fought bitterly over his suggestions and laughed together
about my ultimate disregard of them. Continually, we talked.
Conversation was the art we practiced as a duet, analyzing
the books we read, the plays and films we saw, the jazz we
heard, other people, each other and ourselves, religion, politics, and philosophy. Over dinners with friends we could talk
and talk for hours, both of us loving to laugh and to make
people laugh with us. We talked about almost everything.
We had every conversation, except the ones we didn't have.
Or rather the three we didn't have: we never spoke of the discomfort Tracey had once expressed about his gender—but
those feelings had been resolved long ago, hadn't they? We
didn't talk about having children. And we didn't talk about
sex.

It's not quite accurate that we didn't talk about having
children: Tracey didn't talk. I talked, but rarely, aware of his
distaste for the subject. I brought it up from time to time in
our early twenties and more frequently as thirty loomed.
That Tracey refused to entertain the idea became a festering
source of pain. Much later, he would say that his reluctance to
be a father was his reluctance to be a man. He would imply
that he'd been envious of my female body and what it could
do—if he couldn't have a baby, damned if he was going to let
me have one. But Tracey's position in our standoff on having
a family looked and felt like that of any young guy who just
doesn't want children. Like someone who lacked my lifelong
passion for babies and was loath to take on the responsibility,
the financial burden, the curtailment of freedom, that come

with them—all of which Tracey spoke of when, as time went on, I began to press the issue and that he later complained of when the children arrived.

The spring of Tracey's thaw toward parenting was an especially good period. I had quit a lousy job to write full-time and was publishing a number of my stories. We'd moved across the bay from San Francisco to Oakland to a funky artists' loft complex. Our new perch had drawbacks, but we could ignore them and thoroughly enjoy our stay because we knew it wouldn't be lengthy: Tracey had been accepted to graduate school, and we'd decided to move back East in the fall. In a conversation about the upcoming year, Tracey said out of the blue, "I've been thinking that this might be a good time to have a baby." I was so shocked that I couldn't speak. With this one shy sentence a wall between us dissolved and in its wake came a rush of energy and intimacy, a heady sense of embarking on a new adventure. We were happy and full of anticipation. Yeah—or so I thought.

When he broke up our family, Tracey said, "I only agreed to have a baby because I knew you would leave me if I didn't."

He said something else that haunts me. "When we decided that spring to have a baby, I warned you that I'd read that gender identity issues sometimes flared up in middle age, and that I was worried this could happen to me."

I remember the long walks we took those months around our industrial neighborhood, around nearby Lake Merritt, up and down the Berkeley Hills. The long talks in which we fantasized our family into existence, happily terrified by the prospect of parenthood. I remember it all vividly. What I don't remember is Tracey saying anything about gender issues. Since this would have come in the midst of roughly two decades in which the subject was never mentioned between us, you would think if the conversation had taken place, it would be a standout. But that doesn't mean it didn't happen. The response he attributed to me—"We can't live by our fears"— sounds like something I might have said. Most striking about Tracey's report of this conversation is that his concern was for the future. Just like me, he didn't see himself as having a gender problem. He worried that he might have one later. The way someone in remission fears the recurrence of cancer.

The third source of silence: sex. Tracey was shy about talking about sex, though not about doing it. For over two decades we had an active and, I believed at the time, satisfying sex life. We didn't sleep in separate beds. We didn't forget to touch, didn't find sexless weeks slipping by unnoticed. Whatever the disconnect between Tracey and his body, it didn't result in performance glitches, not one in over twenty years. Sex was physically pleasurable. It was an expression of affection, emotional closeness (continually I feel the need to add: or so I thought); something to wake up to when we didn't have to jump out of bed for work or babies, to spend long rainy afternoons and late nights after the children were in bed, enjoying. Something to be surprised by in the middle of a shower. But we never said much about it.

One day, after we'd been married for some time but before we had children, I showed Tracey a short story I'd written about an encounter between a man and woman.

"Sexy," he commented stiffly.

Just the single word, *sexy*. Not a compliment. Not exactly a criticism. An observation that clearly made him uncomfortable, as if I had gotten myself up in an alluring outfit for a party I was attending without him.

I never felt, not even then and certainly not from my very differently informed perspective now, that Tracey and I had a profound sexual connection. Around the same time as the short-story incident, I found myself in a conversation about sex with several other young women. One of the women said, "Sex is a communication." I remember this now, so many years later, as an "Ah" moment. An instance in our long relationship when, forever skirting the abyss at the center of our marriage, I briefly, vertiginously, looked down. I had never heard sex described as a communication before. I had no idea whether other people, most people, experienced it that way. I knew instantly that I didn't. This was a point in time when I was happy with Tracey. But sex between us was not a communication. We were good to each other and we had a fine time, but our bodies weren't talking, at least not to each other.

"Oh, look," I told Tracey. "This is perfect for you." I was reading the events calendar of the local Jewish newspaper. "A Jewish men's group. Why don't you check it out?"

"I have no interest in that," Tracey snapped. "What would I have in common with them?"

I laughed. He was kidding, right? What did he have in common with his own demographic? Tracey wasn't kidding. He was angry, as insulted as if I'd suggested he join a group for the mentally impaired. "I don't want you making suggestions like that," he said testily.

"Um—okay. I won't."

His response surprised me, but behind his back I was still laughing. How typically male, I thought. Women join groups to connect with other women. Men join groups, when they join them at all, because they want to engage in a particular activity. I thought Tracey needed more friends. I just wanted to encourage him. This conversation took place only weeks before Tracey's June announcement. It never occurred to me that what upset him was that I was suggesting he was a man.

When our marriage began to unravel we were still socializing as a couple, but we didn't have real friends in common. Our relationship seemed to require a level of exclusivity and isolation in order to flourish, an ambience I don't think either of us actually felt at home in and that I didn't like to examine too closely while I was living in it. In retrospect, I see that before I got involved with Tracey I had a number of close friends, male and female, gay and straight. After, I kept female friends at bay and avoided friendships with men altogether. I'm not claiming direct cause and effect, only that this was the way it happened. I did know that male friends wouldn't fit in our marriage. Without anything said between us, I understood that other men in my life were a potential threat. To our relationship. To Tracey. Whenever I briefly, ever so slightly, became friendly with a man, the immediate effect was a chill in our marriage. If I mentioned a man's name at home, Tracey would respond with sarcasm and hostility. If he met a man I liked, it was a given that he would dislike him. We never spoke of this directly. Jealousy was outside the bounds of Tracey's self-image. After our marriage ended, one of Tracey's friends told me that he'd always understood that Tracey didn't want him to know me.

A friend once described the huge distance in her marriage by saying that she had to go outside of it, to a best friend, to "process" the things that happened in her life because she could not do this with her husband. This seemed to me to be a terrible admission. I thought that was what marriage was, the place where two people could take whatever either of them went through outside it. Tracey was my process person, no question. That doesn't mean I didn't miss having close friends, even as my reserve made it impossible for anyone to be truly close to me. When I became a mother, I felt keenly the lack of other women to share the experience with and I sought out friends in a way that I hadn't done before in the whole of my married life. I worried that the mutual experience of motherhood couldn't be a strong enough point of connection with another woman to lead to friendship. But if it wasn't enough on its own, it turned out to be a great starting point. Despite the limits I put on intimacy in my friendships, the attachments I formed with other women during the early motherhood years ended by being the basis for the real connections that would later come into being while my marriage crumbled. But forming these attachments with other mothers brought a different problem to the fore. Tracey was interested in my relationships with other women. Too interested. Whenever I began a friendship, he would edge suffocatingly close. He wanted in.

One day when our first child was an infant, Tracey and I ran into my new friend Alice out in town. Alice looked at Tracey oddly and giggled as though they shared a secret. When I asked Tracey about it later, he smiled. "I called Alice to ask if she had a babysitter she could recommend," he admitted. "I wanted to take you out for your birthday. I asked her not to tell you about it so that it could be a surprise."

My birthday had already passed. "*Did* she recommend someone?"

"No, she didn't know anyone."

"Then why didn't you tell me?"

"I didn't want to disappoint you."

There were several things wrong with this picture. First, I was a ferociously protective first-time mother. Tracey, who knew me so well, couldn't have imagined for an instant that I would leave my baby with a sitter I hadn't thoroughly vetted myself. Second: "How did you get her number?"

"I looked her up in the phone book."

I took a deep breath. "I know you meant well," I said slowly. "But I don't feel comfortable with you calling my friends or having conversations with them that you ask them to keep from me. About anything."

Tracey just smiled a self-satisfied smile. "I was doing something nice for you." The next time he found some pretext—it always felt like a pretext—of doing something nice, he again got his hands on a friend's phone number, again called for advice or information, and again asked for secrecy. When I found out, I tried to explain that it made me unhappy. He didn't get it. He never got it. It felt creepy every time. Now I think I gave up on intimacy with other women rather than share it with my husband. This simple insight astonishes me. More astonishing: How could I have lived that way? Without close friendships? When I think of my connections to men and women now, I can only feel deeply grateful that I live that way no longer.

At the time, though some friends didn't know what to make of him, most thought Tracey sweet, gentle, the sensitive type—qualities that, when I encounter them in my friends' husbands, now cause me, entirely unfairly, to cringe on my friends' behalf. As if I could see the panties, the tweezers, the boat-sized high heels headed their way. This is a passing PTSD-style reaction. I don't really want my friends to spend their lives with brutish cavemen. When they eventually discovered what was going on in our marriage, what Tracey was up to with me and with our children, my friends, of course, took a different view of him. After we separated,

Tracey sometimes insisted that my friends were his friends. As far as he was concerned, he and my friends had been having same-sex peer relationships. He was surprised to discover that he was the only one who saw it this way.

It goes without saying that I've given a lot of thought to the question of why I was drawn to someone with whom I was in many ways ill matched. After we separated, a friend of mine posed the companion query to Tracey: "Why did you stay for so long with a woman who could never accept the person you call your real self?"

"I lived through her," Tracey said without hesitation. Obviously I was what Tracey wanted to be. I had a woman's body, a woman's experience of the world, women friends, all things he could glom on to. But any woman would have done for that. Tracey elaborated on his viewpoint. "She was always in touch with her emotions and desires. I never knew what I wanted. She always knew exactly what she wanted, and wanted it passionately. I felt numb, and she was so alive."

Sometimes people who didn't know our marriage try to tease out whether and to what extent the relationship was an entity they could have recognized as normal. Did we divide our domestic lives, as many couples still do, into his and her responsibilities? Yes. Tracey was much better at earning a living and coping with car maintenance. He could shovel more snow. I was the better cook and home decorator. I was the one responsible for family pictures, by which I mean I was the family photographer, I assembled the photograph albums, and I was the one who kept the big picture in mind. All the big pictures. I organized our social lives, balanced the checkbook, made all the lists, grocery, to do, and otherwise. I knew when holidays were coming and what had to be done to be ready for them. When we were traveling for a few days or a year, I packed for both, then for all of us. Of course, these things became more pronounced once we had children and there were so many more details to keep track of, so many more pictures to hold in mind, so much more money to be earned. Though I worked always, Tracey bore the brunt of supporting us. To date, he has never filled out a school application, scheduled a routine pediatric appointment, or helped a partygoing child select a birthday gift for a friend. Like many husbands and fathers, during our marriage he was able to handle discrete tasks, under direction. He could get tiny arms and legs into the places intended for these appendages in tiny garments, provided said garments were selected and laid out for him ahead of time. He could not do hair, but a child can get through a day with wildly disarrayed hair on occasion if necessary. Competitive with a vengeance, he could engage children in an exciting game of soccer, which he played to win even when his opponents were four-year-olds. On the other hand, he was, and remains, incapable of feeding a child within the bounds of any known civilization's notions of healthful eating. He could get a child to school or home afterward somewhere in the range of the accepted time parameters, but expecting them to arrive at either destination with all the necessary books, lunches, outerwear, and comfort objects was expecting way too much. ("Make up your mind," a preschool teacher advised me. "Do you want him to remember the kid or the teddy bear?") In short, Tracey could not do the things generally, if idiotically, considered hallmarks of feminine dexterity. He still can't.

There were moments over the years when I was aware that on a deep level things were not what they could be between a man and a woman, not what I longed for in a marriage. I didn't lie to myself about these feelings. I just consciously packed them away. If I wasn't going to break up my marriage—and I wasn't—what else could I do? When I imaginatively reenter those moments now, it's with a keen sense that if Tracey hadn't done what he did, I would have remained in that marriage, packing my longings away forever. Living a kind of half-life.

One of those occasions, particularly poignant, occurred during a two-year course of Jewish study I engaged in at our synagogue. The rabbi who taught the class gave a spirited and dynamic explanation of the traditional view of the Jewish wedding as a cosmic collision of male and female, heaven and earth, a generative Big Bang (sorry, I can't resist) out of which life begins. Hearing her describe this joining of masculine and feminine forces, I knew at once that she was describing my own beliefs. I felt the rightness, the sexiness, of this view of marriage. At the same time, I knew that this was something I had never experienced. Something I would never experience. I didn't say to myself that my problem was that I wasn't really married to a man. I just felt that something was lacking. I remembered being more in love in our early years, enjoying our togetherness when there was more of it. I hoped those feelings would return when children and work didn't so relentlessly crowd out the time and energy to cultivate them. But at no point did I kid myself that ours was the ecstatic union of opposites the rabbi described. I knew another sort of marriage. Compromise. You give up some things to get others. You build a relationship, a family, a life, on an all-grown-up acceptance that things can be good, not perfect. With the benefit of hindsight, it looks now as though I gave up the wrong things. I gave up too much. At the time, I understood only that I had never experienced the kind of encounter the rabbi described, and that made me sad. I didn't know that failing to encounter a man in this way, I would never encounter, never really become, myself.

Searching now for these "Ah" moments, I can find them. They were there. But I am wary of my impulse to find them. To say that they formed the only true texture of our lives, that they appeared in the gaps where two segments of utterly false surface didn't quite come together. That the story I thought we were living was entirely other than what I believed it was while it was happening. To say those things would be easier— cleaner, certainly—than to come up with a plausible story that includes these two opposing truths: Before and After. I want to do as Tracey's done and just call it all a lie. Asked by a friend how, if he felt the way he now says he always did, he could have loved me for all those years, Tracey dismisses the subject with a single word. "Testosterone."

I can play either/or, too. I can say Tracey was a wonderful husband, lover, father, friend. He was funny, smart, sensitive, supportive and caring, spiritual, ethical, creative. A man with whom I could share my deepest self, could envision laughing with and loving through the ages. Or I can say Tracey was a fabrication. A fake. A creep who—to quote a transgender information Web site I turned to early on in anguish—didn't want to be *with* me, he wanted to *be* me. When I sat beside him and our children in synagogue on Saturday mornings and read the lines in Psalm 116, *What shall I give back to God | For all God's bounties are upon me!* and thought they had been written expressly for me, I can conclude that I must have been seriously, sadly delusional.

Which is it?

What did I know and when did I know it? It's because I'm asking that question, because I'm digging through the past with the explicit intention of answering it, that I discover random bits and fit them together into a story about a marriage of uneasy compromise. A story whose known ending— failure—creates links between seemingly disparate elements. In my narrative during that marriage the bits would have lain where they fell. Remained disconnected. Wouldn't have figured at all.

I was certain that Tracey had made peace with himself. So certain that, about a year before the June night he told me our marriage was over, I did something I had never done before in all the time we'd known each other: I brought up the subject of gender. *His* gender. It was a sticky July afternoon. Tracey picked me up from the campus of a local elite college where I was teaching a journalism course for advanced high school students. Always on the lookout for things to spark their writing, I had brought my class to a gay-lesbian-transgender panel discussion. As it happened, the gay and lesbian speakers had failed to materialize, and the transgendered visitor had to carry the whole show. Afterward I'd gone up to him, an obviously male retiree in a flouncy dress, wig, and sloppy makeup who tugged at my affection and pity, to thank him for coming and to tell him that I thought he was courageous. Getting into the car with Tracey afterward, I described the encounter. Then I told him, "You could have chosen that life. You could have put me through the hell that man says he's putting his wife through right now. Thank you for not doing that." Eleven months before Tracey would tell me our life together was at an end, I said: "Thank you for choosing me."

Even before the obvious signs of maleness, Tracey's laughter disappeared from our lives. His funny stories, his verbal play, in fact, his words on any but a single subject. His emotional presence. His touch. That June I began to lose my husband. My lover, my best friend, the father of my children, the person who knew me best. The person I trusted and thought I knew above all others. I lost any sense of control over my life. That summer, to paraphrase Hamlet, time went out of joint. For me, the known world spun rapidly, crazily, into a chaos from which, six years later, it can still sometimes seem I haven't entirely emerged. While for Tracey, everything moved with excruciating slowness. His statement that he wasn't going to do anything didn't hold for long. His appearance began to blur, the man I knew not so much feminized as smudged away into an awkward and sickly stranger.

For two years we continued to live together, full-time the first year during Tracey's fellowship and leave of absence from his job, then part-time the second when he returned to that job in another state. Outwardly we were still a couple, but our long marriage and our family painfully unraveled. We entered into a battle of wills. We demanded compromises of each other that, in the end, neither of us could make.

Overnight, it seemed, Tracey stopped smiling. He no longer took pleasure in anything. He said he was ill. He looked ill. He complained of fatigue, stomach ailments, and dizziness. He lost his appetite and began to lose weight. I saw his suffering and at first felt empathetic and concerned. I tried to understand him. Visiting an exhibition of Aztec art with my son, I was struck by a sculpture of a young male warrior staring out of a feathered suit of armor, a body-sized

bird costume in which the boy was intended to go into battle. The slight figure stared out of the headdress of feathers,
eyes wide with anticipation and possibly fear. This must be
what it feels like to be Tracey, I thought. To inhabit a form
that feels like a costume. A second skin in which he cannot
be himself. In which he must do battle.

But sincere attempts to sympathize with Tracey alternated with bewilderment and rage over the close, secret relationships he'd formed with women confidantes, over his
insistence that his urgent need to express his femininity outweighed every other concern.

"I have a medical condition," he insisted. "A fatal condition that's going to kill me unless I get treatment."

"Who decides the treatment?" I asked.

"I do!"

It was hard to understand the sudden, dramatic change
in a state of being he now claimed was lifelong. Not to wonder about the timing of this sudden attack with the start of a
year off from work. (Coincidence, he claimed.) It was hard
not to see him in a friend's description of her husband as a
depressive who needed to suck it up, find the right medication, and do what he needed to do to support his family and
be a father to his children. When Tracey and I both eventually spoke with gender specialists, they agreed that his physical symptoms were extremely unusual to them. These
professionals who spent their lives supporting gender transformations had never heard statements like Tracey's, that
wearing anything other than a dress would cause him to
faint—or die.

The first of those gender specialists entered our lives on a
hot July afternoon that summer. While we waited for Tracey
to return from his initial session with the therapist he'd found

online, the children and I played in the backyard, giddy with mounting anxiety. Well, no. The children were giddy; I waited with mounting anxiety. As the big kids hurled themselves over and over off the low stone wall behind the house and the little one launched herself into my arms, maybe they didn't even feel the tension in the air—at least, not yet. It was still early days for that.

It seemed important that Tracey be received into the embrace of a loving family when he arrived home. When he finally pulled into the driveway, later than I'd expected, we called to him to join us in back. He walked around the house, grim, not exactly unfriendly but also not as though it made him happy to see us. "Daddy, Daddy, watch us!" the kids cried out just as they always did, oblivious or determined to be.

I waved him over and he sat beside me. "How was it?" I whispered.

"It was okay." He sat hunched over, staring at his hands. He didn't look pleased to be home, as he had in the past. He looked uncomfortable. He didn't join in the children's antics, as he would once have; he didn't show any pleasure in watching them. He still looked like himself, though. Blue jeans, white T-shirt. Blue tapestried ritual skullcap. Mustache and beard.

"But—did you like her? Was she nice? Are you going to go back?"

"Oh, yeah," he said wearily. "She seems great."

"But then—" *Then why aren't you cheerier? More hopeful, at least?* I didn't put those questions into words, but Tracey caught the gist of them. He shrugged. "Well, what does she think?" I insisted. As if he had presented a medical practitioner with a set of symptoms to diagnose.

"I told her I don't want to destroy my family," he said slowly.

I gulped. "What did she say?"

"She says she has no agenda about where I go with this."

I have no clear memory of the remains of that summer. But if Tracey didn't want to destroy his family, by fall he came to accept it as collateral damage. A fog of grief and fear—cold, wet, palpable—had begun to fill our house and thicken. With our very different levels of awareness and comprehension of what was happening to us, my children and I were lost in it.

With the support of his new therapist and his women friends, Tracey began to transform himself. For two years I endured the day-to-day drama, by turns infuriating, gut-wrenching, and hilarious, of living with a man attempting to turn himself into a woman. Lacy underwear and high heels that weren't mine began to appear, and the man I knew vanished. I slogged my way through the stages of mourning: denial, anger, deal making, and the agony that comes with accepting the unimaginable. I tried to convince Tracey that he was not a woman. When that failed I tried to convince him that, for our children's sake, he could believe he was a woman and still choose to live as a man. I reminded him of a Jewish folktale about a prince who believes that he's a chicken. Like a chicken, the prince insists on going around naked, scratching in the dust under tables, and pecking grain off the floor. After the series of unsuccessful cure attempts typical of such tales, a wise man convinces the prince that he can be a chicken who wears clothes and sits at a table and eats with a knife and fork.

"Why," I asked Tracey, "can't you be a chicken who behaves like a man?"

For his part, Tracey's perspective was that if I loved him, I would accept that a transsexual has to do what a transsexual has to do—and sacrifice my own identity accordingly. When he wasn't telling me that the person I thought I had known had never existed, he'd say that it was a sign of my limitations that I couldn't grasp the idea of same person, different package.

"After all," he said blithely, "the changes I'm making are pretty superficial."

"If they're so superficial, why do you have to turn all our lives upside down for them?"

Tracey was outraged. "The symbols of gender are the most elemental and meaningful things possible!"

Not so superficial after all. And that was the sticking point. He didn't seem the same. He didn't act the same, didn't sound the same. His values seemed to change along with his personality.

"What if you knew that doing this would destroy one or all of the children?" I asked him.

Ice cold, the man I had once thought a wonderful father replied, "I would do it anyway."

When I eventually got around to reading other women's accounts—that is, the accounts of women who stayed with their transsexual husbands—they said about their partners what my husband said about himself: He's still the same person inside. *Where inside?* I wanted to shout.

This argument reached an absurd zenith on the day he declared: "You only loved me for my gender!"

"Yes," I said sarcastically. "Since nobody else had that gender, I had no choice but to love you."

We fought. I pleaded. Our interplay, previously harmoni-
ous and full of humor, was strained and discordant, hostile.
Our once rich and wide-ranging twenty-some-year conversation about (almost!) everything shrank to a single topic. I
told him how much I loved him in one breath and attacked
him in the next. He told me he was the same person he had
always been in one breath and that I had never known him
in the next. We talked and talked and talked. In mounting
desperation, I came up with one metaphor after another to
describe his dilemma and the alternative ways I proposed he
think about it, as if I had found myself in a game of Extreme
Writers Workshop and the stakes were my marriage and
family. As if I needed only to find the right words, the right
image, to convince him to go on living as a man. He coun-
tered with his own metaphors, trying to convince me that he
could not. I made deals, or tried to, not so much with him as
with the condition overtaking him. Just as I have heard one
tries to make deals with death.

PANTY HOSE:

HIS, MINE, AND OURS

When secrets emerge like Mr. Madoff's financial deceptions or Gov. Mark Sanford's extramarital affairs, the partner suffers profoundly. Post-traumatic stress disorder is the result—being battered by unwanted intrusive thoughts about the betrayal, nightmares, emotional numbing coupled with unpredictable explosions, sleep disturbances and hypervigilance as the partner or spouse searches for yet some other betrayal.

—"The Clueless Wives Club," Julie Gottman,
New York Times, July 5, 2009

It began with a pair of purple cotton underpants. A woman's underpants. I pulled them out of the dryer amid the rest of the usual laundry produced by a man, a woman, two children, and one baby. I had never seen these purple underpants before. Tracey came upon me in the basement, standing before the dryer with them in my hand, staring at them. Trying to figure out and at the same time understanding what they were. We stood there, both of us staring at them, in silence.

"Oh, sorry," he said finally. "Did I put those in the laundry? I've been trying to keep them out of your sight."

"That's okay," I whispered.

This was the first time I had ever seen an item of female clothing that belonged to my husband. It was also the end of Tracey trying to keep women's clothes out of my sight.

I didn't want to see. I didn't want to know. Then again, I was terrified of what I didn't know. I was afraid of what might be happening behind my back. Of what others might see. Each time he did something new, something further, took another step, made another change, each time I discovered that yet another person had been brought into his confidence, I had to suffer all over again. As if it were possible to stop or even to contain this thing once it had begun. I wanted to understand and yet I didn't. Understanding meant believing it was happening. A kind of acceptance. I couldn't accept. I *couldn't*. This is one of the hardest things to remember now and to convey: the difficulty I had bending my mind around this thing.

Generally speaking, people wear women's clothes because they are women. Or they don't because they are not. I can't back my opinion with statistics, so I'm going to go out on a limb here. My guess is that few people announce that they are going to begin wearing women's clothes as a radical departure from what the world has known them in before. I'm going to guess that most people live entire lives without ever becoming recipients of such announcements. To date it has happened only twice to me.

The first time in my life I heard someone announce a switch to women's clothes, I was a child. I was in Catholic school, a Catholic schoolgirl as uneasy in the faith I'd been born to as I would later feel at home in the Jewish world I chose. The speaker was the mother superior of our convent. She came into class one day, presumably a stop on a round of visits to all sixteen classrooms in the school. (Did she repeat her planned remarks word for word from the two first grades through the two eighths? My class was somewhere in the middle.) She stood before us in the floor-length full-skirted habit of her order.

"Children," she addressed us, a thin smile playing around her lips, "do you think that nuns have no legs?" She meant to be funny, but Mother Superior was not a funny person, any more than she was a mother, in the least what is thought of as motherly, or possessed of any perceptible claim to superiority. She was humorless and cold.

We children, stony-faced, responded in unison, "Nooo." We knew that she had legs. Smiling her waxen smile, she told us not only that she had legs, but that we were all going to get to see them. She and the other sisters at the convent would thenceforward abandon the habit in favor of ordinary clothes. In practical terms, what she meant but didn't say was that the nuns would immediately begin to wear polyester dresses, and after we'd had some time to get used to it, they would go completely hog wild and appear in polyester pants suits. In metaphoric terms, what she meant but didn't say was that throwing off the habit, the sisters would reveal the female bodies hiding beneath them all along. Also the legs. Coming from Mother Superior, this abrupt uncovering of bodies sounded almost aggressive.

When Tracey announced to the world that he liked to

wear women's clothes and would now do so all the time, he was aggressive, too. He didn't ask. He told. He *did*. He assembled a treasure trove, a trousseau, of feminine things, and he eloped with himself.

> Currently surgery to remove the 11th and 12th ribs on both sides of the trunk is the only way to permanently minimize the waist measurements and create a more feminine torso. . . . To take measurements of the waist, the hips, the derriere and the breasts is very important. To appreciate progress, even a small amount consistently each time the measurements are recorded is very encouraging.
>
> —*Feminizing Hormonal Therapy for the Transgendered*, Sheila Kirk, M.D.

The unfolding, the ripening, that is female adolescence can be a beautiful thing when it happens to a twelve- or fourteen-year-old girl. When it is embarked upon by a forty-something-year-old man, it is something else again. Female adolescence was Tracey's way of explaining the process he had entered into, an umbrella term to cover the series of things he was doing to himself. Many young girls experience this period in their lives as hellish, and most adult women would rather shoot themselves in the head than go through it again. Tracey was gleeful.

I've been told that when it comes to gender transformation, it is easier to add than to subtract. A small-muscled, not very hirsute woman takes testosterone and finds herself developing biceps and a beard, hears her voice deepening. (This rule can be taken only so far. The adult female-to-male transsexual doesn't get any taller, and the addition of a working penis is another, much more complicated matter altogether.) Estrogen works as grow-potion for the male-to-female transsexual desiring breasts, but it doesn't dissolve obvious signs of maleness. Tracey had quite a few of these to get rid of.

The first and easiest things to ditch were not symbols of manhood. They were symbols of Jewish manhood. Tracey doffed his *kippah*, or skullcap, and the garment called tzitzit, or *tallit katan*, the ritual fringes that he had worn visible at the bottoms of his shirts at all times. We were not part of a religious community in which the wearing of these garments was a given. They represented Tracey's personal commitment to his Jewish identity. In a sense, they represented our family's commitment to our faith, because whenever I or our children appeared with him in public, these bits of cloth and thread told the world that we were a Jewish family who practiced some degree of religious observance. Who were actively engaged in religious life. Everywhere we lived or visited outside of Israel during the years Tracey wore these garments, we stood out in this way; we were different.

Tracey hadn't always worn these things. At a certain point in our marriage, he began to wear the *kippah* when he was at home, then all the time. Then he added the fringes. (It seems typical of Tracey now, a kind of foreshadowing of things to come, that he didn't discuss with me his decisions to wear these garments, not even to inform me that this would now be his [forgive the pun] habit. When I asked him about the *kippah*, it had already dug tracks into the curls on his head and I had more or less gotten used to it.) Tracey explained his decision by saying that according to tradition, as a Jewish man he was supposed to have his head covered when he said a blessing or any other kind of prayer. Which was why he had always worn a skullcap in synagogue and to the dinner table on Friday evenings and holidays. But in fact the occasions for blessings and prayers occurred all the time, everywhere. He had to be ready.

To be prepared, always, for holiness; to acknowledge the divine in a mouth full of bread or first sight of the new moon. This answer struck me then, and strikes me now, as very beautiful. It was also another foretaste: the explanation of a public gesture as a necessary reflection of inner being. When Tracey wore the *kippah* and tzitzit I felt proud of him, proud and happy that we were Jews. When he abandoned them I experienced a terrible sense of loss, the first of many. With this simple gesture, he was throwing off our Jewish family.

Outwardly that family continued. We handled together what we had to: home repairs, the scheduling complications entailed by three children. From paying bills to baking birthday cakes, I had always managed much of our domestic lives on my own. Now "much" gradually became all.

We had dinners together as a family when Tracey was at home, but the noisy conversation that once bubbled over at our table dwindled to a strained trickle. The children witnessed Tracey's undisguised misery, felt the tension they couldn't name. In Tracey's presence I found there was very little I needed to say. Once I would have chatted about work, the events of my day, the endless pleasures and concerns occasioned by the children. Now the stuff of my life, of the children's lives, never seemed to grab Tracey's attention. A single subject absorbed him. When we weren't talking about *that*—and we weren't, in front of the children—it was as if Tracey and I had nothing in common.

Female clothes—tarty and juvenile, conservative and middle-aged—metastasized in our home. After the incident of the purple underwear, our bedroom closet—for a time it was still, excruciatingly, "our" bedroom, until Tracey began sleeping in the living room—filled up with his women's clothing, side by side with his male wardrobe and the female wardrobe, mine, that had always hung there. His new things came from the thrift stores where he openly shopped for himself in our small community and from a growing network of women who saw my closet as the repository for their castoffs. Hanger space grew tight. My clothes were crushed into a corner until there ended up being no room for them. Tracey acquired garments from all over the fashion map, ranging from things (most) that I would know weren't mine if I was struck blind to the occasional item that resembled something I wore. I felt ill handling his women's wear, but sometimes I had to examine the family laundry closely to separate what was his from what was mine. He acquired a black T-shirt that looked similar to one belonging to me; I memorized the label in his so I'd recognize it and could quickly stuff it away. One day I found myself in a particularly agonized wrestling match with a pair of navy blue panty hose. Without thinking, I put them in my panty hose drawer. Then I remembered. I got worried. Took them out again. Scrutinized them. Tried to recall if I'd worn blue hose since the last time I did laundry. Put them away in the drawer with his (men's and women's) underwear. Took them out again and put them on top of the chest of drawers. I went through this routine several times until I finally showed them to Tracey.

"Are these yours?" I asked him.

"Yeah," he said, vaguely apologetic.

On another occasion, we enacted our bizarre struggle in silent pantomime. Tracey was allowing his once very short, mostly gray hair to grow out. It looked terrible, but of course that was beside the point. He brought home a hairbrush to use on it which he kept in the bathroom closet. On the day in question, he walked into the bathroom while I was combing my hair. He took out his brush, positioned himself next to me before the bathroom mirror, and began to brush his hair. When he was done he smirked knowingly at his reflection—as if he liked what he saw and at the same time as if sharing a joke with himself—and, after tracing an exaggerated arc with his hand, very deliberately dropped his brush into a basket I kept for my personal things beside the sink.

Such moments—I could describe so many, two years' worth of them—packed a breathtaking array of meaning and emotion. All at once there was the pathos of witnessing a middle-aged man—that middle-aged man being the husband I loved and had admired—taking pleasure in gazing at the woman he evidently saw when he looked at himself in the mirror. His satisfaction with himself. His in-my-face "I'm going to do this and you have no choice but to accept it" attitude toward me. The painful fact that such moments represented his departure from our marriage and from the person he had been, and that I was forced to watch that departure not once but over and over again. The terrible feeling of intrusion—violation will sound over the top but is actually closer to the truth—into my space, my privacy. Like a rebellious teenager, he wanted me to know: You aren't the only woman around here anymore. He wanted me to know: Absolutely nothing will be left to you. My basket of personal care items had become a public receptacle marked "All Women's Things Go Here." Like womanhood itself, it was no longer my domain. More than one would-be wit has quipped that my husband left me for another woman—himself. At moments like these, it seemed that he'd actually invited another woman to move in with us. A woman voracious in pursuit of my life.

We fought daily, endlessly. I begged him to stop or at least slow down his transformation. Tracey complained that it was already taking far too long. During one such argument, seated side by side on the sofa with all the children off in their rooms, Tracey suddenly and bitterly exclaimed, "We could have been doing this together!"

Now, this was an odd moment. Tracey was right. I—at any rate, a different me—could have accompanied my husband, been his guide, into the forbidden, longed-for world of womanhood. There could have been shopping expeditions, Henry Higgins–esque tutoring of speech, walk, body language. From the glossy magazines he collected, he'd learned that women, young girls especially, used clothes and hairstyles to try out different images of themselves. And that they liked to bounce these images off one another even more than they liked to bounce them off their mirrors. He wanted to become a woman, or at least learn to look like one. He wanted me to help him. What was odd was that I felt sad when he said this. Sad that helping him was entirely outside the range of possibility. At the same time I was astonished, given the well-known strength of my revulsion for his activities, that such an idea could even occur to him, much less that he would voice it.

I couldn't express the sadness I felt. By this point in our marriage's demise, such an admission would have been painfully personal, as only revelations between former intimates can be. So I expressed the astonishment. "Would you like us to be sisters now?" I said sarcastically. "Would you like us to be friends?"

"Yes." He nodded, not ignoring the sarcasm so much as butting against it. "That would be great."

If I couldn't play adolescent girlfriends with my husband, there were plenty of other women who could. In the endeavor to remake himself, Tracey found a circle of women to sympathize, encourage, and dress him. Once he left his laptop open—inadvertently, he claimed—to a message from one of them that read, "Your wife has to accept losing you." He reported that another had urged him to "do it all quickly!" at the very start of his explorations. Even when he was with our children, his cell phone kept their voices perpetually in his ear.

We had always enjoyed making a fuss over each other's and the children's birthdays. Roughly nine months into the first year of his transformation, his birthday fell on a day when he and I were home and the children occupied, so we would have some time alone together. Against the odds, I decided to try to give him a nice day. Since the slow morning in bed that would have begun such an occasion just a year before was no longer in our repertoire, I took him out for breakfast. The meal was strained. The food at a favorite café was tasteless. We, who had always talked and talked as though we could never get to the end of all there was to say, found ourselves unable to carry on a conversation. We stared at each other across the table, each confronted with a person whose company we had recently cherished and now found excruciating. Back home, I drew a deep breath and decided to take on the elephant instead of pretending it wasn't in the room. Tracey had told me he'd been writing down his thoughts about what he was going through. "Why don't you read some of it to me," I suggested. He'd read only a few sentences when we were interrupted by the ringing phone. It was the proprietor of a local florist shop, wanting to check the address of a woman whose first name I had never heard but whose last name was Tracey's. I fumbled the call in confusion. The florist was amused that I wasn't sure who lived at my address. Humiliated, I finally got it. A little later, a bouquet was delivered to the female persona whose name I don't recall but was something other than the name Tracey currently uses—perhaps he was trying on names along with different dress styles. The flowers had been sent by a woman who evidently had a thing for male-to-female transsexuals. Tracey had "met" her online; he wasn't the only transsexual in her life.

"I had no idea she was planning to send me flowers," he protested. "I just mentioned that it was my birthday. I've never even given her my address."

But he had called her from our home phone, and for anyone with caller ID, a published address such as ours was a piece of cake. Some months before, I had read this woman's postings on a transgender support site Tracey sent me to and found her odd enough to comment on in conversation with Tracey. He had agreed that she was weird. We had laughed together. The only thing he'd neglected to mention was that he'd been having a telephone relationship with her for months.

Passover arrived the following month with another delivery. My children and I, preparing for a holiday I was determined to make joyous, ran to the door to receive a UPS package of what we assumed were their yearly Passover goodies from their grandmother. It turned out to be a box of women's clothes sent by yet another confidante who had outgrown them.

From Tracey's cheerleaders I learned that in the new political correctness, female solidarity is out. A man in a dress is in. Among women who consider themselves feminists, a man who declares himself a transsexual trumps another woman any day. Women, feminists, Jewish feminists, rushed to embrace Tracey. I found it peculiarly painful, even when it was entirely impersonal. For example, later on, when the kids and I were newly on our own, we attended a dinner party at which a fellow guest, a close friend of a close friend who was meeting my children and me for the first time, was warmly sympathetic to our single-parent situation, the evidence of the children's traumas and emotional turmoil. When she got wind of the reason behind all the chaos, her sympathy stopped on a dime. About-faced. A divorced woman and a mother herself, she immediately began to moan about poor Tracey, "This must be so hard for him!"

A new twist on women's age-old abandonment of one another.

One of Tracey's supporters, a member of my Jewish community, would eventually sum up this perspective most explicitly. Upon hearing what Tracey had been up to with the children and with me, she had one thing to say: "He's a transsexual. Anything he does is what he needs to do."

Most people stopped short of actually saying these words. Instead it was the implicit attitude of the women who as-

sembled themselves around Tracey in transformation, their
hearts as stirred by his triumphant embrace of femininity as
they were untouched by the actual woman, the three children, in his way. These career women told Tracey, and some
would later tell me, that my wifely role was to support my
man's gender-bending and to get my children on board with
the project. My responsibility was to Tracey. Tracey's responsibility was to Tracey. In the Valley of the Politically Correct, being a transsexual means never having to say you're
sorry.

Tracey's ladies were a various crew. A few were lesbians,
most were straight. Some had husbands or female partners,
children, placid domestic lives untouched by chaos and
destruction. Some were considerably younger than Tracey,
some older. They were local and far-flung. What they had in
common was that they were certain they were right to urge
him on. The fact that Tracey had a family didn't concern
them. They weren't troubled by his state of mind, a rejection
of self I found scary. "Body hair makes me feel like a repul-
sive, furred animal!" Tracey exclaimed during the first
months of changing his appearance.

Not surprisingly, the fur was among the first things to go.
He shaved off the beard he had been wearing when I met
him at the age of seventeen. He shaved off body hair, taking
a razor to obvious targets like calves, then to the chest hair I
had loved to run through my fingers. While body hair made
him feel like an animal, his preoccupation with removing
every last bit of it—even the bits commonly found on
women—struck me as an eradication of humanity, not an
embrace of it. He shaved his forearms, and when we gathered
around the dinner table with the children, his shirtsleeves
fell back to reveal eerily bald, dead white skin, while on

either side of him sat our young daughter and me, our arms covered in normal fine dark hair that had never caused me to doubt our species. One day he came home with his eyebrows plucked within a fraction of an inch of their lives, a style choice I tried unsuccessfully to convince him no actual woman had made since the 1940s.

He paid for a series of laser sessions to get rid of all this hair on a permanent basis. This was at a stage when his transformation was still supposed to be a secret from the world at large, from almost everyone in our geographic area, and in particular from our children.

"Couldn't you at least have gone to a salon in another town?"

My distress shouldn't have surprised him, though it did, when he chose to have the laser work done in our town, refusing even to travel to the next one over. Likewise that he shared his plans for gender makeover with the staff there, including employees we were acquainted with in other aspects of our lives (by this point, were there any other aspects of our lives?) in a small community. Without the beard his face took on an angularity I had never noticed before. Had his chin really always been so sharp? Ironic that facial hair had been softening the contours of his face all along.

In our joint checking account, I saw that payments to a voice coach were being recorded. I discovered that he carried a portable tape recorder with him during solo drives, so that he could work on raising his pitch, eradicating the deep and melodious voice that I had always considered one of his most attractive qualities. I found this out when he let our toddler play with the tape recorder, a button was hit, and out of the machine came a weird, feminized lisp that neither the children nor I had ever heard before: Daddy's new voice.

Did the kids notice Tracey's gradually rising cadences? They didn't say and I didn't dare ask. Many men add or subtract facial hair from time to time, so he just told them he'd decided to try shaving. Neither the kids nor I would actually see him dressed as a woman during the two years his transformation took place under our roof or for many months after. We didn't have to confront him modeling the new threads, but I, for one, couldn't forget that they were there.

Panties that weren't mine were now regulars in our laundry. I also caught glimpses of their lace edges peeking out of his jeans when he bent over to help one of the children. By this point he had long ago stopped wearing the skullcap that wouldn't have sat well on his bourgeoning hair. The ritual fringes were replaced with a bra, whose outline was sometimes visible underneath his (man's) shirts. The bra didn't come of fleshly necessity; he said it made him feel better. Presumably the falsies I found around the house also made him feel better. The only problem was that they made me feel worse. Much worse. Again, I was like a woman encountering the presence of an intruder in her marriage in the traces of infidelity among her husband's things. Only the lipstick smears weren't on my husband. They were my husband.

Each of these things felt like exciting steps in the right direction to him, the direction of his true self. Each of these things felt to me like the willful destruction of a person I loved. One of the many metaphors I employed to explain how all this felt to me, not one of his favorites, was this: A stranger had entered our home, murdered my husband, and expected me to accept—indeed, to welcome—him in substitution. Good luck.

Again and again Tracey promised he would do nothing

further; again and again he broke this promise. To my anguished and outraged, "But you said—," he'd tell me, sometimes in anger, sometimes icily cold: "That was yesterday. I
didn't say anything about today."

Once upon a time, I grew up in an unhappy family. A normally unhappy family. No exploding skeletons. Just discontent, mutual dislike, a general absence of love. I'd spent a
childhood learning that arriving at one's own doorstep didn't
necessarily feel like coming home. Since Tracey and I had
moved into our first apartment together at nineteen, home
had meant sanctuary and affection. Not to put too maudlin
a point on it—*domestic happiness.* These were the connotations I had been certain my own children would grow up as-
sociating with family and home. Now all that changed.
Leaving the house felt like escaping a nightmare. As I drove
back up the curved, climbing roads to our home, my heart
would grow leaden, my foot lighter on the gas. During the
second year of our ordeal, when he returned to his job in another state, his absences for the first time in our long marriage meant relief. Alone with my children I could relax and
enjoy our time together. But whether I was out for a matter
of hours or Tracey was gone for a few days, I dreaded the re-
union, the changes that might have taken place while we'd
been apart.

Easily as painful were the moments when my mood was
lifted by a trick of mind or memory. Once I overheard him
speaking on the telephone in another room to an assistant.
Suddenly, mysteriously, I was caught by a feeling that had
become, along with my husband, a stranger in recent months:
hope. The crash followed hard on the hope when I was able to

put my finger on its source. Talking to his assistant, he had
adopted his old voice. What I would call his real voice. Or,
simply, his voice. The sound of his familiar cadences carrying through our house was like the momentary return of the
man I had loved.

Why did I go on this way?

Here are my explanations, my answers. I will try to make
them sound reasonable. I thought at the time that they were
reasonable. They weren't reasonable. They were decisions
based upon a bedlam of love, grief, fear, and rage—perhaps
I'm leaving out an emotion, but those will do—experienced
all at once and sequentially, over and over again in the course
of two years. I was standing on shifting sands and I kept falling when they caved beneath my feet. Falling and falling
and falling until I finally learned there was no bottom.

I have said, and it is true, that from the moment Tracey
told me he'd been thinking a lot about his gender identity
that June night, I knew our marriage to be over. At the
same time, I never believed that Tracey would actually do
the things that he proceeded to do. I never believed that he
would choose the life of a middle-aged transsexual over his
children, over our family. Over me. I thought that he had
made his choices when we married and had three children. I
couldn't believe those were revocable choices for Tracey for
two simple reasons. Because I thought I knew Tracey. Because they weren't for me.

When people ask how I continued to live so long with a man
who was no longer my husband, the truest answer I can give

is this: a boy, a girl, a baby, aka my children. Day by day and week by week, I begged Tracey to grant our children a little more childhood. For over a year and a half I put off telling them. As anyone who knows kids will guess, this ultimately proved a losing strategy, as their growing awareness, despite my efforts to shield them from it, that their father was changing and that something had gone terribly awry in their parents' marriage erupted in confusion, fear, and stress. Still I couldn't let go of it—the beautiful family I thought we had made, the *intact* happy family in which my children felt loved and secure. I had not lived in this family in a don't-it-always-seem-to-go-that-you-don't-know-what-you-got-till-it's-gone fool's paradise. I had consciously considered myself—us—blessed. Once, having lunch at a now defunct coffee shop in our town, I had looked from my family around the table to the street outside and understood that I had realized my childhood dream. I now had exactly the kind of family in the kind of life in the kind of town I had longed for as a small child. At the point I experienced this revelation, our financial circumstances were precarious and we did not yet even own a home of our own, something that was terribly important to me. It didn't matter. We had everything. I knew it. I didn't want my children to lose this family, this life that to them wasn't *a* life, it was life. I didn't want them to lose their father.

I took it for granted that if Tracey was really going to live as a woman, he would move away, or the children and I would move away, or perhaps he would head off in one direction and the children and I would take another. I couldn't yet reimagine my life alone with my children, but I was beginning to understand that that was what I was going to have to do. I was going to have to re-create myself, ourselves, just as Tracey was eagerly re-creating himself. It went without saying that I wasn't going to attempt a fresh start in the small town in which we had lived together as a happy family, passing Tracey on the street in a dress.

One night during that first year, something snapped. I don't remember what precipitated this particular crisis; there were so many. I only remember lying on the living room sofa after the children were in bed, overcome with grief. Sobbing. Realizing this was it—this was real. I had to believe Tracey when he said that he *must* live as a woman. That he wouldn't do it if he didn't have to. That his happiness, perhaps his life, depended upon it. Even if I couldn't understand it, I had to stop fighting him.

Tracey wandered into the living room. I sat up, pulled myself together, and delivered the little speech I had prepared. "Okay," I told him. "Go for it. If you know you really want to do this, go ahead and start your life over somewhere. If you aren't absolutely sure, go away for six months or a year and try it out. We'll wait for you. I won't even ask you to support us."

I expected him to react with appreciation. Gratitude. Wasn't this, after all, a generous and encouraging offer? Wasn't he relieved that I was finally giving him my blessing to do what he wanted to do?

Wrong. None of the above.

"I'm not going anywhere. I'm not leaving this house. I'm going to do what I want to do and I'm going to do it right here."

"But you want to make a fresh start," I spluttered. "We need one, too."

"You're not making a fresh start!" He was furious. "You have no legal right to the house or the kids. They belong to me. If you want to leave, go right ahead. I won't stop you. But you're not taking the kids with you."

I was—once again!—stunned. This wasn't just the first moment that I feared Tracey's intentions. It was also the emergence of the new Tracey, the one I would come to know very well over the next several years. The one who intimidated and threatened, who laid down the law and expected me to abide by it. If Tracey was becoming a woman, he had never seemed so male—a tyrannical bully he had never been in our marriage. His statement that I had no right to custody of the children or to our joint property was, of course, not factual. I suspected that even at the time, but it was said on the accurate assumption that I knew absolutely nothing about my state's divorce laws and that he could frighten me by saying it, even if only temporarily. It was a statement straight out of an outraged husband's playbook of the past. Spoken like a man.

Many conversations followed from that one, and in this respect Tracey remained consistent—one of his very few consistencies. The new life, the choices and decisions, were his. The children and I would live with whatever he decided.

This is the kind of moment in which a woman with financial resources would have taken the children, moved out, gotten a lawyer, and filed for divorce and custody. Barring that, a woman with parents or an extended family would have gone home to them. I had none of those things. I stayed. I stayed and continued to live in an agony that I shudder to recall. As time passes and I reflect on this period in my life, I understand less and less how it is that I survived it.

Throughout these two years, Tracey's activities and the demise of our marriage were kept largely under wraps. Loosening wraps. He told more and more people. I told a few. He was gradually feminizing his appearance—for example, growing out the hair on his head and removing the rest, but not actually dressing as a woman in our neck of the woods. That wouldn't come until after he moved out of our home, and neither my children nor I would be forced to confront him dressed as a woman for many more months after that. But in the second of the two years we lived together during his gradual transformation, he returned to commuting to his job in another state. There he could cross-dress nights after work. He'd come home each week after a few days away sporting his old casual men's business wear. Or sometimes he'd appear in a style best described as male-with-a-glitch—for instance, khaki trousers and a tailored shirt rounded out by a pair of high-heeled white patent-leather sandals.

Yes. High-heeled white patent-leather sandals. Very strappy. They affected me like objects from a nightmare, invested with the power to make me sick with fear and . . . well, just sick. Later I could laugh, sorta, about these things, at least when I had other people to laugh with. For example, after Tracey went public, a woman I knew slightly told me about a family member who had also taken a middle-aged shine to women's clothes.

"He had terrible taste," she recalled, shaking her head at the memory, "a terrible style." This man, my confidante's relative, had a chronic illness and for the last decade of his life spent his days mostly at home, grooming himself and making his wife miserable. " 'Why don't you wash the dishes?' I told him. 'You want to be a woman? Well, that's what women do.' "

Around our town Tracey began to wear gender-neutral clothes, which in actual fact meant female but not overtly feminine: women's jeans, a blouse kept zipped inside a navy-blue sweatshirt. He could wear this outfit almost everywhere because he didn't go out much. Our public appearances as a couple were rare, dwindling to nonexistent. He socialized very little on his own. In his life outside the house, such as it was, he went about looking pale and dreadful and speaking in an exceedingly odd high-pitched whisper, so some people concluded that he was ill. Others apparently bought his story that he was very tired. Continually tired. For months on end. But what were they supposed to think? The truth?

I wanted desperately to contain the truth for my sake and my children's, and the indications were that Tracey was itching to alert the media. By continuing to live with him, I could at least forestall the day he would appear in full female regalia in front of the children or in our community, because Tracey had grudgingly come to realize that for the time being, forcing me or the children to see him, as he put it, "dressed" would not be wise. Again, my delays were a losing strategy. Tracey was not trying out a possible lifestyle. He was making permanent changes. By the end of the first year, his most valuable beauty tool was a daily dose of female hormones. Which meant that he was growing little breasts. And though I didn't see for myself, my information is that the hormones also do an irreversible number on the penis, shrinking and rendering it useless as a sexual or reproductive tool.

It is inescapable: for me there is something slightly creepy and more than slightly sad about a man in women's clothes. Male legs in sheer stockings. Male feet in high-heeled canoes. A man's face coated with makeup, topped by a wig or feminine hairstyle. A man speaking and moving in a way that suggests not femininity but a man trying to approximate it. I think of the time I've already described when I brought a summer school class of journalism students to hear a transgendered speaker. The man, in late middle age, would never be taken for anything but a man, and I don't think he imagined otherwise. It wasn't about "passing" for him. It was about comforting himself. When he described how he had comforted himself by wearing a flowered bathrobe that morning, I felt sorry for him. When he described how he had walked outside for the newspaper in that robe at just the moment his wife's friend was driving past, I felt sorry for his wife.

Feeling this way, I am a product of my childhood, neither original nor alone. But I am hopelessly retrograde. Hopelessly, viscerally outside the pale of political correctness. These—admittedly terrible—feelings are not especially activated by male-to-female transsexuals to whom I have never been married. Gut-wrenching questions such as "What was I doing for twenty-some years of my life and who the hell was I doing it with?" are not aroused by the outfits of other male-to-females as they are by the sight of Tracey in an exact replica of a skirt that was once my favorite and that, yes, Tracey used to say he thought I looked so good in. It is creepy for one woman to copycat groom herself to look just like another, the stuff of thrillers. Creepier for a man to do the same. Creepier still if that man was your husband.

But aside from the effects of our personal history on my experience of Tracey, Tracey himself was not a poster child for the transsexual lifestyle as good clean healthy fun. He lied, he threatened. He sometimes seemed scarily out of control. Once, he arrived home late at night after several days away. From my bedroom I heard him burst into the house giggling and chatting giddily. It sounded like a party. For some minutes I lay in bed frozen with fear. Thinking of my sleeping children, I finally forced myself to go out and confront him. Lights were shining in the kitchen and dining room. The dining room door leading to the driveway was open and I could see that Tracey's headlights had been left on, the car doors open, and the radio on as well. I heard his excited voice in the basement. The evidence suggested that two or more revelers had made a dash from the car to the basement. Who had Tracey brought home with him?

No one. With echoes of Hitchcock's *Psycho,* I gradually became aware that the giggling and chatting sprang from but a single source. Tracey was talking to Tracey.

The next morning I told him, "I was really freaked out last night."

"What do you mean?" he asked me.

"I mean when you were talking to yourself like that! I thought you had brought someone home with you. Even once I realized you hadn't, I was afraid the kids would wake up and hear you."

Tracey was baffled. "I wasn't talking to myself." Either he didn't remember or he hadn't been aware of what he was doing at the time. Which was more disturbing?

Whatever else went on in the basement, one of its rooms became Tracey's makeshift boudoir. At some point he moved himself to the living room sofa and his fast-growing woman's wardrobe—the gauzy white miniskirt, the dowdy businesswoman's suits, the long flowery dresses—to the basement. His male wardrobe continued to be housed in my bedroom.

When he moved out at the end of these two years, that was where it remained, a collection of slacks, shirts, sweaters, jackets, and ties hanging in my closet, underwear and socks in my drawers. Beautiful clothes, clothes I had loved and in some cases given him: forest-green pleated corduroy trousers, a black suede baseball jacket, an expensive light brown shirt in its dry cleaner's bag. On top of my chest of drawers, two pairs of his prescription glasses. People generally take their clothes and their eyeglasses with them when they move out, but of course the man I had married wasn't moving out. That man was long gone. It was as if he had left the bedroom expecting to come back. As if he had died suddenly. These personal effects were the detritus of his life. Along with the now unnecessary falsies and the dozens of empty pill bottles I found scattered in the basement, the disposal of my late husband's clothes formed a small part of what I had been left to cope with.

GOOD COMMUNITY,
BAD COMMUNITY,
INSIDE/OUT

"So that's basically what's been going on," Tracey summed up news of work and family life in a long-distance phone conversation with his best friend, Michael. "Oh, yeah, one other thing—I'm a woman."

We gradually stopped socializing as a couple. The clumsiness of making excuses for one or the other of us—usually him—to be absent from any gathering was preferable to being in company with others, where I would find it excruciating to present ourselves as still married and Tracey would find it excruciating to present himself as male. We had separate friends the other didn't see. Tracey had many confidantes who were active participants in his life, as cheerleaders, fashion consultants, wellsprings of cast-off clothes. I lived with our ordeal in isolation for many months before I began to let others in, finally telling one friend everything and a few others something, basically that our marriage was a sham and that I couldn't bring myself to say why. There were people who considered us both friends, but by the time our marriage disintegrated there was no one we both felt close to, wanted to be close to, no one we both sought out as an ally. No one except Michael.

Michael had been Tracey's friend for over fifteen years. Over time he had become my friend, our family's friend, our children's honorary uncle. Because he lived across the country, he was long oblivious of what was happening in a marriage he had once admired, as he would not have been after five minutes in our presence. It was during that long-distance phone conversation that he first heard about the little glitch in his and Tracey's claim on male bonding. Michael's memory is that in the midst of routine catching up, Tracey told him, "Oh, yeah, and I'm a woman."

Michael flew out to see us. It was spring, roughly midway through our two years of post-marriage cohabitation. I wouldn't have any idea what time of year his visit happened if I didn't have the photographs Michael took and sent me after: the children and tulips, bright flashes of color against gray skies.

In a packed weekend he spent time with the children, time with Tracey, and time with me. Because he already knew what was going on and I didn't have to be the one to drop the bomb, because he had a better sense than anyone outside our family of what we were losing, Michael was easier for me to talk with at this point than many of the friends I saw regularly.

I took him out to dinner at a little restaurant desperately trying to pretend it was in New York or San Francisco and not on a sleepy New England main street. Over our inventive fish entrées I spilled everything that had been going on— from my perspective. Until that evening, Michael had taken only the trans-eye view of our situation. But now I told him,

"Tracey thinks I'm just going to go along with anything he does. He thinks he'll gender-bend at will and I'll bend myself around it—that we'll stay married!"

"I guess I thought so, too," Michael said quietly. "At first I was just shocked when he told me. But then I assumed you'd stay married and go along with whatever he wanted. I never thought about how this must feel to you."

Michael told me about an exchange he'd had with twelve-year-old Adam that afternoon.

"Have you ever heard that sometimes a man feels like he's a woman?" Adam abruptly asked him.

"Yes," Michael said. He'd heard. He waited for Adam to continue, but after a brief silence Adam changed the subject and spoke of other things. Michael was the sole person to tell me about this brief conversation. Tracey, who was present as well, never mentioned it.

Adam's remark shocked me. Did it spring from his observations? Overheard conversations? I'd been telling myself that though the kids might be aware that something was wrong in our home, they didn't know what that something was. At the same time, I was increasingly troubled by Tracey's erratic behavior with the children, and I shared some of that with Michael now. Among other stories, I told him about a recent incident involving Lilly.

"Guy-woman?" My toddler looked up, frowning, from the lunch I'd just set before her.

I froze.

"Guy-woman?" she persisted. It was a question. At the age of two she wasn't given to speaking in complete sentences. Something had confused, maybe disturbed her. She was asking me to explain it.

I had arrived home minutes before. She had spent the

morning alone with Tracey, who now bustled in and out of the kitchen, getting ready to leave, a little smile playing about his lips. This, actually, is how I always picture the Tracey of those two post-marriage years of living together: getting ready to leave. Sometimes still present in body, never in mind, enigmatically pleased by thoughts and plans only he could know. I looked at Tracey, waiting for a reaction to our daughter's words. He had none. He was oblivious to Lilly's question or was choosing to ignore it.

Meanwhile, she wasn't giving up. "Guy-woman?"

I had no idea what to say. I could only think, How does she know? She seemed to be troubled by something she had seen. I didn't say anything in particular to Lilly that day or on the several subsequent occasions when she repeated her question. I reacted with stupefied silence, then changed the subject, distracted her. Tracey was still living as a man, certainly in our community. It would be a long time before he would begin to present himself as a woman in our neck of the woods and even longer before our children or I would see him "dressed." I had begun to realize that I didn't know what he was getting up to when he was away from home. Now it terrified me to think I might not know what he was getting up to when he was home—and I wasn't.

I brought Lilly's question to the therapist I had recently begun to see. "If she's asking that," the therapist said firmly, "he's dressing up with her. There is no other possibility." Armed with this professional opinion, I confronted Tracey.

"Why is Lilly asking about a 'guy-woman'?"

As had become usual at this stage, he responded with immediate anger. "I've never heard her say anything like that!"

"Well, she's said it to me. You don't know why? You've never dressed up in front of her?"

For a moment, it was clear that he was about to deny that he had ever done anything of the kind. Then he seemed to catch himself. With just as much belligerence as before, he snapped, "Yes. I dress when I'm alone with her. I didn't think she would be able to tell you."

Tracey refused to believe that there was anything wrong with dressing up, secretly, in women's clothes with a toddler who thought of him as her father. With relying on her to be too inarticulate to communicate her confusion. He refused to hear the distress in her repeated question. Like me, he told his therapist what had been going on. As on several other occasions, he reported that she backed him up, condescended to me, and saw no cause for concern. "She said there's nothing wrong with dressing up with Lilly behind your back, but that I should just tell you I won't do it again if that makes you feel better."

If Tracey's therapist wasn't worried about Tracey's judgment, Michael was. The things he heard from me that night, the details of our family life that Tracey hadn't mentioned, made Michael concerned about all the members of our family. It also made him angry. In the property division splitting couples go through, the allocation of friends must surely be most painful. In our case, the political correctness quotient meant that much of what I had thought of as my community went to Tracey. In an unforeseen development, I got Michael.

When we left the restaurant that night and got in my car to drive home, Michael looked dazed by all that I'd told him. But not so dazed that he didn't ask, rather anxiously, if I wouldn't like him to drive.

"Of course not," I said. "I'm perfectly fine. What makes you think otherwise?"

"Just the fact that you had two glasses of wine with

dinner," he explained. "And that you've forgotten to turn on your headlights."

For the first time in what felt like forever, I laughed. Sober, if a bit preoccupied by this first outpouring of my private anguish, I turned on the lights and negotiated the country roads home as smoothly as ever.

The next day, the last of Michael's visit, he and Tracey went for a long walk together. Later, Michael recalled that Tracey took this opportunity to tell him that he refused to leave our home. That he vehemently denied the necessity for our marriage to end. Michael's concern for the children and for me would ultimately alienate Tracey and silence his confidences. But at this stage of the game, Tracey still valued their friendship and could view Michael as his, or perhaps our, mutual ally. Michael is a therapist, an eloquent and persuasive speaker. During this visit he had a profound impact on Tracey. An impact I can now see as a powerful illustration of the benefits of letting people in over isolation. (Okay, duh. But that was me: I needed to have this powerfully illustrated.) On our own, Tracey and I were going round and round. Deadlocked. Dead-ended. Michael was a bracing blast of oxygen into our stale impasse. He found the words to make Tracey begin to see our situation in a new light. He explained to Tracey that I was living a lie. I no longer had a husband or a marriage. I was outwardly still pretending that I did, and the pretense had become untenable.

"The outside has to match the inside." That's what Michael told Tracey.

The outside has to match the inside. With great reluctance, I was coming to understand that this was true for Tracey. In the Valley of the Politically Correct, it was a right that everyone would ultimately fall all over themselves to insist on for him. Michael was the first person to apply that right to me.

THERAPISTS:

HIS, MINE, AND OURS

Wegner argues . . . the loss of . . . joint memory . . .
helps to make divorce so painful. "Divorced people who
suffer depression and complain of cognitive dysfunction
may be expressing the loss of their external memory
systems," he writes. "They were once able to discuss
their experiences to reach a shared understanding. . . .
They once could count on access to a wide range of stor-
age in their partner, and this, too, is gone. . . . The
loss . . . feels like losing a part of one's own mind."
                    —*The Tipping Point*, Malcolm Gladwell

One afternoon driving my children home from their three
schools, we passed a billboard announcing: STRESS AWARE-
NESS MONTH.

"Look," I told the kids. "It's Stress Awareness Month!" I
began to laugh, helplessly and with perhaps the slightest
edge of hysteria. It was one of those times when everyone is
both smiling and looking a little worried about Mama.

I feel as though I could laugh that way when I read that

people going through divorce *complain of cognitive dysfunction*. Cognitive dysfunction. I like that.

If you have ever lost a longtime lover, you've probably had the experience. You're walking past a bar on Polk Street in San Francisco from which you catch the barest strains of a Billie Holiday song that is a favorite with you both. Your child says, "I want too much love." Someone tells what he thinks is a funny story about your ethnic group and expects you to laugh. You look up, physically or metaphorically, to share it—the look, the smile, the shrug, the memory of accumulated occasions that makes this moment mean what it means. There is one person on earth who shivers, grows misty-eyed, or clenches his fists just as you are, at least knows that that's what you are doing and why. But— Oh. No. There isn't. That person is gone. You catch yourself. You have to catch yourself. There is no one else to catch you, and if someone doesn't do it, you will fall.

Cognitive dysfunction. You lose your partner and your access to his memories. One day he comes to you in different clothes, with different hair, and in a travesty of his voice he tells you that his name is something other than the one you have always known him by. He tells you that he has been posing as your partner, a fictitious character of his own and perhaps your invention throughout your relationship. Tells you every memory you've stored needs to be rewritten. This person, the one standing before you now, who looks and sounds and moves in a manner that strikes you as being just about as authentic as a child playing dress-up, tells you: I'm real. The man you knew was not.

It's like losing a part of one's mind.

———

This, though, is what I was determined not to do. I hung on to my own mind, all of it, sometimes by my fingernails.

"You're sick," Tracey told me when I protested against any aspect of his behavior. "You're mentally ill. No one in the world thinks the way you do. Everyone else thinks what I'm doing is great."

"Well," I pointed out, "none of these people are married to you, are they?"

But it turned out I wasn't married to Tracey, either. That is, not to the man I believed I knew, the man who loved me. That man never existed. Tracey told me that the past twenty-odd years of my life had not actually happened. Wasn't the fact that I had lived a fantasy for two decades proof that I was insane?

When he wasn't actively questioning my sanity, Tracey undermined my self-confidence with threats and intimidation, chiefly by claiming that I had no rights, legal or otherwise, when it came to my children. After Michael's visit he began to accept that if he was going to live the rest of his life as a woman, he couldn't live it married to me, but he belligerently insisted that the children and our home belonged to him. He shook my emotional equilibrium by making and breaking promises about what he would and wouldn't do to his appearance, where he would do these things, whom he would tell.

For a long time, his bizarre blossoming took place in a hothouse atmosphere. In self-imposed isolation, I was vulnerable to his bullying perspective. But when he told me I should see a therapist because there was something wrong with me for not greeting his transformation with fireworks and confetti, I resisted.

When Tracey found himself a therapist the summer it all

began, I was frightened, as I was frightened by all the steps he took. I knew he would choose a therapist who was accustomed to working with transgender issues, and I wouldn't wish him to do otherwise. My fear in those first months when I was still grasping at diminishing hopes that he could ride out the crisis and reconcile to being male was that a sympathetic therapist might encourage him to feel that there was no alternative to stilettos and Wonderbras. At the same time, I knew that Tracey needed help. He was losing weight and complained of feeling ill constantly. He was palpably, miserably depressed. Occasionally he spoke of suicide, which was frightening even if it wasn't meant as a serious threat. He was on the edge and I knew the wrong therapist might push him over. He needed someone who was knowledgeable and compassionate, someone he trusted to help him sort out his feelings. Someone to whom he could speak freely and who could be there for him, without his or her own agenda. Someone I could not be. Tracey said he had found all this in the first therapist he went to see. He assured me that she had no fixed ideas about the feelings he was grappling with. She was there just to support him. Because of the concern and caring he said she showed him, I viewed his therapist as my ally as well as his.

I'm not sure when I began to have doubts about the therapist I'll call Dr. Q. That she was there for him was indisputable. At first she was there for him in their once-a-week sessions, then in phone calls in between, then in several sessions a week and phone calls that happened daily or more—I never got a final count. She saw him when he could come up with the co-payment his insurance required and accepted the beaded jewelry he began making, or nothing, when he could not. When Tracey reported that she thought I should have a therapist of my own, I naïvely took it as recognition that Tracey wasn't the only member of our family who needed support. What she actually had in mind turned out to be more support for Tracey, with a therapist for me acting as channel.

As I've already described, Dr. Q didn't share my concerns about Tracey's behavior with our children. She wasn't worried—but I was—when Tracey casually mentioned that he had sent photographs of the children via the Internet to a transgendered person he'd "met" online.

"You sent their pictures to someone you've never actually met?" I couldn't believe this was Tracey's—even the new Tracey's—idea of responsible parenting. "To a stranger? And now they're out there somewhere on the Internet?"

"You only say that because my friend is a transsexual! This is just more of your prejudice and phobias!"

"It has nothing to do with that! How do you even know the person is really a transsexual if you've never met?"

The next time he saw Dr. Q, Tracey reported that she had backed him up. "She said what I did was fine." Adding coolly on this and several other occasions, "She said I should just tell you I won't do it again to placate you."

Dr. Q became so involved with Tracey that I would ultimately hear through the grapevine that her colleagues were concerned that she had breached the emotional barriers usually thought necessary in a healthy therapeutic relationship. Dr. Q and I never met. Based on Tracey's description ("She's an ordinary middle-aged married woman"), I concocted an image of a woman with a Talbots-Burberry look, lots of plaid, short gray hair and pearls, and a trans suicide hidden in the family closet, maybe a son or daughter whose gender identity she could never accept and was hell-bent on atoning for. With my husband. With my family. With me.

Through Dr. Q—by which I mean Tracey's reportage of their sessions, of course—I began to experience for the first time from a source outside my marriage the curious pressure to get on board with the program. His program. Only a hopelessly conventional woman, the message went, would be less than thrilled to watch her husband shrink into a violet. It wasn't that conformity was bad. It was that I was to conform to their particular specifications. My job was to be his wife. To support him, period. To stick with him, whatever, whenever, however. It wasn't merely my own life, my deepest feelings, my sexuality, my very identity, that I was to sacrifice for his transformation; it was my children. According to Tracey, his therapist, and ultimately his other supporters, my role was to strong-arm my children into accepting him as a woman, not when they were ready but yesterday. However this affected them—not that this camp could admit that a child might have any trouble getting over the loss of an adored father and accepting in his place a cross-dressed stranger whose personality had changed more and faster than his underwear—wasn't anyone's concern. What mattered was what *he* needed.

In this bizarrely retro transuniverse, my spluttering insistence that I had a right to make my own judgments—what I quaintly called feminism—was the height of political incorrectness. For the first time in my life, I was landing on the right (wrong) side of liberal. Not long before our odyssey began, one of my children's teachers had taken the kids on a class trip to an event in support of same-sex marriage. Upon hearing that the teacher had received some nervous flak from the principal for this excursion, I'd written a letter praising the decision, and the principal had read it aloud to the entire staff. Now, expressing some delicate feminine reluctance—okay, I was kicking and screaming—to radically alter or give up my own sexuality on command made me a gender nazi. *I support other people's right to be in a gay marriage!* I wanted to shout. *Does that mean I have to be in one myself?*

For months I resisted their pressure—Tracey's and Dr. Q's—to see a therapist. I didn't believe I had a problem that psychotherapy could solve. I rejected the idea that my husband's desire to live as a woman, or my lack of enthusiasm for this desire, constituted neurosis, at least not mine. In the end I decided that I needed someone safe and safely private to talk with.

"These are people Dr. Q thinks won't frighten you," Tracey told me, handing me a list of therapists.

I didn't even bother to point out how condescending this was. At first ignoring Dr. Q's list, I began making calls, putting potential therapists through my prepared privacy drill. Obviously I didn't approach anyone whose name I recognized, but in my rural area there is never more than a degree or two of separation between any two people who think they don't know each other. I didn't want to see someone professionally I would then run into socially. I explained as much and told each of the therapists where my children went to school and what my Jewish affiliations were. They were patient with my questions. One who sounded nice was also someone I might end up interacting with in Jewish contexts. While debating the risk, I decided, in lieu of other options, to try one of the names on Dr. Q's list. As soon as I heard N's voice on her answering machine, I had a feeling she was my girl. When we met, I knew it.

After fielding my questions, most of the therapists, N included, had one for me in our initial phone conversation: "Why are you seeking therapy?" I refused to answer. "I know you may not be able to help me with my particular issues," I explained, "but I need to discuss this in person." At this point, eight to nine months after Tracey's momentous June announcement, I had yet to tell a single soul what was happening in my marriage. I had a strong conviction that saying the words aloud for the first time—breaking the silence—would be a powerful experience and that I needed to be looking the person I told in the eye when I uttered the words.

When we met, N repeated the question I'd declined to answer on the phone. "Why are you seeking therapy?"

I couldn't put it off any longer. I took a deep breath and said it: "My husband is a transsexual."

N looked startled. The subject isn't shocking in her neck of the woods; she's a transgender specialist. I took, still take, her reaction in two ways. First, as a mirror of what I was feeling myself as I spoke these words for the first time. Second, as a reflection of a thought process probably identical to what she would have gone through if Betty Crocker had uttered this sentence. Something akin to, Sitting before me is clearly the most conventional wife and mother in the world. Her husband is trans? Poor girl!

Ultimately, hearing my side of the story became part of a reevaluation of N's received wisdom on gender dysphoria. Although she wouldn't tell me this for a long time, her expertise in transgender issues—her training in the field, her reading of the literature, and her experience with clients—made me a challenge for N. Until I walked into her office, she had been in the habit of taking the transsexual's point of view for granted. Not surprising, given that it was the transperson coming to her for empathy and counsel, not to mention a psychological visa stamp to hormone treatment and gender surgery. For the first time in her practice, she was being asked to consider the ramifications of switching gender not for the person who chooses it, but exclusively for the partner and family members he leaves reeling in his wake. The people without choice in the matter.

N's clientele range from soft-skinned boys with hips who have never developed masculine personae to begin with to middle-aged macho Republicans agonized by their desire to dress up in women's clothes. It includes lesbians who have decided that what they really want is to be men, and among this demographic she has worked with both partners in couples, female-to-male transsexuals and their female partners.

Of course I asked her, "How do the women in these couples feel about their partners becoming men?"

"They usually hate it," N told me. "They say they've chosen to be with women because they want to be with women. If they had wanted men, they would have been in heterosexual relationships."

Some of the women end up leaving their partners and some end up staying, but none had a vote in the gender change and none would have ratified it if they had. Sounded familiar. Also funny, since I had it on Tracey's and Dr. Q's authority that I was the last pigeon-brain on earth to have trouble with her partner's gender makeover.

Talking to N took this thing that had consumed my life out of the realm of nightmare and made it real. Not that it hadn't been real all along, as N made sure I understood at the end of that first conversation, with a question spoken in the matter-of-fact, pull-no-punches style that was already becoming my lifeline into the future. A question to which I responded in the affirmative and with equanimity but that in actual fact skillfully sliced away the very last clinging strands of hope connecting me to a twenty-plus-year marriage even as it confirmed my sense that Dr. Q was not the agenda-free mental health professional Tracey claimed. I can still hear N's exact words:

"You understand that if he's seeing Dr. Q, he is going to transition?" she said. "You know that train has left the station?"

For me, Tracey was Tracey. I didn't know if or how he was typical of transsexuals or entirely his own . . . er, man. "Whatever I feel and whatever I choose to do about it is dictated by my condition," he insisted.

I remained skeptical about many of his claims but had no idea what was *normal* in the realm we had entered. N was able to offer me a perspective on Tracey. For example, whereas he had once brought caring and intelligence to the dialogue about our children that we'd begun sometime during my first pregnancy, he now had only one thing to say:

"What's best for me is what's best for them. The kids need me to be happy. They need me to be a whole person. When they look at me they need to see my true self."

Actually—wrong, wrong, and wrong. Children don't care about these things. On the contrary. As a parent, and in particular as a single parent, it is tempting to believe that what is good for me is good for my kids. Within tight parameters there is some truth to that. Put your own oxygen mask on first, airlines tell parents, and in our house the oxygen mask is the first cup of coffee it is in everyone's interest that Mama have. That's because a parent who is not conscious and func-

tioning can't meet *children's* needs. *Their own* needs are the
business of children. Their happiness, their wholeness, their
true selves. That's just the way it is. It isn't personal.

I reported Tracey's assertions to N. "Intense narcissism
comes with the territory," she explained, voicing an opinion
later echoed by others on the sidelines of gender transformation.

N said she tries to get the transpeople she works with to
speak about why they want to change their appearances,
their bodies. "Why do you want to live a cross-gendered life?"
she asks them. "What does being the other gender mean to
you?" Few of her clients are articulate about why they are
doing what they are doing. Over the years, she has distilled
what they do tell her to two constants. "What I've found is
that when women decide to become men they want power,"
N noted. "When men decide to become women they want
beauty. Both are envious of what they perceive as the special
access to these qualities enjoyed by the gender they weren't
born into."

When N told me this, I recalled an early moment in our
odyssey when Tracey said with intense poignancy, as if this
were the most tragic risk of his endeavor—as indeed to him
it may well have been—"I might not be beautiful. That will
be okay."

On the other hand, N had never heard or witnessed anything like Tracey's physical symptoms: his claims that not
wearing a dress in a given situation could cause him loss of
consciousness or even death. At a point when our children
knew how Tracey dressed when he wasn't with them, but
weren't ready to see him go all the way, his costume for parental visits—women's jeans and the like, no makeup—was
female but not overtly feminine. His now long hair and

pierced ears remained constants, his voice was the high-pitched whine he preferred. In other words, he dressed the way women all over America do to care for children. But Tracey said that dressing this way—not being who he really was, as he described it—made him ill. Dizzy, on the verge of fainting, on occasion actually blacking out. And suicidal: thus the threat of death. To Tracey, I think, this was proof that he was *really really* feminine. To N, it was proof that there must be something else going on with Tracey.

Many people who listened to me describe the new Tracey's unstable personality posed this question: "Could it all be female hormones?"

Like the laws that once banned women from giving (unreliable!) testimony in court, this explanation didn't sit well with me. I resisted the suggestion that to introduce estrogen into a highly intelligent, rational, moral being is to create a mental and ethical jellyfish. There was also the problem of timing. Tracey began to display dramatic personality changes prior to his first prescription. He has now been taking hormones for years and, like all transsexuals, will continue to ingest them daily for the rest of his life. Were the meds acting on him like the female adolescence he says he was embarking upon at the start. Do all transsexuals undergo radical personality shifts?

N offered a different view of hormones. "Apart from their physical effects," she said, "in my experience a man taking estrogen is likely to become more emotional. Possibly cry more easily. He won't become a different person."

But she added that she had encountered a lot of instability among her trans patients, both male-to-female and female-to-male. "Sometimes this is because they have intense fantasy lives and resist coming into contact with reality." N recalled

the sixty-four-year-old client who was dissatisfied with the
A-cup breasts his estrogen pills produced. N tried to warn
him that he might find big implants a lot weirder than he
imagined. He poo-pooed the warning and had the implants.
A month later, hating the sudden appendages on his chest,
he had them removed.

Did Tracey's unbalanced personality lead to his decision
to start life over as a forty-something woman? Or did he become unbalanced by suppressing a desire to be female all
those years? N didn't speculate about cause and effect.

One result of Tracey's transformation that took me by
surprise was that in the process of feminizing he began to
exhibit some of the aspects of femininity he'd once decried in
his family—namely, weakness, emotionality, and illness, particularly mysterious, often incapacitating illness. He suffered from lingering malaise and lingering doubts about the
nature of his ailments. He also adopted small foibles of (feminine) familial behavior with our children, such as offering
them continual shopping as a pastime.

Well, duh, N said—she said it more eruditely, but that's
what it amounted to. "When Tracey was with you and was a
man," she pointed out, "he was strong, healthy, and successful. Now he's weak and unwell all the time." On the other
hand, even N had no guesses as to why Tracey, bullying and
blustery, simultaneously seemed more male—more like his
father—when exiting our marriage than he ever did in it.

More important, I told N that Tracey said our marriage
had never happened. She was dismissive. Refreshingly so.
"Of course the marriage happened. It was a good marriage.
You loved each other and took care of each other for over
twenty years. You built a family and a life together. Then
Tracey changed. The marriage ended."

This statement gave me back my past.

The ending of the marriage didn't negate what had gone before. If Tracey needed to rewrite history to justify what he was doing now, I didn't have to accept his edits. It was my history, too. I'd been there.

I wasn't insane.

I don't mean to give the impression that N has merely served as a reality check when Tracey and transgender issues were at hand.

Trusting people. Trusting people to be what they seem to be. To mean tomorrow what they say today. These have become problematic for me. I trusted N when I was able to trust no one else. From the beginning I relied on my direct experience of N, ignoring the fact that she had been referred by Dr. Q and was intended by both Dr. Q and Tracey to serve Tracey's ends. This wasn't easy to ignore: when I started seeing N, Dr. Q took to phoning her regularly to complain about me and demand that she convince me to do whatever Dr. Q and Tracey thought best—best for Tracey. Her complaints dominated the twice monthly sessions that were all I could afford, squeezing out time I desperately needed for myself (while Tracey, of course, could rely upon daily contact with Dr. Q). She became increasingly intrusive and inappropriate until N, who considers Dr. Q a friend, finally had to ask her to stop calling.

N became not just the first person I could talk about Tracey with, but one of the first people I could talk with *instead of* Tracey. Tracey had once been my go-to person for chewing over (almost!) everything. From the quick chats about day-to-day parenting concerns to the rich twenty-some-year conversation about politics, art, and God. All the other conversations in between. A therapeutic relationship couldn't replace that kind of deep communication, but it could and did begin to fill the gap. And so much more: for the first time I experienced a talking partner with whom I had to hide not *almost* nothing but, simply, *nothing*. In contrast with the enclosed, exclusive, even claustrophobic rapport in which conversation with Tracey had thrived, talking with N led beyond itself. Became a model of openness. A demonstration of the possibilities for connection everywhere. Convinced me that I didn't have to be limited to knowing and being known by just one special person. Communication and connection could happen simultaneously with a motley and unlikely crew of disparate souls. Talk therapy indeed.

One of the reasons I trust N and one of the reasons I like her: She tells me what she thinks. She tells me things she knows I don't want to hear. She is not a therapist who sits in tranquil silence nodding sagely, smiling, saying, *Yes, you really need to look at that, don't you?* Saying, *You have to figure that out for yourself.* She thinks therapists who do that are wasting their clients' money and time. I have gone into her office moaning, "I want you to tell me what to do!" To which N has calmly replied, "I'm *going* to tell you what to do." And then did. This is real life, so often I didn't do it. At least not right away.

Among the things therapists do, at least therapists who have to answer to insurance companies, is diagnose. N would not consider herself to have diagnosed Tracey when she uses certain terms to describe him—narcissistic, as I mentioned earlier, also borderline (borderline what? it seemed to me that whatever Tracey was, he was it wholeheartedly, no borderlines in sight)—but I like to think of it that way. At some point early on, I saw the diagnosis of me that N was offering to my insurance company. "Husband a transsexual" is not one of the recognized categories. Instead, N had written that I was suffering from grief reaction. As with stress awareness and cognitive dysfunction, I found this phrase initially startling and ultimately helpful, even comforting. The phrase carried simple recognition of loss and simple recognition of sadness. Sadness it was quite usual to feel. In fact, when I looked it up in medical literature, I could congratulate myself that I was really doing quite well. There were so many symptoms of distress to which I was not prey, from breathlessness to loss of muscular power to inability to stop sobbing. Physical symptoms, behavioral symptoms. Occurring in the immediate wake of a loss or long after. Lasting a few weeks or years. Acute but normal, or pathologically morbid. In other words, have it your way. An umbrella called sorrow. What I liked about my diagnosis was not its specificity. I liked—I was surprised by—the word *grief*. It made me feel seen. Understood. Drawn into the normal human realm of anguished survivor-spouse. The way I had lost my husband, my children's father, was not common. The reaction was. Talking about the dead person might resolve the crisis. Alas, the diagnosis had nothing to say about my stickiest complication. The dead person wasn't really dead.

I didn't have an especially high opinion of therapists and therapy before I met N. I had very little patience with people who raved about their therapists. A statement such as "My therapist has saved my life" would have had my eyes rolling. Now I am one of those people. N has saved my life many times. Or it feels that she has, which amounts to the same thing. A religious person who takes the idea of God very seriously, I have been known to claim minor deity status for

N and to refer to her as a goddess, small g. At my absolute lowest moments, I have told myself that I owe it to N not to turn my story into something she'd have to chalk up to a professional failure. That may be a pathetic hook in survival, but survival is survival and a single mother of three will take any hook she can get.

Speaking of those three children. At various points throughout our—their—odyssey, my children have spoken with private therapists I've found for them and with counselors at their various schools. All of these people have been intelligent, caring, well-meaning individuals. All have attempted, under varyingly pressured conditions and with varying degrees of success, to support their clients—the children—while simultaneously coping with the fears and demands of two hyperverbal adults at war with each other—the parents. I don't kid myself. It's been rough. Rough on the therapists, I mean. (Even rougher on the children, but that's a separate story.) I don't kid the therapists, either. I try to tell them what they are letting themselves in for (me! Traccy!) when they take on any member of our family. It's like trying to describe combat to a raw recruit who has never seen a battlefield. We all start off on good, if uneasy, terms. Then one of us (generally Tracey) begins to feel that the therapist is siding with the other parent's concerns. Complaints and demands are made. The therapist, overcompensating, goes out of his or her way to show sympathy to the slighted parent, with the result that the other (usually me) accuses the therapist of caving under pressure and putting fear of the offended parent ahead of consideration for the child. Tensions ensue.

To the therapists around at the time of our divorce, however, nothing we brought to the couch caused so much as a butterfly flutter compared with their dread of the law. The court dismayed all the therapists with the threat of sub-poena. Evidently mental health professionals are extremely reluctant to appear in court and make legally binding state-ments about their take on the experiences and condition of a child of divorcing parents, thus laying themselves open to malpractice suits from any and all sides. My suspicion was that the therapists who had seen my children would have skipped town before allowing themselves to be dragged into court. It never came to that. My attorney's view was that having the therapists make statements would help my case and harm the children. (Tracey, perhaps advised that the therapists would not help his image, stayed out of it.) As mi-nors, my children have no right to confidentiality under the law. I could have given my consent to the court to subpoena their therapists, utterly violating their privacy and the trust they had placed both in the therapeutic process and in me. It was a no-brainer.

It will be clear from all this that as our marriage turned to dust, our ability to parent our children together through present and future crises disintegrated with it. It was a hope-less situation, but we had to go through the motions of doing something to improve our chances of co-parenting without acrimony. We tried to communicate about the children with a third person in the room, two separate third persons at dif-ferent times. At least, I thought we were there to communi-cate about the children. In both situations, Tracey was there to rehash our relationship. To make his case, as he was doing over and over again to me, that our breakup was entirely my doing and none of his. Yes. According to Tracey, "I developed an illness, or I decided to switch jobs, some kind of change happened in the course of my life—and you dumped me."

Again, N provided a much needed perspective:

"Tracy says I am breaking up our family, not him. That there is no reason we can't go on together."

"You can't just change your sexual orientation." N shrugged. She was breathtakingly matter-of-fact about it. I didn't have to—I *couldn't*—simply give up being who I was because Tracey told me to.

So we made two stabs at facilitated communication, one with a therapist, one with a rabbi we'd known and admired in our past lives as a couple. To call the situation with the rabbi facilitated is a bit of a stretch. Let's call it less-is-more facilitation. The rabbi agreed to let us speak to each other in her presence. This was her offer precisely. She would not counsel, mediate, tell us what she thought. Wouldn't intervene in any way except to hold a kitchen timer in her hand and try to get whoever was talking to stop when the timer dinged, signaling that two minutes (it might have been three) were up and it was the other person's turn. We went back and forth this way for something like an hour on two separate occasions. I remember nothing about the first session except that it was utterly useless. The second session was useless, too, but I remember the details. For that occasion, in the middle of a hot Sunday afternoon at the rabbi's home in our summer-deserted town, I showed up in a pair of my son's outgrown khaki shorts, a T-shirt, and gender-neutral walking sandals. Tracey wore a floor-length velvet skirt, a bodice-hugging V-neck long-sleeved black sweater, high heels, and lots of jewelry. This was the second time I was seeing Tracey "dressed." The first time had also been

our first meeting in court, and he had gone all out in an effort to rattle me (not hard!). My attorney had kept me as far
away from him as the situation allowed, had had me keep my
eyes on her and my back to him, lest I get hysterical or lose
my cookies. When she greeted me at the door, the rabbi was
clearly entertaining similar fears. She murmured, "Someone's already here," which would have sounded oddly coy if
it was not so obviously strained. This time, as I sat opposite
Tracey in the rabbi's small living room, there was no looking
away.

We were supposed to be reaching consensus on high-
stakes issues like child custody so that we could finalize our
divorce. Every time he spoke, Tracey made lengthy and
heartfelt statements about our relationship. I played it cool.
I can't claim that playing it cool is my usual style, but I
brought it off, to a point.

Tracey spoke.

I said, "Look. What matters right now is completing the
divorce negotiations."

Tracey spoke.

I said, "Look. We disagree, but that doesn't matter now.
We need to hammer out an agreement so we can go forward."

Tracey spoke.

I said, "Look. I've moved on. We need to conclude this
process so that we can both go forward with our lives."

Every time my turn dinged to an end, I ceded the floor to
Tracey. Every time Tracey's turn ended, he kept talking.
"Just a minute," he said. "Let me finish this thought." His
turns went longer. And longer. The rabbi started waving her
hand, a little more frantic each time. I tried to gesture that it
was okay with me. Let him talk if he wanted to. It wasn't

okay with the rabbi. Guarding our equal time was the limited role she had assigned herself, and she took it seriously. We were getting nowhere.

I said, "Look. We aren't going to work all this out now. Maybe someday we'll be on better terms. We'll get along, maybe. Not now. Maybe in the future we'll be able to have dinner. Maybe we'll be friends, even. Of course we'll never forget—"

That, it turned out, was the wrong thing to say.

I had tripped myself. I had been doing so well. I was tough and calm and collected, eyes on the prize of finishing the divorce, no emotion, no rehashing. And I'd said the wrong words and tripped myself. *Of course we'll never forget.* The *we* who would never forget, the *we* I had in mind, was the children and me. We would never forget the father and husband we'd had. The family we'd been. Even when we were all such great friends and had those chummy dinners together. I choked on my words. Everyone sat in silence. I tried to regain control. Failed. After a moment, I said I was sorry but I had to leave. I got up and left. I never heard from the rabbi again, and Tracey and I never referred to these two conversations. They had no impact on anything.

At another point, Tracey and I tried seeing a therapist together. We lasted three sessions.

"Can we agree that while we're in this process you won't do anything like take out a restraining order against me, or try to get custody of the kids?" Tracey asked at the outset of the first session.

These were actions that, amazingly enough, I might actually feel forced to take. To explain why I couldn't agree, I related an incident (which I'll detail later) in which he had terrified me that he might make off with one of our children.

"I did nothing wrong," he protested.

"I'd like to hear what you think," I said to the therapist. She demurred.

I insisted.

Under pressure, grudgingly, she said, "Ideally things like that should never happen."

After this session, Tracey phoned the therapist (without telling me) to complain that she seemed sympathetic to me and that if he saw signs of that again, he'd walk. He never saw it again. The therapist, a sharp and caring person, clearly felt she had to be very careful to toe his line thereafter. After two more sessions, realizing that she couldn't find a balance between us—likely more than any human could accomplish—I called it quits.

In a phone conversation following our final session, I told her that what I had needed was to hear her tell him: *You destroyed her dreams. You have to take responsibility for that.* He wouldn't have taken it in, I knew. He would have brushed it off as he brushed off the few nonprofessionals—my son, me, one or two friends—who suggested he take responsibility for what he did to our family. Still. I would have heard it. I would have heard someone outside myself saying that I mattered, too. That the children mattered. Saying it to *him.*

To her credit, the therapist apologized. "I wish I had said it."

What the therapist had said in that last session she had said to me. "You need to stop agonizing about what he does. You need to go on with your own life. You have to accept that you can't control his actions." Tracey would soon be leaving our home and going public in his female persona, something he had not yet done at the time in our community. "You can't keep this a secret much longer," the therapist told me. "You need to hold your head up high and stop caring what anyone thinks about it."

The freedom of *not caring* that she suggested—the possibility for a new life, a new *me* that it contained within it—rocked me to the core. She was right, of course, and even at the time I knew it. I also knew that I was absolutely not ready to hear it.

TRANSPARENT

What do you call a mom or dad you can see through? A
*trans*parent!

—Bubblegum wrapper riddle that
disturbed my eight-year-old

Last night Adam said that he likes our friend Michael
because Michael is "solid," that he trusts me because
I'm solid too, like Michael and himself. "Daddy," he
said, "is not solid." To which his sister immediately
added, "No, Daddy's transparent." Adam readily agreed
and they moved on, in complete understanding of each
other, leaving me sort of stunned.

—Journal entry

It was the kind of gritty gray winter afternoon when it seems
that there is nothing beautiful in New England. Tracey had
taken our youngest child out while the older kids were at
school. I was planning to take Lilly to an appointment with
her doctor later in the afternoon, and I called Tracey on his
mobile phone to confirm that he would have her home on time.

"Where are you now?" I asked. It was a routine question, and I expected Tracey to answer in kind.

But what he said was, "I won't tell you."

"What?"

"No, I'm not going to tell you where we are. I have the right to take my children anywhere I please."

Suddenly vague, hovering fears—that he would use the children to get at me, that he would endanger or run off with them—took on solid shape. Cold with fear, gripping the phone tightly in my hand, I insisted Tracey tell me his and Lilly's whereabouts. Getting no results, I begged, "Please tell me where you are. Where you have her."

Again he refused. "If I tell you," he said, "you'll just come and make a scene."

Me? Make a scene? The woman he accurately accused of an obsessive concern with privacy and keeping family secrets? This should have been funny, but I wasn't laughing. I was trembling. Though Tracey's recent talk about his rights as a parent—he no longer wanted to think of himself as my children's father—had troubled me, nothing like this had ever happened. I tried to imagine the sort of place they could be that he thought would trigger a scene. Victoria's Secret?

"Tell me where you have my baby," I pleaded. "I won't come there, wherever it is." I thought if I could convey my distress, I might manage to connect with him; with the old him, anyway. Like a hostage trying to connect with a madman holding a gun to her head.

In the end, after what felt like an impossibly long standoff, he grudgingly relented. "We're at the library," he told me. The library. Five minutes from our home. Of course, he could have been lying. But I felt at once that they really were at the library. This wasn't about hiding a particular location.

It was about power. The power to separate me from my three-year-old, something he could not do so easily with my older children, to make me beg even to know where she was. Of course, I wanted to race to the library and reassure myself. I knew I couldn't. Tracey might claim to fear that I would make a scene, but if I showed up having said I wouldn't, he was sure to make one. I pictured a Solomonic battle over my child, and I wouldn't subject her to it. "*I'm* taking her to the doctor appointment," he said. "If you want to come, too, I'll see you there."

I arrived at the medical offices a few minutes early. Tracey and Lilly weren't there yet. Unable to keep still in the waiting room, I walked out to the front doors. I paced the lobby. In a state of mounting anxiety, I watched the time for the appointment come and go. Should I call the police? When should I call the police? As he kept reminding me, he had every right to be with our children. By the time they finally walked through the door, I was on the verge of all-out panic. "Can't you imagine how this frightened me?" I asked him. I tried to reach him, to get him to empathize with my fear. I tried that afternoon, before the appointment and after. I tried many times in the days and weeks to come. I returned to this trauma over and over in an attempt to make him understand. He never did.

More than anything else that had happened up to that time, this incident blew away the same-person-different-package party line. Tracey was not the same person. Not the person I knew. The story of that afternoon became a kind of litmus test when repeated to others. It was the incident the therapist we saw together grudgingly admitted should never have happened. To my friends it was a dramatic illustration of the potential danger posed by an emotionally unstable father (transsexual or not) willing to use his children to wield power over an estranged wife. When Tracey came out to our Jewish community a few months later, I shared this story with some of its members who were determined to take his part. It silenced them. They were visibly shocked although they didn't come out and say so. They couldn't justify Tracey's behavior, but they wouldn't condemn it, either. They couldn't even offer me sympathy. To do so would have been to suggest that a man who dressed in women's clothes could do something ill advised. In the Valley of the Politically Correct, this is not possible.

Life in a war zone is rough on the noncombatants, too. All may be fair in love and war, but children have a way of suffering the fallout from both. Our deteriorating relationship took its toll on the children who lived with us, witnessed the fighting, felt the tensions even when nothing was said.

Nothing was said because I had no words with which to say it. Because I didn't want it said. For a long time I took it for granted that Tracey wouldn't want it said, either—wouldn't want our children to know that he was changing into someone who wasn't going to be their father. Wasn't going to live in their home. I cohabited with him long after I had accepted that our marriage was over to extend the illusion of an intact home for our children. I begged him not to take the children to the playground sporting an obvious bra under his polo shirt, not to return from a few days' absence accenting his men's clothes with necklaces and high heels. Over and over I begged him to let them have one more day of seeing themselves as part of a secure family that would go on forever. I thought he would want this for them, too. As with so much else, I was wrong. He was eager to share his news.

"When the children look at me, they don't see the real me," he lamented.

"Young children never really see their parents," I tried to explain. "They see their own needs and desires and the extent to which they are or aren't being satisfied. They don't care about seeing the real you!"

But Tracey was way past discussing what was realistic, much less good for children.

I had grown up with a mother and father who were unhappy with each other, united by a shared conviction that neither had anywhere else to go. I created my own family confident that my children would witness something very different. I had once thought my children lucky to have parents who loved and kissed and touched and teased each other in their sight, who thought well of each other, and who worked out conflicts to everyone's advantage. As much as I dreaded exploding their world with the news that we were breaking up, and why, I also began to hate the thought that my children would think that what we had now was a marriage.

Of course, it was naïve to think that not telling them meant they were being spared, that they didn't know—something, at any rate, enough to feel baffled and frightened. Signs of stress along the lines of Lilly's "guy-woman" worries were leaking out all over. Like lots of kids, they adjusted without direct comment to their father's relocation from marital bed to living room sofa. To a home that crackled with discontent, to parents who didn't look each other in the eye and never appeared together in public. Never touched. Unlike most kids, mine also had to adjust to the changes in Tracey's appearance and voice, his chronic unwellness, the stashes of women's clothes, clearly not mine, filling the house. My eldest began to blurt out bizarre remarks about gender—that is, remarks that might have been bizarre if their source wasn't clear. My middle child developed eating and sleep disorders. Even more pressing than the signs of stress, things were emerging that made me worry about Tracey's judgment.

He had dressed up with Lilly. He had sent photographs of the children to someone he'd "met" online. Now he told me that the pressure to appear male—what he termed "in boy mode"—was so painful that it made him light-headed and dizzy and that he sometimes briefly passed out. "I blacked out for a second on the way home today," he reported matter-of-factly one afternoon. "The car went off the road and I regained consciousness and came to an immediate stop. No one was hurt, everything was fine, but a lot of people saw it happen and ran over to see if we were okay."

"But maybe you shouldn't be driving the kids. Maybe it isn't safe for you to drive at all."

"Of course it's safe! You're so prejudiced you think children aren't safe with transsexuals!" Tracey was enraged. "*No one* thinks the way you do. I tell you this and you attack me! I'm only even mentioning it because the kids might tell you."

Then Tracey began to talk about his rights, a subject dear to his heart to this day. "I have the right to drive my children!" he asserted.

If I had to boil down my relationship to parenting to a single word, that word would be *responsibility*. Tracey's is *rights*. Some days Tracey said he had as much right to our children as I did; other days he said all the rights were his.

He had no intention of giving up any of his rights, including the right to drive them around (conscious or unconscious!). He was never going to move out of our family home, and if I didn't like what he was doing, I was welcome to go—provided I left him the children (he eventually changed his mind about this detail, influenced by Michael and by the realization that his freedom of gender expression would be entirely unfettered on his own). When he was out with the children, I dreaded a car accident. After the day he wouldn't tell me that he and Lilly were at the library, I feared that he might take all three children and run away. According to Tracey, and by report his therapist, my apprehensions just reflected a loopy bias against the transgendered. In any case, the status quo could no longer be maintained. Even I had to admit it.

Finally, eighteen-plus months after Tracey's original June revelation, we sat the older children down one at a time and served up the double whammies—Tracey, our marriage. We started with Adam, twelve, deep in preparation for his bar mitzvah, the ritual that would mark his passage to Jewish manhood. There was practically no literature available to us about the children of people who change gender and nothing useful to the parents breaking the news. What we could find we'd read, so Tracey and I had both come upon the information that our son's age and developmental stage—preteen, budding adolescence—were precisely the worst possible to receive this information about a same-sex parent. But Tracey was excited about sharing his news with Adam and didn't want me present to spoil it. I refused to be cut out of the picture. My own therapist and the therapist we'd found for Adam some months before in anticipation of this event backed me up, and even Tracey's therapist apparently advised him that this was a battle he wouldn't win. After weeks of wrangling over it, he finally accepted that I was going to be there, like it or not. I did agree not to say much in this initial conversation, to let him present his case his way.

We went together into Adam's bedroom one January evening. I thought at the time that I should write down the date, the date that my son's childhood came to an end, but I couldn't bring myself to do it. "Come into the living room and sit down with us," we told him. "We want to talk with you."

He looked at us warily. "Are you mad at me about something?" A heartbreakingly childish question.

"No, no," we assured him. We settled stiffly on either side of him on the living room sofa.

"I know you've noticed some changes in me lately," Tracey began.

"No," Adam said quickly. "I haven't noticed anything."

"Well," Tracey said, "there have *been* some changes."

We were convinced that Adam already knew. Knew but didn't know what he knew. It had been more than six months since the conversation in which he'd asked our friend Michael if Michael had ever heard that "sometimes a man feels like a woman." Much more recently, during an improvisational theater performance at school, he had uttered an odd, hostile remark about another player's gender identity that had caused a sharp intake of breath across the auditorium.

"I've shaved off my beard," Tracey pointed out. "I've been letting my hair grow out. The reason I'm doing these things is probably going to sound funny to you. You see, for a long time I've felt like I'm really a girl inside."

Tracey told Adam that though his body was male he felt as if he was really female—a girl, as he said—and that the

alterations to his appearance were part of a process of preparing to live as the opposite gender. Tracey explained at
some length—his feelings, his plans. He was excited and
happy. Telling Adam was the realization of a dream, and it
was hard to cut it short. With one statement he addressed
feelings that Adam, a male child on the cusp of puberty who
explicitly thought of his father as his role model, might be
supposed to have. "Even though I'm not going to be a man
anymore," he told Adam, "being a boy and a man is still part
of my experience. I'll always have that." To me, it was as if
my son's father were telling him: *I'm vacating the job of being
your father, but I'll still be available for consultation.* When I
recall this now, four and a half years later, my grief at that
moment wells up as if it could still engulf me.

As for Adam's emotions, he expressed none. Not directly.
He said almost nothing, asking just two questions after
Tracey had talked for a long time. Evidently struggling to
place the changes his father spoke of in the context of our
family, he looked at me in confusion. "Will you be changing,
too?" he asked.

"No," I told him firmly. "I'm going to stay exactly the
same. You can count on it."

Adam's face registered the reassurance and at the same
time the question it raised, the one he wouldn't ask in this
conversation: What, then, did Tracey's "change" mean for
our marriage? The second question he did ask, with a look of
utter exhaustion, was, "Could we please stop talking about
this now?"

When we told Bibi, some two months later, we sat on either
side of her on the living room sofa, just as we had with Adam.

Bibi, who was then seven, recalls this vividly. She says that her favorite thing in the world was to be hugged and cuddled by both Tracey and me at the same time. She says she thinks of this moment as the last time we ever did that. Though in fact she realizes that we didn't hug her together on this occasion. We wouldn't have gotten that close to each other.

Bibi also recalls a night some two years earlier when we were tucking her in together at bedtime. A school friend's parents had just separated and Bibi was shaken by this introduction of uncertainty into her emotional world. "Promise me that you guys will never get divorced," she insisted.

"We promise," we both said without hesitation. Blithely certain—at least I was blithely certain; if Tracey's story is to be believed, it's hard to see where his certainty was coming from—that this was a promise we would have no trouble keeping. Now, two years later, while Adam was perhaps subliminally aware of his father's steps to feminize, his sister was tuned in to the tension between us. Directly and indirectly, she had been expressing fears about our fighting; about our marriage.

Tracey told Bibi that he knew she had been worried lately that something was going on in our family and that she was right. Something was going on. Then he said the same words he'd said to Adam: "I feel like a girl inside."

Bibi giggled.

"It does sound funny, doesn't it?" Tracey agreed. "You've noticed that I've been changing some things about the way I look," he went on. "Like shaving off my beard."

"Oh, yes, I've noticed."

"There are going to be more changes. I'm going to change all kinds of things about my appearance so that I can live outside the way I feel inside."

"Really?" Bibi was surprised, but in contrast with Adam's stunned silence, she was also amused. It was as if her father were announcing an elaborate role-playing game and she was curious to hear all about it. Then she remembered the worry that had been nagging at her for weeks, if not months. "But what does this have to do with you guys fighting lately?" she asked innocently.

"Well," I said gently, "Daddy doesn't want to be a man anymore. He doesn't want to be my husband."

Bibi stopped laughing. To this day she describes this, quite accurately, as the moment we broke our promise to her that we would never split up.

In those two initial conversations Tracey offered assurances, said he knew Adam and Bibi might have many different feelings about what he was doing—anger, fear, pain—and expressing them all would be fine. In the weeks that followed, the children did have a range of feelings—anger, fear, pain—and went about expressing them all with punches and kicks and a noticeable lack of subtlety. Tracey was stunned. He had been so sure the children would share his joy. Fortunately, he knew whom to blame for their distress. Long before, he'd told me that a father's gender-bending didn't trouble children unless their mothers conveyed that there was something wrong with it: it was always the mother's fault. Sound familiar? Mothers have been blamed for everything under the sun. Though Tracey presented his argument as psychological opinion, my therapist scoffed and my common sense told me it was hooey. Tracey was going to do what he wanted to do. Why couldn't he simply own up to the effect on his children?

The kids' right to free expression turned out to be as revocable as our marriage vows. One Saturday morning a few weeks after Adam and Bibi were both in the know about what was going on, Tracey walked into the kitchen and announced, "I want to have a family conference."

The children and I were in the middle of a pleasant and relaxed breakfast, but suddenly the meal was no longer palatable. We abandoned our plates and followed Tracey into the living room.

"I can't believe the way I'm being treated by this family," Tracey seethed. "I'm sick! I'm very, very sick, and instead of supporting me you're all angry. You're abusing me! You should be accepting that whatever I do is what I need to do to treat my condition. Anything else is the moral equivalent to denying chemotherapy to a cancer patient."

I was astonished. Until now I had thought that Tracey would be reluctant to risk alienating the children. That he would conceal his anger at me, not widen its scope to include them. That he would keep to himself his view that he was critically ill. How much did the children get out of his statement? Bibi, not much. She kept out of the conversation and slipped off to her room as soon as she could. Lilly, nothing. She ran around the living room with her toys, watching our faces, knowing only that the nice Shabbat mood we'd been enjoying was at an end and no one wanted to play. Adam, too much. His father was angry. For the first time, but not, alas, the last, he knew the experience of being pulled in two directions by competing loyalties, to his father and to me. During the "conference," which went on for hours, he came up with a procedure to resolve our family conflicts. "Let's have a trial!" He brought out a little videocamera someone had given him and asked Tracey and me to state our cases:

testimony. I didn't want my son to film me listing griev-
ances. Tracey did. When Tracey talked to Adam's camera, I
heard for the first time the statement about our marriage
that he would later make in a different context to me: "For
me divorce has always been an option." It was also the first
time he uttered a question he would repeat many times in
future. "Why," he asked with pathos and bewilderment,
"aren't you celebrating the new life that is unfolding for me?"

My children's experience of Tracey's transformation and the
breakup of our marriage is hands down the ugliest and most
painful aspect of this story. It is when I confront what my
children have gone through that I find it hardest to forgive
Tracey. Not just for deciding to do what he's done, but for
many smaller decisions about how to do it along the way. For
his refusal to admit responsibility for his actions' impact on
the children's lives. I have no hesitation about my responsibility: I blame myself for my children's anguish. When the
ground our family stood on started quaking, keeping our
children away from the fault lines turned out to be a lot
harder than I had ever imagined.

Adam's bar mitzvah took place the very day he turned
thirteen. Some thirteen-year-olds look like children when
they wrap themselves in a tallith, a prayer shawl, for the first
time, climb the steps to the bimah, the raised platform from
which the Torah scroll is read, and assume the starring role in
this peculiarly American Jewish coming-of-age drama. A
year before, Adam had been singing a part for a boy soprano
in a local composer's opera. In the months before his thir-
teenth birthday, his voice plummeted. He grew several inches,
facial hair appeared. He was informed that a few weeks after

this celebration of his Jewish manhood, his father would move out of our home and stop calling himself a man. Adam didn't look or sound like a child that spring day. He did the things bar and bat mitzvah kids do, chanting from the Torah and delivering a talk he had written. Somewhat unusually, he and I led the entire service together, something neither of us had ever done before. We practiced for weeks. The hours we spent singing together during that last hellish stretch of cohabitation with Tracey kept me sane. They gave me joy. The only joy I had known for a very long time.

Tracey played no role in the day, just as he had played no role in handling the many details of preparing for it. He told me he was furious that he would not be attending his son's bar mitzvah in a dress. He said the lack of a dress would likely cause him to take ill or faint during the service, and he threatened to make a scene in the synagogue. Despite everything, I was astounded that Tracey didn't feel he owed Adam better. He said this day was as much about him—Tracey— as it was about Adam. I thought the day was about God, Torah, and several thousand years of Jewish history, and Adam's embrace of all three. The Tracey of the past would have agreed with me. In the end, for our last public occasion as a family, Tracey was a silent, ghostly presence. The rabbi and some of the friends who came that day knew what was going on. Other friends, Tracey's mother, our Jewish community, did not. Because we had stopped going out together or doing things as a family so long before, a few of my friends had never met Tracey and couldn't believe that I was married, could ever have been married, to this person. People who'd known him in the past and hadn't seen him for a while were shocked by his pale withdrawal. Some thought, not incorrectly, that he was dying.

It was a Tracey reborn who loaded up his car and said good-bye to his children a month later. This Tracey was upbeat and energetic, eager to set off on his new life adventure. He had rented a room in a house in another town, and we'd vaguely agreed that he would visit with the children several afternoons a week during the summer. I sat at my computer, trying to keep my eyes and my mind on the dull editing job before me, crying unobtrusively. The children ran manically in and out of the house, confused. Their father moving out was a bad thing, right? But he looked so happy! A moment after we thought he'd gone, he burst back into the house.

"Come out, quick!" he urged. "Come see what's happening! This is amazing!"

I followed the kids out the door and down the driveway to see the fascinating thing happening behind the car Tracey was about to drive away from our lives in. A midsize snake was swallowing a large live frog whole. The children were horrified. I thought I was going to be sick. Tracey was gleeful. The snake and the frog were like characters out of a folktale: evil swallowing good. Was this really the symbol of him leaving them that he wanted the children to carry into the rest of their lives?

It was. A year later, I would overhear him remind them that it was the first anniversary of his moving out. "Remember the snake swallowing the frog?" he gushed. As if a rainbow had appeared in the sky.

LAST KISS

Two weeks after Tracey moved out, I had a birthday, not the best one I can recall. A friend brought me flowers and chocolates shaped like frogs wearing tiny crowns.

"Because," she said, "you married the prince who turned into a frog."

When I think of our intimate relationship at its best—say, making love on the rug in front of the fireplace the winter we lived in Oregon, as we spent any number of evenings after our older children were in bed and where we conceived our youngest child—I see it in hazy, soft focus. I see the flames, the glow of firelight. I don't feel the heat. I don't taste raw sexual desire. I don't hear—anything. Tracey didn't talk, during or about sex. Talk about sex made him uncomfortable. Because he didn't, I didn't.

During one of our early conversations about his relationship to his body the summer our lives unraveled, I blurted out, apropos of nothing, that when we got together in our late teens I expected him to relax over time. "I thought you'd get more comfortable and eventually we'd be able to talk about sex the way I did with my friends and boyfriends in high school. I waited for it to happen. But it never did happen. You never relaxed. After a while I realized that we would never have that kind of openness. It made me sad, but I accepted it. I gave up on it. I stopped waiting."

Having blurted this out, I felt confused. I added, "I don't know why I said that."

Tracey nodded.

For me this felt like a major admission. Even to say we didn't talk about sex was talking about sex. It felt taboo to say it. To admit there had been a barrier all along in our relationship. To say what amounted to: *You're sexually uptight.* If our marriage had been a place where Tracey's true gender identity went unrecognized, it had also been a place where my sexuality had not found full expression.

I don't know what Tracey thought of this because he didn't say anything. It didn't seem to make him uncomfortable or defensive. On the contrary. If it made any impression at all, it would have bolstered his argument that he had in some way never been present in our marriage. It could have made him feel that he had failed me, but failing me was no longer his concern. Much less to his liking was another conversation in which I protested that he had been an obviously willing partner in an active intimate relationship with me for over twenty years, that it wasn't hard to tell when a man didn't wish to engage sexually with a woman, and that such indicators had never occurred between our sheets. Tracey didn't want to hear that sort of observation. The reality that he had noticeably been with me *as a man* for over twenty years didn't fit into his new story about himself.

In truth, I don't think any of this much mattered one way or the other. To Tracey, that is. It mattered to me. I was caught up in parsing our relationship. Tracey was busy re-creating Tracey. What did the man he had been for over forty years have to do with that?

The way Tracey saw it, he was changing one little rule of play (his gender) and I was running away from the game. My sexuality was not at issue. That is, not for Tracey. His vague implication was that we'd work things out in bed—or not. Tracey offered as a model a woman he'd heard about who stayed with her trans husband and gave up on intimacy alto-gether, inside or outside of the marriage.

"Why couldn't we continue to live together like that couple?" he wanted to know.

"What if you decide you don't want to be with a woman?" I asked him. "What if you end up wanting a man?" I had read that the post-operative sexuality of transsexuals is dif-ficult to predict, with roughly a third continuing to be at-tracted to the gender they were always attracted to, a third switching gears, and a third having no sexual inclinations whatsoever. "What if I bend and twist and wrap myself around this thing just to stay with you and in the end you don't want me?"

Tracey smiled and without hesitation said, in a bemused tone, the words he'd already said to our son: "Of course, di-vorce is always an option."

My therapist, herself a lesbian, assured me that my sexu-ality was not something I could switch on demand. My feeling was that if I had been a lesbian, I would have been a lesbian—I wouldn't have been with a man. And if I did want to be with a woman, then I would want to be with a woman— and that was what Tracey was not. Though it proved remarkably difficult for me to do it, at some point in this process I had to admit to myself that Tracey was no longer a man. He also wasn't, for me never will be, a woman.

So why couldn't I just give up on a sexual life for the sake of an intact family? Though usually for different reasons, people do it every day. There's a lot of support for giving up on one's sexuality, as a woman, as a married woman, as a long-married woman. There is very little support, very few models, for not giving up. I myself had relinquished the hope of the kind of intimate connection, communication, passion, that I knew on some not quite conscious level I really wanted and was capable of. That should have made it easier to give up on sexuality altogether. Shouldn't it? But it didn't. Maybe I'd given up too much, too easily, without anyone asking. Now someone was asking.

I've always had a problem with people telling me to give up. Telling me that wanting something I want is wanting too much. I'm not talking about wanting the moon and I'm not talking about wanting a Porsche, not that there is anything wrong with wanting the moon or a Porsche, these just don't happen to be the sorts of wants I'm talking about here. I'm talking about wanting something that is elemental, something that, when I look around me, is quite ordinary to want and indeed to have—for other people. I grew up working class, and my parents did not have upwardly mobile dreams for their daughter. They didn't get why I needed to go college. If I had to go, what was wrong with secretarial courses at a local community college? "Why isn't that good enough for you?" My parents couldn't understand ambition as a driving force, a force to which things like pessimism are sacrificed. There were family stories—to be sure these were short stories—of relinquished dreams in both their distant pasts. They were only telling me that I didn't need what they had shelved themselves.

Tracey turned everything in our lives upside down and inside out to get what he wanted. To be himself, he said. So it's ironic that he expected me to . . . er, cut off an essential part of myself, leave behind a vital part of life, in order to stay with him. But another way to look at it is that Tracey was asking me to give up on something that at this point he didn't feel the necessity for himself. I realize this now. He had lost what sex drive he'd once had. Sexuality is lodged in the body, and Tracey was an unhappy camper in his. He had probably never been a fully realized sexual being. He had ceased to be a partial one. He couldn't understand sex.

None of my friends have had even remote experience of anything like my specific situation, but for a long while it wouldn't have mattered if they had—I couldn't bring myself to tell anyone anything anyhow. Knowing no one who'd been where I was, I went where everyone in need of information about (or fellow sufferers of) anything goes these days: online. At first I found nothing but sites advising men about where they could find women's shoes and hosiery to fit them. Then I tried a site where transsexuals and their family members communicated with one another. For a while I read the postings on the bulletin board for people who had been known as husbands and wives before being reduced to significant others, then further marked down to "SOs." Actually, "SO?" seemed an apt designation for my role. With the exception of a single, elderly man, all the participants were women. In a fringe twist on "Stand by Your Man" (Even When He Isn't One), the women told themselves and one another that they owed it to their spouses to eat whatever was dished out. Yes, their husbands were putting them through hell. Yes, they seemed to care only for themselves. Yes, they could be emotionally abusive. But didn't their husbands really have it much worse? Wasn't it a wife's job to be supportive—no matter what? One woman protested that she couldn't stay with her husband, he'd told her that he was really a heterosexual woman and planned to look for a man after the great transformation. From a fellow sufferer she got this response: Stay with him anyway. Huh? I wanted to tell them, *Stop taking this on yourself!* But I never entered the fray. Not just because they wouldn't want to hear what I had to say. The almost unendurable grief they described was too familiar. And who was I, after swearing no more, no more, to tell anyone else when it was time to move on?

When I did start talking with friends about Tracey and the how and why of ending our marriage, no one said, *Oh really? Guess what: My husband wears lace panties, too!* Not one. But when I talked about the impossibility of remaining in a loveless, sexless marriage, of my astonishment that he would expect this of me, friends—mostly but not exclusively women—had stories to share.

"My husband and I don't sleep in the same bed," more than one friend confided. "We have separate bedrooms and once in a while when we feel like spending a night together, we do."

"My wife and I don't have a sexual relationship," another friend told me.

"We haven't had a sexual relationship in years," confessed others.

No one ever said: *I don't have a passionate relationship—*

why should you? Nevertheless, these kinds of admissions from friends made me sad. They made me uncomfortable about insisting on having a romantic, sexual marriage or not having one at all.

"Wow," a friend mused one day. "I don't know what I would do if I loved my husband and he did something like this."

I laughed, shocked, and gave her a do-you-realize-the-first-part-of-what-you-said look. But she was fully conscious of what she had said, and she meant it. She and her husband get on reasonably well and neither is looking for an exit out of the marriage. But it isn't love. She makes no pretense that it is. Nevertheless, she was able to look at me, at my marriage, to hear what I was saying. She got it. My marriage was about love. It certainly was for me.

This was a small, important moment with one of the first friends I told the truth about my marriage. My friend responded empathetically even though my take on marriage is so different from her own. Not everyone needs sex or romance. Not everyone wants them. But there are times when I'm urged to pour my passions entirely into my children or to cultivate my friendships and leave men behind, and I know the advice isn't about me. It's about what the person pressing it has given up. I don't hear this from friends who are sexually and romantically engaged or who've made peace with their lack of engagement. It takes a generosity of spirit to meet a friend where she is, rather than where you are coming from, rather than where you want her to be. Judaism teaches that God pulls it off every time. Therapists are supposed to be capable of this kind of emotional omnipotence, but most probably aren't. (I'm lucky, mine seems to be.) The rest of us have to strive to be there.

My friend's matter-of-fact revelation about her marriage

was painful. It's the kind of thing that I almost never used to know about my friends and that I now hear about all the time. I've been offered so many such glimpses into my friends' intimate lives that I've come to feel that good marriages are not the norm. At my blackest moments, I've wondered how it is that people can exuberantly, extravagantly celebrate weddings that set the happy couple off on a path that will likely end in a place with which I'm now all too familiar— divorce court. This doesn't mean I'm antimarriage. After a period of disillusion, I am, alas, more of a romantic than ever.

In the good times, once in a while I used to dream of losing Tracey, and we would laugh together at my fears. The scenarios proposed by my sleeping mind of a Tracey coldly indifferent or unfaithful struck the real man as so absurd that he couldn't even take them seriously. Which was, of course, reassuring. Then, during the two years when reality became nightmare, I occasionally had cruelly happy dreams that Tracey came back to me. In his old face and his old clothes, that's what he'd say: "I've come back to you." I'd wake to the knowledge that this person was dead. I had to retrain my thoughts, even my sleeping thoughts. I had to leave him behind. After a while I stopped dreaming of Tracey. I stopped dreaming. I slept very little. One day I was visited by a waking specter, the image of a face, eager, receptive, open, full of laughter and compassion. The face of the friend I wished I could tell what had happened to my life, the one who would understand what this loss meant for me. His face. Gone forever.

Serving witness to the dismantling of the face I had loved, there was no step that didn't sear. No stage was passed without mourning. But even in the course of watching someone die, there are moments of special agony when the pain is so acute, the reality and totality of the loss so stark, that it occupies a special place in memory. For me, such an occasion was when Tracey told me he was going to shave off his mustache. The beard was long gone, his hair had grown out, clothes and voice were changing, and still I begged for the life of a mustache. Because of the way I'd reacted to surprise changes in appearance, and because he knew how hard this one was going to be for me, he warned me that one day soon the mustache was going to go.

Months before, I had said to him, "If you knew you were going to break up our marriage, why didn't we go away for a weekend alone together first? Didn't all our years together deserve a real good-bye?" During the spring before the June night of his momentous announcement, we had spent a weekend in a fancy hotel with a beautiful marble tub in our bathroom. I had wanted to take a bath together in that tub, but with three children sleeping in our room it hadn't happened. "Why didn't you make sure we took that bath?" I'd asked him. He never responded to these questions, beyond looking baffled. He had gone so far down his rabbit hole that I don't think they made any sense to him.

Now, in this moment, I understood that I had a chance to bring our love affair to a proper end.

He was on his way out somewhere when he told me about the mustache. I was sitting on the living room sofa.

"Kiss me," I said to him. "One last time."

He thought that I was threatening to kill myself. I couldn't explain that the last time he would kiss me with his mustache was the last time he would kiss me. I had said all that I could say. He kissed me. His mustache brushed my lips. We had not kissed lately, but before lately there had been twenty-some years of kisses. This one was the last. It was a real kiss. It was a good kiss.

I wish I could say it was over then, that he walked out the door and I never saw him again. It would make for the perfect ending. It didn't happen that way. But in a very real way, that was the end. It was over. I would never be married to this man again.

I went into a deep freeze that would last a long time. In some ways, it seems in retrospect that this freeze predated the dissolution of my marriage. In some ways, it seems as if it had no beginning, as if it were always. However it began, I do know exactly when and where it ended. I know who I was with when I melted.

OKAY. WEIRD.

The summer was a kind of bubble. The four of us operated in shock. Having waited, longed, so many months for Tracey to leave, I was surprised by how bad it managed to feel when it finally happened. Because it was summer, we could largely avoid people we didn't know well, explanations. One day I ran into an acquaintance from synagogue in the grocery store.

"You must be feeling so relaxed now," she said cheerfully. I can only imagine the look on my face from the uneasiness that suddenly crossed hers. "I just mean—now that your son's bar mitzvah is behind you." This was the only fact she knew about what was happening in our family.

"Yes," I agreed, "very relaxed," and hurried away.

We kept busy. I had operated as a single mother part-time for much of the previous thirteen years but was still surprised by how seamlessly I stepped into running the whole show full-time. I was available, emotionally and physically, to the kids all day, staying up late nights to complete freelance

writing and editing jobs with a new level of fiscal urgency. I
sent Bibi to two weeks of the least expensive day camp in our
area, driving forty minutes there and forty back mornings
and afternoons, and took all three kids to every community
activity I could find. Adam, in the first throes of an interest
in the law (remember his trial idea), attended a week of free
police department camp. While there, he dropped Tracey's
half of his hyphenated last name for the first time, something he's gone in and out of doing since.

In the middle of that summer, for the kids' sakes and
against my own inclinations, I agreed to go along for a weekend stay at the Cape Cod vacation home of one of the couples
in the small Jewish group, or *havurah*, with which we'd been
worshipping once a month on Friday evenings and on holidays for the past two years. As my marriage disintegrated,
I'd felt increasingly invested in the *havurah*. Tracey rarely
attended the gatherings. He disparaged the group as a whole
and didn't feel personally close to its members. Although
they knew nothing of what was transpiring in our family, the
havurah was very supportive around Adam's bar mitzvah. I
appreciated the members' involvement more than I could
tell them at the time. When Tracey moved out I thought
that for me, and especially for the children, the continuity of
being part of this group was going to be a key source of stability and spiritual sustenance through the rocky times
ahead.

I hadn't expected the Cape Cod weekend to turn into a
marathon support group. Still, it came as a surprise when *no
one* spoke the words *How are you? How are the children?* in
my direction. Those of the group who were able to make it to
the Cape traced wide margins around me. They threw themselves into summer sports and board games and the raucous

group singing of funny songs about breakups. They laughed their heads off. I laughed my head off, too. They wanted me to so badly. I've said that in the months before Tracey moved out, I went around feeling as though my husband had just died and that it would be a breach of decorum to mention it. Now it seemed as if I had been anticipating this very weekend. Everyone knew what was going on. No one spoke of it. I wasn't allowed to. I was a cheerful, compliant houseguest and never referred even indirectly to what was happening in my life.

On Sunday, the self-appointed group leader, a rabbi, called a meeting to discuss the need for fresh faces. The group, as she saw it, was being disrupted by changes (!) in the membership. She wanted new members, and she wanted them now. She had brought up the issue previously, and I'd indicated my discomfort with new people joining the group at this particular point in time. I hadn't known before the weekend that this discussion would be part of the fun. I'd brought off good cheer for two days. Now it began to crack. By which I mean that I sat in the circle of deck chairs quietly sobbing. The meeting rolled on. So did my tears. Everyone pretended my grief wasn't happening. Later on, I asked them how they could have ignored my sorrow.

"It was for your sake!" they protested. "We were giving you a break from your situation! We were letting you have a weekend to forget!"

What did they imagine I had forgotten, sobbing before them? Did they think I had a toothache?

Now (groaning permitted) I get to the hard part. A few weeks later, one of my children was diagnosed with a heart condition. There is no good moment to discover that your child's health is threatened. Adjusting to single motherhood

and a husband going around town in skirts, feeling economically insecure in the extreme and short on resources of all
kinds—that was a bad moment. A moment for spiritual sustenance if ever there was one. The *havurah* members all knew
that my child was undergoing tests. Knew that during a certain week I was awaiting test results from one minute to the
next. I expected that some or all of them would call. E-mail,
at least?

Sure enough, S, a medical professional, called on my cell
phone one afternoon as I was getting out of my car in front of
a friend's home. (A friend who would ask about the test results and cry when I told her the news.) When she heard my
voice, S became embarrassed. "Actually," she said, "I meant
to call *Tracey*. I guess I saved your number in my phone under his name." Having called, she felt the need to chat for a
moment. "So, what's new?" S asked in the upbeat tenor of
the Cape Cod weekend.

"Well," I said, "I got those test results."

"Oh, right," she said. "So what were they?"

I told her.

She had nothing to say. She had meant, after all, to phone
Tracey. She got off quickly.

None of the other members called. No e-mails. A couple of
weeks later, it was my turn to host the group. I made an elaborate meal. I knew this would be my last occasion with the *havurah*. I decided to make it perfect. As each couple arrived, I
braced myself for the too-little-too-late questions about my
child's health that I still, somehow, expected. No one asked.

I resigned from the *havurah* by e-mail not long after.
Needless to say, no one tried to convince us not to go. The
group's abandonment in those first months as a single-parent
household was a source of such pain and bitterness that it

constituted a kind of trauma in itself, layering the primary loss as we struggled to go it alone. To this day, my children cringe when they run into any of its members.

That last evening with the *havurah* was representative of a rocky autumn. The children and I dreaded the looming New England winter. We were daunted by the school year with its many demands, not least of which was that the kids begin to cope in public as well as in private with our separation, Tracey's gender-bending, and the notoriety it can bring.

While maintaining his sweet, goofy demeanor at home, Adam spent eighth grade wandering around classrooms during lessons in a daze, sometimes defacing the papers pinned to his teachers' bulletin boards or lying on their desks. When I asked him why he had done these things, he looked at me with genuine astonishment. "Did I do that?" he asked. His behavior was so bizarrely disassociated, his personality so changed from the funny, polite, engaged boy he had been, that teachers thought he had become either mentally ill or a drug user. Neither. I had told his previous year's guidance counselor about our family, but the information wasn't passed on. Once unable even to speak the words aloud, I now became adept at bearing personal tidings to school personnel, as well as to pediatricians and therapists, all against Adam's will. Of the three children, Adam has been the most reluctant to let people know about his father, particularly—no surprise—other teenage boys, but teachers and other adults as well. I respected Adam's privacy, having been rather attached to my own. When Tracey decided to change our lives, privacy became a luxury our family often couldn't afford.

We set up a visitation arrangement in which Tracey would pick up the kids a couple of times a week for a few hours. Though Adam generally refused to speak with Tracey on the phone, he was usually amenable to seeing him. What was troublesome was what happened during the visits themselves. I've heard a secondhand tale of evolving and variously expressed hostilities: bitter fights between the children of a kind I've never seen; knock-down-drag-outs between the children and Tracey. That first year, Adam often attacked Tracey physically. Obviously an expression of anger and aggression, this was also Adam's way of trying to keep his dad a dad. Tracey still presented himself to the children in an androgynous style, gradually adding more feminine touches as the months went by. He was sickly, shrinking. Adam was spurting, taking on weight and inches and stretching into great big boyhood. He wanted to wrestle. He wanted to make Tracey wrestle. Tracey complained to me about Adam. He complained to Adam's therapist. "Thanks to the hormones I'm taking, I'm losing muscle tone," he reported, obviously taking a pride in lost muscle no woman I know would feel. "I'm afraid Adam is going to hurt me." Recognizing Adam's need for an alternative outlet, I signed him up for martial arts classes.

Adam liked to confide in me about some aspects of his emotional life (girls!), and I was surprised that he didn't talk more about Tracey, his feelings about Tracey, during that first year of our separation. Didn't cry, never fell apart. When, with a little encouragement, he did open up, I'd be astonished by his rage. Not that it was there, but that he could be so aware of it, so articulate about it, and yet so closemouthed day to day.

"Daddy," he said one day, "is a female monster."

"Daddy is no longer 'there.' He just pretends to be during our visits," was his biting comment on another.

In his therapy that year he staged another trial, with Tracey the defendant and his therapist the judge; the point didn't seem so much to be to determine guilt as to try to place court-ordered limitations on his female expression around Adam and his sisters, at a time when Tracey was pressuring them to see him fully "dressed."

Still other days, Adam heart-tuggingly insisted, "Daddy is still a guy to me."

In psychospeak, Adam is "parenticized." Literally. By the time Tracey physically removed himself from our home, Adam had come to see himself as his sisters' father. His sisters' protector around Tracey. My protector in some way, too. I didn't want him to carry this burden. I told him I could handle things. That I was in charge. I told him the girls weren't his responsibility. It didn't seem to matter much what I said. Adam saw how vulnerable, emotionally, socially, economically, Tracey's unfolding new life left us. He experienced his sisters' intense desire for his time and attention. He looked around and saw that he'd become the man of the house. The only one available.

Tracey amazed me that first November—we were barely on speaking terms—by asking if we wanted do Thanksgiving together. (That is, invite him for Thanksgiving. Tracey usually spends holidays with friends. This is the only one since moving out that he's suggested being with the children. Maybe this was an occasion on which he had no other options.) After Lilly was asleep one night, I brought the suggestion to Adam and Bibi, who looked at me as if I'd taken leave of my senses. "No way," they both said at once, a rare moment of unanimity. Then Adam made a leap entirely mysterious to me. "Although," he said abruptly, as if it weren't a non sequitur, "I do remember the nickname he used to call you. He doesn't call you that anymore."

Adam said the nickname, a term of endearment that dated from our freshman year of college. I couldn't believe he knew it. Remembered it from what had to be more than two years before. I was floored. So much so that I did something I've managed to almost never do throughout these years: I teared up in front of them.

"Oh, I'm sorry," Adam said quickly.

"It's okay," I told him.

And it was. The three of us hugged. Adam and Bibi comforted me. I comforted them. We embarked on a beautiful, wrenching conversation about sadness, theirs and mine. I felt as if I were glimpsing my son's heart, big enough to carry grief for a lost father and for his parents' lost love as well. He had been a silent witness, not only to the destruction of our marriage, but to the good things that had come before. The parents he'd once had.

At seven, Bibi already had a keen sense of the divided loyalties between Tracey and me. She and I have always been very close. Before he told Bibi about himself, Tracey said something distinctly ominous to me: "I've left Bibi to you— until now." In the immediate aftermath of his revelations, Bibi and I were closer than ever, as she looked to me for stability, reassurance—in short, to remain her mother—in the bizarrely shifting landscape that had become home. Then quite suddenly she changed. During Tracey's last weeks in our house, Bibi pulled away from me for the first time in her life. She and Tracey started spending a lot of time giggling and whispering secrets together like preteen girls. I tried to reach Bibi, careful not to push. To speak to her as if I weren't frantic. I knew that she was anguished and bewildered and that she needed to negotiate a new relationship with her father that she could hang on to throughout the changes that lay ahead. I didn't want her to feel she had to choose between us. By not pushing, I hoped she would see that she didn't have to. Meanwhile I felt as if I were losing her.

She was remote throughout the summer, deflecting my attempts to make contact. In early September, with school about to resume, she began to thaw. We talked with excitement about the year she was embarking on, the old friends she would see. Always a very social being, she felt now an even more intense desire to be close to those friends. At the same time, she dreaded them finding out about Tracey. Would they tease her? Reject her outright? The idea of her peers seeing Tracey dressed as a woman, something she would not yet witness herself for a long time to come, was too appalling for her to contemplate rationally. We discussed strategies to mediate between her conflicting needs for privacy and friendship.

The week school was to begin, Tracey arrived one afternoon to pick up the children. Doing an abrupt about-face, Bibi became distraught and refused to go with him. She said she was *afraid* to go with him. I wasn't sure what to make of it, but it was a beautiful late summer day, so I invited her to take a walk with me. We live in a very small town of thickly wooded hills, houses, a few remaining farms. No commerce, no sidewalks. I can see us side by side on the road around the bend from our house, loping uphill in a mix of sunlight and dense shade. I can see the glow over Bibi's long light brown curls as she walked on my right nearest the shoulder, away from infrequent but fast-traveling trucks and cars. Out of harm's way.

"What's on your mind?" I said, offhand, expecting to be rebuffed once again. Not this time.

"When I go to Daddy's he gives me his shoes and jewelry to try on. I do his hair. Sometimes we put on makeup." In a spill of detail, Bibi poured out the story of the previous months.

She told me that when she and her brother and sister visited Tracey's apartment, he set Adam and Lilly up in front of the television and took her into his bedroom. There he would open his closet and drawers and show her his wardrobe of feminine things. At this point, when the thought of seeing their father dressed as a woman was unthinkable to the children and still months in the future, he would hold up dresses and skirts in front of himself and ask Bibi to imagine how he would look in them. He gave her his high heels and jewelry to try on, had her play with his hair and makeup. Bibi reported that these activities, which she called dress-up games, had begun while he was still living in our home; there they had taken place in the bathroom, while I was out.

"When we play the dress-up games I feel like I want to," Bibi told me. "Then afterwards it seems creepy. I feel dirty. I can't believe I did it. Then the next time I go there it happens again. I feel like I'm under his spell!" Bibi burst into hysterical tears. "I feel ashamed," she cried. "It's my fault!"

"It is *not* your fault," I said calmly. Those were the first words I spoke into Bibi's torrent. I remember her look of disbelief when she heard them.

Under his spell. I was in shock. I knew my little girl to be precociously verbal, but even so her words added shock to shock.

These things had been happening, for a time in my own home. How could I not have known?

Bibi's story had the ring of confession. A confession she had longed for and understood she was not allowed. "We call it our girly girls club," Bibi told me of these sessions with Tracey. "We say we both want to be girly girls. Daddy didn't say I couldn't tell you, but I knew I wasn't supposed to. I knew I was supposed to keep it a secret."

Through her sobs, Bibi insisted on describing her secret activities with Tracey at great length that day, adding more bits and pieces in the days that followed. Her hysteria kept me calm. "You aren't to blame," I kept repeating. "You haven't done anything wrong and nothing that's happened is your fault." She never seemed to believe me. But it was a relief to her, telling me her story. She returned often to the issue of exactly how she had known that the things she did with Tracey were to be kept secret. A few days after that first outpouring, she told me, "Daddy was counting on me being too ashamed to tell you." And she returned often to the difference between the way she felt when she was alone with Tracey and the way their activities felt to her when she thought about them later. "He tempts me," she said. "He puts me under his spell."

I was still calm when I confronted Tracey. "Bibi says this stuff has been going on," I told him, repeating her story.

"Yes." He shrugged. "She likes to see my things. There's nothing wrong with it. She could have told you about it at any time. These are normal activities with a same-sex parent," he added.

Huh?

What he meant was, mothers typically spend hours playing dress-up with their seven-year-old daughters. Alone, in their bedrooms, while their other children watch television outside.

"I never shut the bedroom door," he volunteered. It seemed that he had thought this point through in advance: if he could claim to have left the door open, he couldn't have been up to anything he wouldn't want to be walked in on. (Adam, it turned out, was very much aware that Tracey had private activities with Bibi. He understood that his own role was to keep four-year-old Lilly busy so that they would be left undisturbed. When Bibi began refusing to be alone with Tracey, Adam added to his other burdens the sense that it was his responsibility to protect both his sisters.) The other point Tracey insisted upon was that the dress-up sessions had taken place at Bibi's insistence. His exact words were: "She asked for it. She could have stopped it at any time."

Tracey never acknowledged that there was anything wrong with the dress-up games. But he told me, "If Bibi doesn't want to do these things or if you don't want us to do them, they'll stop." Bibi reported that he promised her they would stop as well.

But the very next time Bibi went along on a visit, she told me later that the moment they were in his car he began to talk about the lovely new things he had bought himself. "I'm dying to show you some new jewelry I have," he gushed. "Why did he say that?" Bibi asked me in confusion. "I thought he wasn't going to say those things anymore. He's trying to tempt me to try on his things!"

No surprise that Bibi often refused to go with the other kids when Tracey came to see them at this time. "I don't want to be alone with him." One day she became distraught at the idea that he might attempt to play dress-up games with Lilly.

Once, very carefully, I asked Bibi, "Are you afraid that Daddy will try to force you to do something you don't want to do?"

"He might make me try on his clothes."

"Are you really afraid of that happening?" I asked her.

"I don't think it will happen, but I'm afraid of it. He'll get angry if I refuse to play dress-up." According to both Bibi and Adam, Tracey frequently flew into rages, chiefly over their reluctance to see him or their (quite normal!) expressions of anger toward him. Bibi said she feared that he would hurt her. Again she said she didn't think it would happen, but she feared it.

When Bibi did choose to go on a visit with Tracey, she would phone me continually, often in tears over their blow-ups. Tracey would tell the children it was his right to see them and threaten to make them come to his home even if they chose not to. When Bibi began resisting his hugs and kisses, he got angry at that. He said that it was his right to kiss her and that he would make her accept his affection whether she liked it or not. Of course it was me Tracey was actually enraged with. That didn't make it any better. Rather the opposite. He knew that there was no better way to attack me than through the children. When he trashed me to the kids, Adam would jump to my defense, and a screaming match would erupt. Afterward Tracey, who had taken to writing me long and regular e-mail diatribes, would send a screed against what he saw as the kids' lack of respect for him, demanding that I get their behavior in line.

Then suddenly, Tracey denied that the dress-up sessions with Bibi had ever happened. He denied that our earlier conversations, in which he had freely admitted everything, had happened as well. This happened one day while we were talking on the telephone. I recall holding the phone in one hand, feeling once again that I had entered a world in which none of the rules of life as I knew them applied. I expressed astonishment at this turnabout and repeated the things Bibi had told me, things Tracey and I had already discussed.

"Bibi," Tracey said icily, "is a liar."

Tracey frequently changed his story about a range of things and sometimes seemed to genuinely forget today what he'd said yesterday. Over the coming months, he would flip-flop more times than a dying trout, sometimes saying the dress-up games had never happened, other times claiming they were a normal same-sex activity that any female parent might engage in with her daughter.

Whether or not Tracey was admitting it, the dress-up continued. During that first year of our separation, not long after she turned eight, Bibi came home distressed one day about a makeup kit she and Tracey had purchased together, used at his place, and then agreed to keep hidden from me. Another day she was agitated because Tracey, who had promised to put off appearing in overtly feminine clothes with the children, showed her the blouse he was wearing under his sweatshirt. Telling me these things, Bibi would say she was frightened of Tracey's anger and beg me not to say anything to him. Saying nothing, of course, wasn't an option. That would only have encouraged him. So I'd tell him I knew what was going on, making Bibi even more vulnerable to his anger the next time she saw him and risking that if he frightened her enough, she might go back to shutting me out.

Following visits with Tracey, Bibi began to wake screaming in the night, describing nightmares about him. She'd stop eating or throw up in the middle of a meal. She began to have problems focusing in class.

That fall, Bibi asked Tracey not to come to her school. His response was to show up randomly at the beginning or end of the day. He told her to get used to it. He told her that as her parent it was his right to march into her classroom at any time, pull up a desk, and sit there through lessons. She grew preoccupied with watching for him, anticipating his arrival. She said she spent the entire bus ride fearing that he would be at school when she got there. Whenever the door of her classroom opened, she cringed, thinking it might be him. On top of her other fears, she began to worry that if he would show up like this when she had begged him not to, what would stop him from coming to school "dressed"?

"School," Bibi lamented, "was my safe place. It was the one place where I didn't think about what was going on at home."

No longer. When I repeated this to Tracey, I expected him to be moved. To back down. Instead, it seemed to strengthen his resolve. Fortunately, the school administration vehemently disagreed that it was Tracey's right to take up residence in her classroom. Seeing Bibi's distress, the principal asked Tracey to stop appearing outside the building as well.

In the secret dress-up sessions, I understood that Tracey was offering Bibi a way to hold on to him, to enter into his newfound girlhood instead of losing him to it. The reality, of course, was that these activities only emphasized the loss of the man who had been her father. Like her brother, Bibi desperately wanted to keep that man alive. While Adam tried to get his dad to wrestle, Bibi began to flirt. In Tracey's presence, she developed a manner that would have been dismaying to watch a girl of any age employ with her father and that was deeply disturbing in a seven- or eight-year-old.

One evening that winter, I went outside to replace a light bulb in the lamp at the bottom of our driveway while Tracey was visiting. From my vantage point, boots sunk in the deep snow that covered our sloping lawn, I looked up into the brightly lit living room at the back of Tracey's head on the other side of the window. He was sitting on the sofa and Bibi stood before him as if onstage, giddily talking, laughing, gesturing. She couldn't see me in the dark outside. From my side of the glass, I watched a little girl attempt to charm the middle-aged man she loved. But there was nothing straightforward or simple about any of her feelings, and as happened with Adam's very different attempts to make his dad be a man, Bibi's fits of flirting would often spin off into violence. She'd start kicking him, and he'd pick her up and put her in a bedroom. She'd phone me in hysterics. Until he stopped letting her phone me during visits.

All this happened during the first year of our separation, at a time when I hadn't yet filed for divorce, didn't have a lawyer or the money to retain one. Tracey and I had no formal separation agreement, and as he constantly reminded me, I had no authority to prevent him from seeing the children. I spoke to the local police about the possibility of a restraining order and was discouraged by what I heard. Tracey's activities with Bibi fell into a gray zone. The law was not particularly inclined to enter that zone. At my wits' end and certain I was failing her, I had no idea how to protect her, either.

To my therapist, the secret games were yet another instance of Tracey's narcissism, his insistence that what was good for Tracey was good for everyone. Now it was left to Bibi to make sense of the dress-up sessions, the secrecy. The experience of being used by the father she had trusted, for his own ends. Bibi needed a therapist of her own.

I found one for her, actually the second therapist she was seeing after an earlier, unsuccessful try. In the first sessions, Bibi—who looked a couple of years older than her age and at eight was as tall as the petite psychologist—curled up in my lap, whispered what was on her mind, and told me what I was and wasn't allowed to repeat. Then at some point she'd look at the therapist and come out with some clear, articulate zinger that would leave the woman floored. Speaking of gifts from Tracey, she commented matter-of-factly, "The things he gives me are like duck decoys, used to lure prey." In another session she said, "Most kids wish their parents would get back together when they separate. I don't. I wouldn't feel comfortable living with Daddy again."

Gradually I eased her into being alone with her therapist for part of each session. After a few months, in what was scheduled to be a fifty-minute visit but turned into two and a half hours, she edged up to the subject of the dress-up sessions with Tracey. Hoping to make it easier for her to talk, I suggested I wait outside. She agreed. We were the last appointment of the day. I sat in the deserted waiting room. The receptionists went home. The medical center emptied. Offices darkened and maintenance people with vacuum cleaners could be heard down the hall. Finally I was called back in.

"It's okay," the therapist reassured me, seeing the look on my face. At Bibi's request, she started to tell me that they'd been working to understand Bibi's feelings about the secret activities with Tracey. "Bibi feels that her girlhood has been violated," she began.

But suddenly Bibi found her voice. I had never seen my daughter so angry before. "He told me I had to show him how to be a girl!" she spat. "He said he'd never gotten to be a girl, so he wanted to experience what it was like through me!"

When it comes to comic relief in our family, the blue ribbons go to Lilly. One day when she was five, she and I were alone in the car together. Lilly, in a typically chatty mood, related something she found odd: On an outing the previous day with her father, she'd seen him enter a ladies' restroom. "He said he had a *girl's* brain and a *girl's* body," Lilly told me.

Whereas once I might have driven my car off the road at this point, I now murmured neutrally, "Oh really?"

"Sometimes," my daughter concluded, "I just have to say, 'Okay. Weird.'"

Okay. Weird. If I had to sum up our lives in two words, I could do much worse.

At the time Lilly watched her father enter a ladies' room, Tracey wasn't wearing makeup or dresses in front of the kids. He had been feminizing his appearance since Lilly was two. She didn't remember a father who wore a beard and men's clothes. To Lilly his odd, androgynous look was just his look. To Lilly he was an average dad. Or rather I should say as far as *I knew,* this was her perspective. The biggest difference she talked about between Tracey and her friends' dads was that, having left our home before she turned four, Tracey didn't live with us. Before the Okay Weird phase began, she wasn't terribly articulate about her feelings, beyond wondering aloud why her father had his own home. She exhibited her distress mostly in immature or regressive behavior (think potty training). Once when she came home from a morning at preschool expecting to grab some mommy and me time while the older kids were still out, she had a crying jag when I told her Tracey was coming to pick her up. But this wasn't typical; I generally saw a happy child. Tracey saw something different. He reported that when she was with him she would often cry uncontrollably, then seemingly lose the ability to speak. He was sure that this behavior, which neither I nor her teachers witnessed, had a medical cause, and he wanted to speak to our pediatrician about it. The doctor laughed at the notion that Lilly's problems were physical and said she would be happy to explain this to Tracey.

Over the years, Lilly has become more articulate about her feelings. When she was six she began to pontificate on the subject of having a dad who is a girl. She felt the need, often at inappropriate moments (whose idea of inappropriate?) and to inappropriate peers (ditto), to confess about Tracey. Typically she'd choose her moment while riding in a packed car or among a crowd gathered in the kitchen. She was fond of speaking to an audience that included but was not limited to the members of her family, preferably with her own and her older siblings' friends in attendance. Heavy sighs would signal the lament. Then the announcement would begin, in a voice laden with pathos and the desire to instill guilt:

"My parents are divorced." A deep intake of breath allowed everyone in the room to start paying attention. "Of course I'm very unhappy about it. They don't live together—*because they're not married*." Dramatic pause before the kicker: "And there's another thing." Older brother and sister start to groan. "*My dad's a girl*."

Calling Tracey a girl, Lilly has adapted his terminology. In the past, anyone would have described Tracey as responsible, mature. Whether it reflects an awareness of or a desire for a regression of his own, he now prefers the words *boy* and *girl* to *man* and *woman*. He speaks of himself as having once been a boy and now being a girl. Thus Lilly asks him, "When are you going to go back to being a boy?" He tells her, "Never." One morning Tracey brought her to school. Another child, overhearing Lilly speak to him, asked a teacher, "Why is she calling that woman Daddy?" Lilly explained, "My dad's a girl."

It is exceedingly difficult to know what Lilly really makes of all this, but it is fascinating, as well as heartrending, to watch her process the facts of our family. One morning she told me that she'd dreamed she'd married a boy she liked. He wore a white gown and she wore a tux. (She didn't say tux. She said the white-and-black thing with the bow tie. She meant tux.) Bride and groom kissed. Lilly was giggly and silly on the subject of the clothing switch.

In first grade, her class was shown a film about the diverse makeup of families. For homework the kids were asked to produce two pairs of sentences and drawings, the first illustrating how their own families were similar to, the second how they were different from, a divorced lesbian couple featured in the film. I sat with her in the kitchen that afternoon and watched her write her "similar" statement: "My parents are divorced." Then she said she wanted to draw a picture of her father and me kissing.

"I don't think that's a good choice since we *don't* kiss," I told her.

"It could be a picture of when you first met."

I knew I should just let her draw the picture she wanted

to draw, but I couldn't bear the thought of it. "Do you think maybe you could draw a different picture?" I asked her gently.

"Okay," she agreed amicably. "Then I'll draw you walking away from each other."

She didn't discuss her "different" statement or image with me. She just wrote, "I don't have two moms," and drew a picture of me.

A few months later, she fell into a discussion with an adult friend about different kinds of families. Our friend pointed out that one of Lilly's cronies has two mothers. Lilly asserted that *she* would never have two mothers. "Even if my dad marries his girlfriend," she asserted, "she'll never be my mother." It so went without saying that Tracey would never be her mother that Lilly didn't even think of it.

She thinks of other things. In another conversation with the same friend, she confided, "I want my dad to be a man and my parents to be married. But if I can't have both, I want my dad to be a man *or* my parents to be married." Enough's enough, and a dad who is a girl and divorced parents is just too much.

Because Tracey told her the divorce was my idea—"Mama decided she didn't want to be married to a woman"—Lilly went through a period of asking me, "Why don't you want to be married to a woman?" She told me, "Some women are married to women."

Once she reported that Tracey had told her about a child who was forced to choose between his trans and non-trans parents. She worried for days that she would similarly be forced to choose, as I told her over and over that she would not. Another time she told me how much it upset her when she saw a piece of mail addressed to her father as "Ms.

Tracey." "Fathers aren't supposed to be Ms. or Miss!" she said.

After a visit to an Orthodox synagogue where women's roles are heavily restricted, I overheard her on the phone with Tracey. "Why do you want to be a girl?" Lilly demanded. "We just went to a synagogue where women can't even touch the Torah!" One day she urged her recalcitrant brother to do something she wanted him to do, saying, "Come on! Be a man!" On another occasion, observing a male friend, she said wistfully, "He's a manly man."

Despite the sadness, one of Lilly's strengths is her adaptability. Her bounce. One night when I was putting her to bed, she told me that she might like to marry a certain male family friend when she grew up.

"That might not work out," I suggested.

Lilly shrugged, plan B on the tip of her tongue. "Oh well," she said. "If he doesn't want to marry me, me and my best friend can just be gay."

Part Two

TRANSWORLD

Once upon a time, I had no interest in "gender issues." In my retro, Edenic worldview, I was content to divvy up human beings—at least, human bodies—into two neat categories. I knew not everyone fit the categories and felt vaguely sorry for their affliction. I had no particular curiosity to know more. When I was forced to accept the presence of transsexuality in my life, I felt that understanding it with my head wasn't really going to help with what was happening in my gut. Actually, I was right about that. It didn't help. After a while, I realized I'd better understand it as well as I could anyway. Raising three children who didn't have the luxury of avoiding this terrain demanded it.

The literature on transsexuality is limited and contradictory and often seems to reflect the biases of those turning it out more than any sort of data. I had to overcome a considerable reluctance to delve into it. Which is a nice way of saying that once I was forced to think about Tracy in these terms, any reference to men in skirts made me feel faint. As faint as Tracey said he felt when *not* wearing them. To this day, a Scot in a kilt makes me a teensy bit queasy.

When I did take a look at the material on transsexuality, I brought three basic questions to my inquiry: What did it mean that Tracey felt he was the wrong gender? What had caused this mind-body disconnect? And, oh yeah—What exactly is gender?

Transgender is an umbrella term used to cover an array of gender stances. These genderful days, there are almost as many designations as there are transpeople. "If someone calls himself a tranny boy," commented G, a transgendered activist I spoke with, "first of all what the heck does that mean? If two people use the term, it probably means two different things." To name just three transgender subcategories: There are *cross-dressers,* formerly known as *transvestites,* people who don't want to change their bodies but who dress up as the gender they aren't for a miscellany of reasons from political shock value to sexual stimulation. There are *gender-queer* people who don't feel they fit solidly into either the male or the female half of the great divide. And there are *transsexuals,* people such as Tracey who feel they were born in the wrong body. A transsexual identifies as the gender that doesn't match his or her body—sexuality is an independent issue. That's something a lot of people have trouble grasping. When friends heard that Tracey had proudly announced to my children that he was a lesbian, there was a lot of laughter and eye rolling. Some people reacted with a kind of outraged bewilderment. As one person expressed this (heterosexist!) view, "Why does he want to be a woman unless it's to be with a man?"

No one knows what causes someone to develop a sense of him- or herself as male or female in contrast with the evidence of anatomy. My sense that Tracey's rejection of manhood grew out of his deep psychological scars wasn't unique. Gender identity disorders are still classified as psychological conditions, and the endocrinologists and surgeons offering hormones or genital reconstruction to transsexuals generally require their patients to be approved for treatment by therapists. But now gaining traction is the thought that transsexuality is more likely rooted in the body than in the mind. It seems that the prenatal process of gender formation is complex and highly vulnerable to mishap. According to one theory, gender disorders are the result of hormone imbalances during fetal development.

In *The Tell-Tale Brain* (Norton, 2011), neuroscientist V. S. Ramachandran suggests the brain is imprinted with a map, or image, of the body. When something happens to damage this map—something like a stroke—patients may experience an intense aversion to an arm or leg, to the point where they might wish to have it amputated. Tracey viewed body parts as ripe for amputation, too. Ramachandran speculates that for a transsexual, anatomy and body image go separate ways in the womb.

There are more and more transsexuals. I for one see them everywhere. I see transwomen behind the wheels of oncoming cars, particularly in the rain. I see them every time an apparently female person is the least bit taller than average. Worse, I see Tracey. Like a trans Forrest Gump, his peculiar feminized visage has been known to appear on anyone in clothes vaguely similar to his, even to turn up under Jacqueline Kennedy's pillbox hat in black-and-white photos, beneath towers of dusted curls in eighteenth-century museum portraits.

Okay. Seriously. More and more people are coming out as transgendered. It's important to distinguish between visibility and incidence. As activists like to point out, transgendered people have been recognized in diverse cultures throughout history and have sometimes been accepted and accorded special roles within communities. In the West today, there is obviously a much more accepting climate for coming out than at any time in the past. That's enough to explain an increase in people seeking services for gender transformation. But it doesn't appear to be the whole story. Gender lines are being muddied in the animal world as well as in the human. Presumably transgendered fish weren't staying in the closet until the political waters warmed.

From California to Washington, D.C., male fish are turning up with high levels of estrogen and female ovarian tissue in their testes. In 2004, *The Washington Post* reported that in the south branch of the Potomac River, 42 percent of male bass were producing eggs. While noting that the cause is unknown, the article pointed to speculation about pollutants in the water, most likely hormonal waste from humans or poultry. Environmental groups are also raising the alarm about estrogen, particularly synthetic estrogen from sources like birth control pills, hormone replacement therapies, and pesticides. Storm water, agricultural runoff, and flushing toilets all send these chemicals into streams and rivers, where they alter the environment in which fish develop and reproduce. And fish aren't the only creatures operating in a chemically compromised world. Similar stories are surfacing about frogs and other species. Tracey told me that he had made friends online with a transsexual who lived in a small, remote Canadian town in which the incidence of gender identity disorder was well beyond the norm. Transgendered folks weren't coming out in unusual numbers there because the town was so darn trans-friendly.

Traccy certainly believes that his female identity is a

physiological fact. He describes himself as having an illness. As being sick. Very sick, sick unto death if he did not alter his appearance to match his internal sense of himself. He maintains that he has a birth defect, a female brain in the body of a male. He means this literally, subscribing to the opinion that there are male and female brains, and transsexuals possess the wrong kind. For most of human history, there was little dispute that men and women were as different above the neck as below it. Women supposedly lacked men's mental as well as physical strength, so it followed that they would be excluded from so much worldly endeavor. Then for a time the two-brain notion was largely left behind. Remember the uproar when Harvard president Lawrence Summers suggested that women were innately less equipped to excel in math and science? But curiouser and curiouser: The new acceptance of transsexuality entails a return to the old belief in his and her brains. How else to understand the kind of violent self-loathing Tracey expressed for his physical being? His own explanation was mind-body mismatch. Since the mind couldn't be altered, the body had to be.

What caused Tracey's birth defect, if birth defect it is? Early on, I suggested to Tracey that there might be a link between the DES his mother took while pregnant with him and his gender identity. He didn't discount the possibility. He simply didn't know. DES, diethylstilbestrol, is a synthetic estrogen that was given to women from 1938 to 1971 in the mistaken belief that it would prevent miscarriages. Doctors stopped prescribing it when it was linked to a rare form of vaginal cancer in the daughters of women who had taken it. DES daughters have an increased risk of vaginal, cervical, and breast cancers as well as infertility. Much less is known about its effect on sons. At the time I proposed the idea to Tracey, I was shooting in the dark. Later, searching for information about gender identity disorders on the Web, I was startled to come across a site linking DES exposure to transgender issues in men. Later still, I read a book titled *The Riddle of Gender: Science, Activism, and Transgender Rights* (Anchor Books, 2006) by Deborah Rudacille, a science writer, who reported that the best evidence that transsexuality has a biological cause comes from DES research. Men whose mothers took DES while pregnant with them describe themselves as transsexuals in numbers way beyond the general population.

Not all transgendered people identify with the illness or birth defect model that resonates for Tracey. But if DES or some other environmental pollutant damaged what would otherwise have been a typical development of male identity, then describing the result as a birth defect is not so far off target. Being transgendered isn't like other medical conditions, though. Transgendered people wouldn't necessarily want a cure if one existed.

Early in Tracey's explorations, I asked him, "What would you do if you could take a medication—say, a hormone— that would let you feel right in your male body?"

The question took him aback. He had no answer.

Whatever the cause of gender identity disorders, people have them. They need legal protection and equality, medical care, dignity, understanding. They need to make their own decisions and live, like everyone else, without harassment. Demanding protections and inclusion is a political stance. Being trans is not in itself a political stance—right? For some people, gender would seem to be more about politics than it is for others.

Tracey wanted to look like a woman: to pass. Other trans-

gendered people make a political decision to present themselves as trans rather than as a single gender of choice. Some
speak of the tyranny of the gender binary. Huh? In other
words, the assumption that there are two genders. Male and
female. They argue that not everyone fits one of these two
narrow molds. For some, breaking the molds is clearly a political position. Others just feel that they could be quite comfortable inhabiting a space between male and female if the
world would let them be. G, the activist already quoted, inhabits that space. Tall and rail thin, with long hair worn in a
man ponytail, G is a biological male who presents as a biological male, albeit one with an unusually smooth face. Facial
hair removal is G's sole physical gesture toward a transgendered appearance. An academic who never felt male, G began
to use the label *transgendered* about ten years ago, around the
age of thirty. At that time, "The transsexuals I knew were
more stereotyped transsexual women, women in their forties
and fifties who did everything, hormones, surgery, to look female. They didn't see me as trans. I got more support from
my non-trans colleagues." G didn't feel a burning desire to
disappear into a female identity and perhaps didn't see it as a
realistic option. "When you transition there's almost an un-
learning process," G says. "I see this a lot with transwomen in
particular. There's a certain male privilege that's there, that
they have to unlearn. I see so many women where I think,
Gee, you act just like a guy. Just because you now look female
that doesn't mean that gets lost."

Tracey fits nicely into G's definition of the "stereotyped
transsexual woman" affirming conventions more than breaking them. But for some, cross-dressing is a revolutionary act,
meant to trans-gress. To bend gender. It might be retro for
women to wear makeup and high heels, but in this view it's

cutting-edge for men to do the same. According to press materials for *Virtuoso Illusion: Cross-Dressing and the New Media Avant-Garde,* a 2010 exhibition at the Massachusetts Institute of Technology, male artists from Man Ray and Marcel Duchamp to their contemporary descendants dress as women to "shock the bourgeoisie" and to express anxiety about feminism. They aren't men who want to be women. They are men who want to be bad boys.

So a handful of male (non-trans) artists wear drag to make a political point. But no one identifies as transgendered for political reasons—right? Actually, I've been told that at certain women's colleges it's become political fad to be trans. This news-of-the-weird item aside, I think we can assume that most transsexuals are actually at odds with their bodies, not saying they are because it's cool.

To recap: Being a transsexual is not about sexual orientation and not about psychology. It runs deeper than politics. And it's not about social roles—right? When Tracey began his transformation, I tried to understand if there were things he felt he couldn't do as a man—ways he felt he couldn't be. There's confusion, in my mind for sure, but among transsexuals as well, about body versus gender role. A few years ago, Oprah Winfrey interviewed transsexuals on her television show. According to the show's Web site, Oprah.com, one guest, Denise (formerly Don) Brunner, felt "feminine since kindergarten."

> I couldn't really say that I wanted to be a woman, but I didn't want to go out and play in the sandbox. I wanted to play in the kitchen with the other girls. I didn't want to go out on the jungle gym. I wanted to be inside doing hair and makeup.

Taking it at face value, this is a statement, pure and simple, about social roles. We can deduce that Don grew up in a neighborhood that took a breathtakingly rigid approach to gender conventions, where even the sandbox (!) was male turf. If children were allowed to play wherever they damn pleased, he wouldn't have had to take estrogen? If he could have chosen to *act* like a girl, he wouldn't have needed to change his body? Presumably, a transsexual in any time and place will feel drawn to the artifacts of the opposite gender's domain specific to that culture—as *symbols* of the gender they carry within. Yet I have repeatedly read and heard that biological men are much more likely to take surgical and hormonal steps across the gender divide than biological women. The explanation for the imbalance is that it is more socially acceptable to be a butch woman than it is to be an effeminate man. That social roles for women are more fluid than they are for men.

What about bodies? Transsexuality is about gender—right? What is gender?

Gender seems to be a deep, internal principle by which we organize ourselves. If your gender identity and your body are a good fit, you are likely not even aware of it. "Do you think I walk around thinking about how great it is to be a woman?" I once asked Tracey. If your gender identity and your body do not fit, you can't forget it. Why should it only be so terribly important if it's wrong? I understand it by going back to the notion of illness. You don't walk around thinking about your head unless it's splitting. Even the day after a headache, how likely are you to consciously experience the pleasure of not having a headache? Of the *rightness* of your head?

Again: What is gender? If it's the fit between an immutable identity and the body it inhabits, then changing one's social role, one's presentation, can't be enough. Is gender an absolute and unchangeable attachment to a particular set of genitals? So that the brain says, for example, *female* to someone like Tracey, who then experiences a kind of vertigo when he looks down and sees it ain't so? And that sense of vertigo is intolerable, simply not to be borne? And because the brain can't be changed, the body has to be?

A gender identity disjunction is tough to understand if you've never had one. Maybe it's tough to understand even if you have.

Tracey, hell-bent for femininity, admitted that he couldn't really comprehend the longing for masculinity felt by some women. He said that when a young woman told him she wanted to become a man, he was horrified—much as his feelings had horrified me. He said he saw the irony.

One day he told me he'd had a telephone conversation with a woman rabbi who was planning a gender change to male. "The rabbi's speaking voice was very feminine and incredibly beautiful," he said. "And when I thought of her changing it, masculinizing it, I felt so sad that this beautiful voice would be lost forever." He went on to say that he had reported these feelings to a friend of his. "She said to me that if I could feel that way after a single phone call, I should try to imagine what you must feel about the destruction of the voice, the body, the man you've loved for so long."

Tracey repeating this conversation to me was a rare instance of acknowledgment that I had any kind of right to a viewpoint. To an experience of loss. Having said this, he then went on with his merry program. His momentary acknowledgment wasn't enough. But I remember it.

GOOD COMMUNITY,

BAD COMMUNITY,

TELLING

"No. We're not okay. We're over. Our marriage is over."

With these words I started on the slow road out of myself.

I wasn't ready, or maybe I just thought I wasn't. Maybe I was so ready that I couldn't wait another minute. I hadn't planned on telling anyone about Tracey or the state of our relationship. It was early spring, about nine months into our long good-bye, nine months after Tracey's June announcement. I was standing outside a YMCA on a small playground messy with cakey sand and black, melting snow. I was visiting with my friend Dawn while our children visited with one another. Dawn said something about her life. (Little did she know this would be her last chance to get a word in edgewise. Okay, I'm kidding. But only just.) Then she asked about mine. I said something about being unhappy. Something about finances or my work, something to throw her off the marital scent. No one ever asked me about my marriage. It was a given. I wasn't really worried that I was going to be asked anything now. But I was.

Dawn said, "But you and Tracey are okay."

All I had to do was agree. She would have dropped it. Unexpectedly, I couldn't. The moment was at hand. I plunged. "No," I said. "No." It was the best word I could have said. It was a step, a step off the ledge into free-fall.

Dawn was shocked. Her reaction would be the first of many times that I would realize if I had been deluded about my marriage, I hadn't been the only one. Onlookers had thought we had a pretty good thing going, too.

Despite my having kept her at arm's length, the same distance I kept every friend I had, she had periodically observed my stresses and strains, working freelance, teaching, raising three children more or less solo while Tracey constantly traveled. She had made the fairly humongous offer, not once but several times (she was serious!), to take care of my children so that Tracey and I could go away for a weekend alone. Now, with tears in her eyes, she said, "Won't you let me take the kids for a few days so that you can get away together?"

"Thank you, but no," I said. "At this point, a weekend at a B and B isn't going to rekindle our flame."

Of course, my friend wouldn't have made such an offer if I had told her why my marriage was over. But to speak *those* words was, at this stage, beyond me.

I didn't change overnight. Many months would pass before I could tell Dawn the whole story. Along the way, she became an amazing source of emotional and spiritual support. Even more, she became a friend who is invaluable for telling it like she sees it. Dawn is a straight shooter. Forced to choose sides between Tracey and me, she chose the kids— and told me she would always let me know if she thought I was doing something that wasn't in their best interests. This could have been a threat, but I took it as a promise. I felt deeply grateful. In contrast with my old, discreet self, I now let it all hang out and trust that Dawn and friends like her will tell me what they really think. (They do!) Possibly more than any other friend, Dawn has also been a strong advocate for starting over. Urging me to go after new life and love. Not get stuck in the absence of old.

This business of *telling* was repeated over the next fifteen months or so, following that afternoon on the playground, with notable variations.

The next September, I had coffee one morning with three women I knew slightly at the home of one. As is true of many of the friends I've made in recent years, I'd met Indira, Nina, and Laura because we had children roughly the same age, in this case youngest or only children just starting preschool. We had chatted while our children joined in a town-sponsored play-group, but none of us had ever said anything very personal. Now, five minutes after I'd arrived, while Indira took muffins she'd baked out of the oven, Nina indulged in some light-hearted and good-humored griping about her marriage. Then she turned to me and said, "*You're* happy with your husband." And again I abruptly found that I couldn't make myself agree.

"Actually," I said, "my marriage is over."

In retrospect, it's surprising that at this stage I was seen as someone in a happy marriage. My marriage had been se-cretly over the entire time I'd been acquainted with these women. I would arrive at the playgroup feeling like a visitor from Planet Nightmare. I would exchange pleasantries with the other parents, every moment feeling the mounting strain of impersonating a married, stable adult with a more or less normal family life. Feeling that if I didn't hold on to myself very tightly, I would fly apart, my very atoms would lose the struggle to hang together and explode. Once, though, talking with several women, I spontaneously and uncharacteristically offered the information that I had discovered that week that I could sob and clean venetian blinds (my bathroom sports some *very* dirty venetian blinds) at the same time. The other mothers enthusiastically agreed. They, too, managed to perform household tasks while crying. The facilitator of the playgroup looked at us nervously. Decided not to ask. The rest of us laughed, changed the subject. Playgroup went on.

Why was I assumed to be happy with my husband? I'd never before breathed a word of the truth (nothing about why I might be sobbing!), but surely I didn't go so far as to say positive things about Tracey, our relationship. I couldn't have. Could I? I had a long-standing habit of marital contentment. Perhaps its veneer had yet to wear away. Perhaps my policy of not complaining (indeed, of saying nothing) when friends complained about their husbands or female partners made a statement of its own.

I barely knew these three women when I informed them that morning that, actually, my marriage was over, though we were still cohabiting, still keeping up the appearance of an intact family. I didn't tell them because they were my friends. They became my friends because I told them. They became, in fact, the day-to-day emotional supports that at that moment I still didn't know my life would come to depend upon. The people most likely to make the "just checking in" phone call. Those most likely to respond to my call with the four most wonderful words to hear in a crisis: "I'll be right over." They didn't become these people the moment I told them—it takes time, friendship. But that was the moment it began.

It would be months later, during a telephone conversation with Nina, that the reason for my marriage's demise would finally out itself. We were talking about Tracey's then imminent removal from my children's home life. Nina said, "He's still going to be their father."

To which I replied, "Well. Sorta."

"Hmm," she said. "Is this about gender?"

I was floored. "How did you guess?" I gasped.

"Well, look, if he isn't going to be their father . . ."

But that first morning in Indira's kitchen I said very little, and the conversation moved on. That was just right—if I could have foreseen how much conversational airspace I would eat up in the near future, I might never have opened my mouth in the first place. Nina hugged me. Outside my mama role, I wasn't much of a hugger. Too shy to initiate physical contact, too stiff in response. The hug said simply, *I see you. I understand that something big is happening behind the scenes in your life.* I believed the world would end if I told people what was going on. I was right. End it did. Life as I had known it slipped into the past. Every time I said the words, even just some of the words, another crack appeared in my woman-who-has-it-all carapace, the carapace encasing a woman people would later say they never felt they could get close to (well, duh). I felt the cracks. Others saw them. I began to reimagine raising my children beyond my marriage. Beyond the crisis it had become. I began to reimagine myself.

Several years later, Indira would tell me, "When I invited you that first morning I didn't even like you. You always wore a long black coat," she complained. "You never smiled." She told me this on a cold Sunday afternoon in my dining room, while we were bundling up to go for a walk on my road. I was shrugging on a red thrift store find I'd bought after Tracey moved out. "If you'd worn the red coat back then," she said, "I would have liked you." We were both howling with laughter, but she was dead serious.

I'd told my therapist because I had to. I'd spoken with Michael because he already knew. And I'd blurted out part of my secret—that my marriage was over, not why—on these two occasions. A different kind of telling happened with a friend I'll call Clarice, not her name, to protect her family's privacy.

I've been friends with Clarice for years, which, being me, meant that our connection wasn't all that personal. We talked about politics and social issues, about our work. As women who met when we were both nursing babies, we talked above all about the intricacies of growing children. I didn't know Clarice all that well and hadn't allowed her to know me. Coming clean to her was unique in several ways. It didn't just happen with Clarice. She was the first person I knew socially whom I deliberately chose to tell. I chose her because she is exceptionally intelligent, insightful, and caring. And because while Tracey was U-turning on what I'd considered a one-way street, something similarly momentous was going at Clarice's house. One of her daughters was turning into a son.

The same fall that my friendships with Nina, Indira, and Laura were beginning, more than a year after Tracey's June revelation, I sent Clarice an e-mail. I wrote that I wanted to

talk with her about something and asked if we could meet. I
was grateful that she didn't ask what. Given her experience
in these waters, I couldn't tell Clarice that my marriage was
ending and then choke up about why. The whole point was to
tell her everything.

One early evening we met at a local pub. Seated across a
table, we made small talk for a couple of minutes. But Clarice watched me carefully and I knew that she was waiting.
Finally she asked, "What did you want to talk to me about?"

I took a deep breath and said, "You know, I have my own
experience with transgender issues." During the shocked si-
lence that followed, I had time to realize that Clarice thought
I was revealing something *really* unexpected about myself.
"I mean, I'm not transgendered," I hastened to explain. "It's
Tracey."

Needless to say, Clarice was still surprised by my news.
Like virtually everyone who knew us, she thought of us as a
tight couple, a happy family. She hadn't picked up so much
as a whiff of gender change in the air, nor of marital discord.
But talking it over recently, Clarice recalled that what
shocked her most was that I could have kept this elephant
out of sight for over a year—from the circle of friends of
which she and I are both a part and, given what I knew
about her family, from her most of all. *How* had I kept such a
secret? It was a good question. Within it I also heard the
echo of *why*. I struggled to explain myself, how I'd been
brought up to be intensely private about family matters and
intensely black and white about gender. How my marriage
ending this way had called into question my entire adult life,
my sense of myself, and made opening the story up to even
close friends feel scary. Looking at Clarice as I spoke, I suddenly realized how bizarrely withdrawn my old self seemed

to her. How bizarrely withdrawn my old self now seemed to me.

In that initial conversation, I sketched the rough outlines of Tracey's activities and what had been happening in our marriage. Covering all the details wasn't important. Opening up the subject was. Clarice became my confidante that evening, someone I could speak with freely who was closer to the subject than anyone else I knew. Since that evening I've heard many bits and pieces of her family's journey along with sharing my own. But recently I asked Clarice to describe the arc of her experience as the mother of a transgendered child. It was my turn to be surprised.

"It really all started that day at your synagogue," Clarice began. "When you had the ceremony for Lilly and there was a transgendered speaker."

A few weeks after my third child was born, we invited friends to join us in synagogue for the regular Saturday morning service, during which we engaged in a brief ritual to celebrate our daughter's arrival in the Jewish community. Clarice came, by chance bringing with her the then twelve-year-old child whose gender identity was beginning to concern her. Each week the rabbi, or sometimes a member of the congregation, offers a short teaching. On this Saturday, a young man I didn't know rose to speak. About eighteen or twenty years old, he said that he had grown up in this congregation—grown up as a girl. And it was here that at age thirteen he had celebrated his bat (literally "daughter") mitzvah, the coming-of-age ritual at which a Jewish child formally becomes an adult member of the community. He was back now to make a coming-of-age declaration once again, this time as a young man.

"That was the first time we'd had any contact with someone who was transgendered," Clarice recalled. "The first time we put a name to it, had the language to talk about it."

At this point, my own cataclysmic encounter with gender identity issues was still more than a year and a half in the future. I was comfortably situated in the belief that Tracey had long ago made peace with any gender issue he might once have felt, caught up in being newly the mother of three children and the new mother of a medically fragile baby only recently released from neonatal intensive care. Excited to be celebrating our first post-hospital event as a family of five. I had no buttons for the young transman to push. Clarice had confided that her daughter, whom I'll call Pat, was unusually agonized by the onslaught of female adolescence, and I may have been aware, dimly, that the two of them could be listening to the speaker with rather more interest than I felt. I'm sure Clarice said something to that effect after. But I had never grasped the importance of the occasion.

Clarice went on. "I remember as we drove away from the synagogue I asked Pat what she thought of the speaker. We talked for a while and then I said, 'If you could be a boy, is that what you would choose?' Pat said yes immediately. I told her I would support her no matter what she wanted, but that it made me sad to think that she felt bad about who she was. And Pat said, 'I don't feel bad about *who* I am. My problem is with *what*.' I thought that that was so profound— that she could make the distinction at the age of twelve between who and what she was. It had a huge effect on me."

The power of Pat's clarity enabled Clarice to serve as Pat's advocate in the years that followed with far less anguish than she might have felt otherwise, and to help her husband adjust to Pat's choice to live his life as a man. When Clarice told me this story, it struck me as ironic (*ironic* is too weak a word, but it will have to do) that the fork in Pat's road was stumbled upon that morning in my synagogue, a place he had never been before, has never been since. Was led only by his mother's friendship with me.

In the Valley of the Politically Correct, it's easy to support a transgendered friend or acquaintance. Better than easy. It gives one a sort of panache, for some people a kind of frisson. Not so easy to live this profound transformation as a mother. Many Valley residents would later argue that their tenuous connection to gender identity issues through friends, family, or community members made it impossible for them to express even basic human sympathy for me or for my children. Impossible for them to object to any aspect of Tracey's behavior for fear of appearing less than fully on board with his gender project. Given her unconditional love and support for her child, Clarice might well have felt those qualms. My very different experience of Tracey's transformation could have alienated and offended her. Extraordinarily, it did not. There was never any confusion in her mind between Pat and my problems with Tracey. We can't all be Clarice. But it would be nice.

From the moment I revealed my situation to Clarice, she became one of the people to whom, quite simply and seriously, I attribute my survival. Aside from all that I've gained from my friendship with Clarice, observing Pat's journey from the sidelines has also played a crucial role in the evolution of my thinking. It allowed me to separate Tracey's specific actions—not just what he did, but how he did it—from gender transformation in general. What happened in my family became for me the sharpest argument possible in favor of supporting young people to express, rather than suppress, their gut-sense gender identities. It gave me an

opportunity to realize I neither objected to nor feared transgendered people. As long as I wasn't married to them.

Tracey had told me that our marriage was over immediately
after I'd returned from a weekend away with friends. We'd
sat around a hot tub and sympathized while one woman related the agonized state of her marriage. Two years later, we
sat around that same hot tub. Tracey was about to move out
and I still had trouble telling. One of the women knew all
about what was going on in my life; the others, nothing. "Tell
them!" my confidante insisted. "If you don't tell them, I
will." With great difficulty, I told.

"Tracey is moving out this week," I announced. "Our
marriage is over. He's a transsexual and he's going to live as
a woman."

After I'd spoken I noticed that one of the women, whom
I'll call Joan, said nothing and turned away. I'd been afraid
that my revelation would somehow make me an outcast.
Now it seemed as if my fears were coming true. (In the Valley of the Politically Correct, you *might* become a social pa-
riah because your husband dresses as a woman or, much
more likely, because you refuse to be gung ho about it.) Joan
can't even look at me, I said to myself. Then I noticed that
she wasn't so much looking away from me as at another of
the women sitting on the other side of the hot tub. "Tell
them," the other woman said to Joan. "Tell them." Joan was,
in fact, gathering the courage to share a secret of her own.
Her story isn't mine to tell, but it turned out I wasn't the
only woman married to a sexually interesting man.

———

Tracey was moving out, and my friends Oriole and Sid were trying to invite us for dinner. We went back and forth via e-mail. Oriole suggested a date. I wrote back that Tracey would be out of town, but the kids and I could make it. She suggested a couple of other dates. I wrote that they worked for the kids and me, but Tracey would be away.

Finally, exasperated, she wrote, "Well, would you please name some dates that Tracey *will* be in town?"

Why was it so hard to tell? I mean, why in this specific instance, beyond all my usual reasons? Maybe, though I have never thought of them in even vaguely parental terms, the fact that they are a generation older than I am caused me to project in their direction the sense of failure I would have felt delivering this news to parents, if I'd had parents. Maybe because they are gracious, highly cultured, decorous—I can hear them laughing—I dreaded shocking them.

Following my usual pattern, I half told. I e-mailed Oriole: "There is no date on which Tracey and I are available for dinner together. Tracey and I are no longer on dinner-eating terms."

Oriole wrote back that she wasn't surprised. "I saw Tracey recently for the first time in a long while. He looked so different. His hair was so long. I tried to tell Sid that something was up, but he said I was crazy."

While so many supposedly savvy people had been clueless, Oriole, who didn't even have a word to describe Tracey ("It's not 'gay,' " she ventured when we finally talked), understood what was happening.

What a relief.

I started laughing as I read her first e-mail responding to my news. We had dinner, them, my children, and me, at a loud pizza restaurant where people go with kids because they (the kids) are given wads of dough to play with and can scream at the top of their lungs and not disturb diners at the next table. I told them as much of my story as was possible, speaking around the children's attention. I told them more—lots and lots more—on the many occasions there have been since. They've been patient, sympathetic, and, I sincerely hope, amused by my melodrama. We're still laughing.

THE TURN OF THE
CORKSCREW

The unusual part of this entire scenario is not only does she not have a mate and a protector and the burden of these three cubs, but she also doesn't have a pride. And that's very, very unusual for lionesses.

—*Fresh Air* interview with Beverly and
Dereck Joubert, filmmakers, *The Last Lions*

At the time she was assuming the role of Speaker of the House, much was made in the press of Nancy Pelosi's "mother of five" voice. As the two years Tracey and I lived together posthumously, no longer married, wore on (and on and on), I began to wonder what a "single mother of three" voice would sound like. An incoherent howl? A cackle of madhouse laughter? A shriek of blind terror? Or would it be the sound of silence, the emptiness of much too busy much too tired to say much of anything? I had been a single mother part-time almost as long as I'd been a mother. It had been a long time since I'd had a husband to share parenting or any other concerns with. To share an emotional or social life, to share intimacy. Yet I feared true full-time single motherhood even as I longed for it. The kind where no one is coming home tomorrow or next week. Or ever. Where there is no one to wait for. Or dread.

Then Tracey moved out. It was June, so that we had the relatively simple months of summer to adjust. In the fall there was the return to three different children's schedules, three different schools in three different towns. New England winter on the way, the usual story: dark days, snow, ice, clogged nasal passages, a long, steep driveway to shovel. One September evening, though I couldn't think of anyone who'd care to read such a document, I sat down to make a record of that (typical) day's events. With adjustments for ages, schools, and schedules, it could have been written long before Tracey left or any time since.

A Day in the Life of the Busy Single Mother of Three

Rose at 4:30 a.m. on the dot, finished making my bed by 4:33, turned on lights, coffee, spent 20–25 minutes in the bathroom, arranged the lunchboxes and breakfast table, along with other miscellaneous tasks. Brought coffee to the couch, finally read a section of the Sunday *Times* (it's Tuesday) while listening to the news on NPR. Checked email while exercising, finishing up just in time to wake a 13-year-old boy from a deep, exhausted slumber at 6 sharp. Ran back to bedroom, dressed, woke 7- and 4-year-old girls from deep, exhausted slumbers. Cuddled (coddled) and dressed 4-year-old, who refuses to leave babyhood behind, calling to 7-year-old to get up, use bathroom, dress. Listened to trope practice of Mr. 13, who is to chant from the Torah at the bar mitzvah of another 13-year-old boy next

month, made girls' beds, did hair of Ms. 7, got everyone to
the table, tried to sit at table while they ate and at the same
time run around the house doing what needed to be done.
Was planning to use the morning to work on the copy editing project I'm engaged in, but when the phone rang before
7, agreed to sub at one of the public schools (fortunately, Ms.
4's school) that morning: I'll do the editing in some other
time slot (when?!) and I need both these minute sources of
income. Just before 7:30, got the girls in the car, leaving Mr.
13, who would be picked up any second by his carpool, and
drove the 10 minutes to the center of town to put Ms. 7 on
the van to her school, a further half hour away, at 7:45. If all
went according to plan—were more dangerous words ever
written?—that leaves *exactly* enough time to race most of
the way back home to the parking lot of our town's public
school, where I put Ms. 4 on the van to her public preschool
program in the adjacent town, the town that *has* a preschool program. All did not go according to plan. By the
time we reached the center of town, Ms. 4, who refuses to
toilet-train, admits she is in need of a change (she is wearing
underwear, as required by her class). I call the school bus
office, ask them to tell the driver we won't make the preschool van. Ms. 7 gets out of the car. I attempt to get a bag
of donation food for the survival center out of the car so
that it can go with her on the van for her school's collection. The bag tears. All the canned goods have to be left
strewn over the floor of the car. Put Ms. 7 on van and race
back home, engage in very lengthy poop change (including
bath and clothes washing), race to Ms. 4's school, install
her in her class, race to school office to sign in, race from
office to assigned classroom. Spend the morning attempting to take care of a first grader with Down's syndrome

who only understands Spanish and is decidedly out of sorts with me for being an unfamiliar face. Throughout the morning I am asked by every adult I encounter, "Do you speak Spanish?" "Are you bilingual?" and have to admit my hopeless limitations again and again.

I never made it beyond the morning. When I sat at my computer to write this, late in the evening, I didn't have enough time to describe an entire day. I didn't have enough energy.

A haunting sound track thrums throughout our house, our car, an a cappella chant for three voices. Goes like this:

Mama. Mama. Mama. Mama. Mama. Mama.
Mama. Mama. Mama. Mama. Mama. Mama.
Mama. Mama. Mama. Mama. Mama. Mama.
Mama. Mama. Mama. Mama. Mama. Mama.

Three voices chanting in unison. Harmonizing. The primal, incandescently beautiful repeated syllable of need, of want, of the desperate life-and-death struggle for attention. My attention. Mine and mine alone, all three, at once, while I'm attempting a hazardous left turn or cooking dinner, writing an urgent e-mail, talking or listening on the telephone. I love this chant. It leads to crazy laughter (particularly when I echo it back to my trio of singers). It fills our home with the sound of life itself. And it creates in me the extraordinary sensation that my brain is being skillfully chopped into small, wet pieces of sushi, manipulated around balls of sticky rice, and offered up between the pointed ends of delicate lacquered daggers.

Somewhere I once read a story by a student of Zen medita-
tion who was criticized by his teacher for engaging in ani-
mated dinner table conversation while reaching to serve
himself food—rice, no doubt—at the same time. Sounds like
a good time at my house, but for this Zen master it was sym-
bolic of everything that was wrong with the student. "Do one
thing at a time," she admonished him. One thing at a time? I
thought. This woman has clearly never been a mother.

Single motherhood has changed me. It has revamped the
pathways of my brain. Along with greatly increased self-
confidence and other benefits that my scattered thoughts, at
the moment, can't quite bring into focus, a constantly divided attention has made me brittle. Sometimes I juggle the
multitude of tasks and enjoy doing it. Sometimes in a moment of calmly abstracted silence, I respond to a single voice
saying "Mama" as if a mob had been yelling in my face all
day. I jump. I snap. *What!?* I don't want to learn to do one
thing at a time. I want to do it all at once and do it better.
Without snapping.

On one layer, the most mundane and familiar, mine is
simply a story about motherhood. Single motherhood. Spe-
cifically being the single mother of three children of widely
divergent ages, all with the multiple needs to fall apart, be
reassured, be rescued, that one might expect of children in
the thick of crisis and loss, two with "special needs" of the
learning and/or health variety. And, oh yeah, all the usual
needs to be fed and clothed and driven to school and tae
kwon do and playdates and doctor visits and to celebrate
birthdays and holidays. Anyone who has had more than one
child knows that family dynamics complicate exponentially
with the addition of each new member of the family. When
children outnumber adults three to one, that one is walking

a tightrope without a net. I've learned how to walk it alone—
and sometimes how not to. With difficulty I've learned
(sometimes) to reach out to others. To accept the hand that
is offered. I've discovered friends ready to catch me when I
fall.

Shortly after Tracey moved out of our home, the Great
Recession began. I wouldn't dream of claiming cause and effect. Still. The bursting U.S. housing bubble is generally con-
ceded to have been the trigger that brought about national
and international economic mayhem. There is no consensus
about what burst the bubble at this particular moment in
time. Kinda gives one pause, doesn't it?

In any case, my life as a single mother has coincided with
a time of widespread economic doodoo. What I read in the
paper and hear on the radio and from friends exacerbates my
financial insecurities, solidifies the none-too-nebulous pros-
pects of penury. It hones my already sharp sense of gratitude
for the variable-rate (but not subprime!) mortgaged roof
I still have over my children's head and my own. It reminds
me daily that I'm not the only one walking a tight-budget
wire strung across roiling seas. But then, I don't need news
stories to tell me that. I'd know that anyway. I have a
village.

We help one another mainly with emotional support, but
we're also there with groceries, sometimes cash. Aside from a
loan that enabled me to begin the process of divorce (To
Those It Concerns: I remember! I'll pay you back! Someday!), I've been offered help a number of times. I haven't
taken anyone else up on their generosity—yet. I tell people
I'm filing away their loan offers for a rainy day. Or, okay, not
a rainy day. If I called on my friends every time it metaphorically rained, they'd be cleaned out. In the meantime, I'm

pleased to be able to help out friends with small sums myself on occasion. We all pass on the books we've read, the still wearable clothes we feel done with, the children's clothes our own have shot out of.

An economist I know was asked during a lecture Q & A, "Do you think hard times are good for building community?"

By way of answer, he told his audience about my friends and me.

Best of all, the village mentality isn't limited to our generation. Indira tells me that her six-year-old daughter was so pleased to see my youngest in the sneakers she can't wear any longer. When she got new shoes, she said, "I'm going to take really good care of them so that I can give them to Lilly in good shape."

How great is that?

As those on the ground in battle or single motherhood say, there are logistical challenges. Sometimes I have to be in three places at once. Sometimes I actually figure out how to be in three places at once. Sometimes I get help: from another parent, from a friend, occasionally from Tracey. Sometimes, rarely, someone has to miss something. Then that child is disappointed but gets over it. And I feel guilty, not for a little while but forever.

Tracey doesn't help raise the children much. He is often unwell, and he travels even more than he used to, with frequent weekends away in addition to his workweek, plus longer trips to Europe, Israel, Africa. I don't mind. A week without Tracey is a week without someone my children can be with for a few hours, be driven to school or picked up by on the odd day. But it's an easier week for me, hands down: no stress of worrying about the children while they are with him. Easier for the kids: they don't have to make the adjustments most (all?) kids of divorce have to make when they go from one parent to another. Especially when the parents have very different styles and values. Probably because he doesn't see them all that much and because they live entirely with me, my children's time with Tracey has the quality of visits with an out-of-town relative who drops into their lives, buys them lots of treats, and goes away again. Once my youngest told me, with panache and a touch of belligerence, that Tracey had said that not only did she not need to eat healthy food when she was with him, she didn't need to eat healthy food when she was with me, either. I knew Tracey hadn't really said this. (Right?) He did laugh when I repeated the remark to him as an example of how I take the kids' reports with a grain of salt. Even so, Lilly's statement came not out of left field, but out of some vague awareness that food is one of our (safer) areas of skirmish. It's gotten a little less worrisome. In contrast with the early days of their visits with Tracey, they don't come home and report that they spent an entire beautiful spring or summer day in the library, on computers, and were given no food at all. Now they say they spent entire beautiful days in his apartment, on the computer or in front of the TV, and were given unlimited junk food. Progress.

I would love to say that I have behaved well through all of this. I have not. I have behaved badly, often, though not so much anymore. Shortly before Tracey moved out, I confided in the divorced dad of one of my children's friends that I would soon be wearing his shoes. Among the good pieces of advice he gave me was this one: "You can never criticize the other parent to the kids. It's really hard not to, but you have to try to avoid it at all costs."

It was clear that he was speaking from personal experience. Wow, I thought but didn't say aloud. You mean you've actually dissed your ex to the kids? I would never do that.

Looking back, I find it hard to believe my optimism.

My children refuse (mostly) to blame me for the tensions between Tracey and me, to admit to anger toward me. I fear this is partly because at some level, having lost one parent, they dread alienating the other. But mainly their attitude toward me is protective. I suspect this is due to their perception (well, Adam's perception, which Bibi shares a bit of and Lilly doesn't share at all) of my vulnerability. Their awareness of how hard I work just to keep us all standing in one place.

My youngest child was blessed with a preschool teacher who struck me as a paragon of grace and intelligence. During a conference in our first year as a solo-parent family, she said to me, "You could give up, but you don't. You keep going."

I shrugged. "I'm just doing what I have to do. What anyone with children would do."

She disagreed. "My husband was seriously ill a few years ago. A friend told me what I'm now telling you: You could refuse to get out of bed. You could pull the covers over your head. You could fall apart. People do. You're choosing not to."

I heard this at a low point in my life. I didn't feel proud of getting out of bed every day. Of delivering three fed, washed, dressed, homework-accomplished children to the school system on time each morning. I don't feel proud of it now. Still. At a time when I felt nothing but shitty about myself and the hands I was dealing out to my children, it was nice to think it might be possible to feel good—at least not shitty—about something. Racked by guilt, low of self-esteem, I could harbor visions of pragmatic grandeur. Aspire to the do-what-you-need-to-do-to-get-through school of parenthood and survival even if I couldn't ever really feel at home there. Know, if not admit to it, that at the end of some days a single mother's most important tool is her corkscrew.

THE WORDS

When my marriage fell apart, the situation entailed a whole
new lexicon, in some cases a new spin on old words.

For roughly two and a half years, I woke with the word
gender in my ears and felt as if it had gouged a crevice in my
brain. I am not exaggerating for comic or any other effect. I
literally heard this word, *gender,* when I woke, it echoed
through my day, and snagged on my punch-drunk consciousness when I attempted to sleep at night. Gender, gender, gender. Lots of related thoughts, obviously, but always
the word itself. Over and over. Until I thought I would go
mad. (Luckily it stopped before madness ensued. It didn't
gradually fade away. It ceased. Like the worsening hip and
leg pain that had for several years made walking difficult,
running impossible, and finding a comfortable position for
sleep an agony—it ceased. There is no mystery about when.
It was displaced, some months after Tracey's exit from our
home, when another word took up residence in my mind. A
name. A name that wasn't Tracey. The hip and leg pain were

nudged aside by other sensations at precisely the same time. But that's another story.)

The word *woman* made me cringe. Woman was now a designation anyone could claim, an equal access club to which everyone might belong. My husband and I were both women, just different kinds. You had your *transwoman* (that would be him) and your *genetic* or *biological woman* (that was me). The transwoman was no less genuine, no less a woman, than the genetic model, which was, if anything, beginning to look a touch obsolete, reduced to a mammalian plane a cut above cow, a creature who owed her femininity to a dumb chromosomal crapshoot, not on the level of those who made a conscious, willed choice.

She. Pronouns, of course, become problematic around a person crossing gender lines. I still use the male variety to refer to Tracey because even now I can't think, speak, or write about this person any other way. This results in minor conversational oddities such as the following:

Acquaintance: "Have you asked Tracey about this? What does she say?"

Me: "I have asked him. He says . . ."

Since these exchanges nearly always seem to be about Tracey's relationships with my children—one he and a pair of shes—a simple interchange is quickly ensnared in pronouns and no one knows who anyone is talking about. As I say, a minor inconvenience. Particularly in contrast with the political issue involved.

It is politically correct to refer to people the way they want to be referred to. I'm probably not telling you anything you don't already know here. A man says, Call me she. You do, or he and his friends call *you* terminally retrograde. I don't know if this trend has its limits. I'd like to assert that if your co-worker asks you to call her Your Highness, you'll decline; but maybe you won't. If you are African American and your white friend instructs you that he has decided to become African American, that you are no more African American than he is, and that to suggest in any way that you are is deeply offensive, not merely to him but to all the politically correct of this earth, do you tell him to go to hell?

To those offended by the comparison of gender and racial identities (yes, I know you're out there!), I offer this semi-apropos anecdote. *"I'm Rosa Parks!"* Tracey declared at one point, equating himself with the civil rights heroine with typical modesty. *"I'm a hero!"* Okay, sure. Why stop at wanting to be a woman? Why not choose a specific woman? Once he had just been a white man frustrated to have no claim on victim status. Now he was courageous. A martyr, a trailblazer. All he'd had to do was put on a dress.

Immediately after Tracey announced to our religious community that he was leaving our family and proposed to begin living as a woman, the members of this community referred to him as she. I mean immediately. To me. In their very first communications. It felt as if I were drowning in loss and they were sharking around me, yelling, "She! She!" I suggested to the group that though they were free to refer to Tracey any way they liked outside my presence, it was a bit insensitive to insist on this with me. I asked that they refrain from doing so. They went nuts. I had offended their deepest, which is to say most politically correct, sensibilities. They could not consider that the very public, very painful demise of a twenty-some-year marriage was not an opportunity for grandstanding for transgender rights. It was my life. And speaking of my life, I also became politically incorrect for being unwilling to rewrite it in retrospect. Tracey is supposed to become female even in the past. I hear things like "When you married her, was she . . . ?" I explain that when Tracey and I married, he was neither her nor she.

Of course, to my children and me Tracey isn't her or she now, either. With one exception. Bibi, a couple of years ago, came home from a visit to Tracey and exclaimed that she had left a book in *her* car. I talked about the missing book with no outward reaction to the pronoun choice. Inwardly I felt oddly glad and sad. Glad that after three years she had made the colossal adjustment necessary to refer to her father as she. (Unconsciously? Impossible to say. A moment after saying it, she looked consciously unhappy, and she's never referred to Tracey with a feminine pronoun again.) Sad as if something had been lost. As if, childlike, I had been holding on to the belief that if none of us said it, we could keep it from being real?

While I'm on the subject of what my children call Tracey, *mother,* in all its permutations, isn't it. Again that's something that doesn't sit well with everyone. I applaud those who fall all over themselves to embrace Tracey's right to change. I regret that this camp doesn't recognize mine to stay the same. Just as my status as a woman now requires a qualifier, my relationship to my children is open to redefinition. Other people's redefinition. *Bio mom* is the term a school counselor chose until I kindly (okay, snappishly) steered her away from it. Aside from the unfortunate echoes of biohazard, mothers are categorized as biological when they've given their children up for adoption, *when they have limited their mothering to the biological role* and there's another kind of mother in the picture. However you frame it, our family portrait includes only one mother. (Among the many families I know who comprise two women and their children, I have never heard either partner called the biological—much less bio—mom by the children or their teachers. In these families, both women are acknowledged mothers, and if there's a name differential, it's on the order of Mom and Mama.) Occasionally people actually get this. One day after a staff meeting at my daughters' school, a teacher took me aside. At the meeting, she told me, Tracey had been referred to by another teacher as one of my daughters' moms. My confidante had questioned the designation. She'd pointed out to her colleagues that my girls call their father their father, their dad, Daddy, he, him. Shouldn't their teachers follow suit?

Declining the M-word for anyone but me does land my kids in sticky situations. Once he began appearing with them in public dressed as a woman, Tracey had his own concerns about being called Daddy on the playground. He asked them to come up with another name for him. They refused. He asked them to call him "D." The older kids made a halfhearted attempt, but it didn't stick. Lilly didn't even try. As I've mentioned, this leaves her open to questions from peers that are becoming more uncomfortable for her as her social awareness grows: "Why is she calling that woman Daddy?"

During a visit to a new friend's home, then nine-year-old Bibi was asked by her friend's mother, not once but repeatedly, "You have two moms, don't you?" Unwilling to say she did, unwilling to enter into intimate family details with a stranger, my daughter had no idea how to respond. She settled on, "It's complicated." And repeated it each time the question was asked. In this instance, the mom had seen two women's names listed in the school's parent directory, not Tracey in the flesh. But though friends who knew Tracey "before" insist he couldn't possibly pass for born-female, my impression is that he often does. Even presented with an odd-looking woman, most people don't jump to trans.

As a result, my kids and I both need to parry the inevitable questions about our family.

One day while I was standing around on the playground at school, another mom asked me, "Did you carry Lilly?"

I was thrown by the word *carried*. I stared back at her, baffled.

"Did you carry her?" she clarified. "Or did your partner?"

I was still in the dark.

The woman was getting nervous now. "Ex-partner?" she tried.

Finally I got it. I rejected the first response that occurred to me—*You don't seriously think that guy you've seen with my daughter has a womb, do you?*—and went with the second. "Oh," I said. "I'm the mom."

What she made of that is anyone's guess. What I made of it is that I'm going to have to face more of these kinds of questions. I probably should try to prepare for them. How the hell do I do that? At least I can learn to expect them.

More recently, another mom at school introduced herself to me. "And you're one of Lilly's parents?" she inquired.

"Yes," I said brightly. "I'm her *mother*."

Tracey expressed a great deal of anger at being male, at the people who made him be male. Above all, at me. One day when we were still living together, he hurled this accusation: "You're *transphobic*!"

I'd never heard the term *transphobic* before. My first impulse was to retort with vehement denial. Instead, I agreed.

"Yes," I admitted. "I am afraid of transsexuals. Well, not all transsexuals. You."

This was one of our lighter moments. "You're not alone," he assured me. "Transphobia is endemic in Western culture." He pointed to old Hollywood portrayals of the transgendered as twisted serial killers (*Silence of the Lambs*) and pathetic losers (*Dog Day Afternoon*). We were still sometimes capable of laughing together, and we laughed now. Had I known about the *hijra* at the time, I would have introduced them as a countercultural—equally feared but non-Western—juxtaposition to his victims of Hollywood. The *hijra* of India, Bangladesh, and Pakistan are considered a caste of their own, a "third sex," but they are most often men decked out as women who want to be recognized as men decked out as women. Economically marginal, they manage to make an occasional buck by showing up uninvited at weddings and birth ceremonies, where terrified hosts pay them off in an effort to avert their curses.

I didn't know about the *hijra* at the time, but I did know what I had in my kitchen. "Look, look!" I told Tracey gleefully, pointing to the food labels promising the absence of *trans* fats. "Trans is bad!"

"I've noticed," he said ruefully.

Tracey's process of appearance alteration carried with it a trans term of its own: *transition*. This was a word to which I strongly objected. Transition implied to me something ordinary, something gentle, something—dare I say it—natural. Children transition—from breast milk to lattes, from elementary to high school, from xylophones to iPods. Everyone, sooner or later, transitions to death. Deciding you are female when, to put it indelicately, you are not, employing falsies and a falsetto—false! false!—didn't strike me as ordinary, gentle, or—I have to say it—natural.

Speaking of falsies, *breast* became another of those words to take on entirely unlooked-for connotations. To possess the real, fleshly thing is apparently one of the male-to-female's fondest wishes. When Tracey began arriving at his job à la femme, the flap at his workplace spilled over into the public sphere. A tabloid ran an article on the story, and my family was temporarily inundated with calls from television stations. Bystanders from all over the sociopolitical spectrum weighed in on Web sites and blogs, calling Tracey everything from victim to hero to devil incarnate. What troubled me most about it all was the fear that the noise would reach my children. What troubled Tracey? The blogger who accused his breasts of being implants.

I came up with a word of my own, *transwidow,* to capture my bereft status as the woman left behind in the wake of his transformation. *Single mother,* a term I'd never imagined applying to myself, became a painfully correct fit long before Tracey removed himself from our home. I remember the first time that I referred to myself as a single mother in conversation with Tracey, who was still living with us at the time.

"You aren't a single mother," he said at once.

"Well," I responded, "I'm single and I'm a mother."

To that he had no reply.

As a single mother, I met up with the term *transitional assistance,* which might refer to food money given by the government to help an indigent single mother feed her children—or might mean assistance for the family whose prime breadwinner has left them to transition.

No-fault divorce is a term I'd never thought twice about until I found myself in the middle of same. It is an oxymoron if ever there was one. Divorce is all about fault. Or maybe you like the sound of *no fault* when the fault is, in fact, yours. Another oxymoron I began to reflect upon in the course of my no-fault divorce was *family law.* A seemingly innocuous category of court activity, it allows the offending . . . er, practicing attorney to self-designate as an advocate in family law, as opposed to saying, "I'm a divorce lawyer." Or maybe, "I'm a no-fault divorce lawyer." For the sundering couple in the courtroom and for the children who hopefully never have to enter it but whose lives will be shaped by what happens within its four walls, these two words ill fit together. Joining them creates a little black hole of language, on the order of, say, Nazi doctor. To add "law" to family is to destroy it.

Another notable word of our divorce was *boundaries,* as used by mental health providers (mine, my daughter's) to identify something Tracey needed more of. That is to say, he had trouble knowing where he ended and I began, where his needs ought to stop dead in their tracks because other people's—in particular the children's and especially my older daughter's—well-being demanded it. During our divorce and custody battle, Tracey told the court that I was insufficiently *feminine* (another word that will never sound the same) to raise my older daughter. Bibi needed Tracey because he was more feminine than I was. In Tracey's words, "Bibi wants to feminize." The idea, of course, could never have occurred to Bibi. As applied to a girl of seven, eight, nine years of age, what could it possibly mean? Tracey had simply forgotten whom he was speaking of. He had forgotten that Bibi is a girl. She doesn't need to "feminize" to become a woman. All she has to do is grow up. Preferably with as little gender-related interference as possible.

Tracey's boundary issues seemed to me to be symbolically expressed in his new use of *boy* and *girl,* not to describe the children, but to refer to himself. I thought the thresholds of age could be crossed in only one direction, but if gender lines are fluid, why not life stages? As I've mentioned, while he once called himself a man, he now says he used to be a *boy* but can't operate in *boy mode* any longer because he's really a *girl*. Even these youthfully innocent single syllables now bear freight they weren't meant to hold.

"Boy or girl?" shouted a gas station attendant one day while I worked the pump.

Huh?

"Boy or girl?"

I stared at the man in disbelief. I couldn't get away from gender. This man was questioning *mine*. I looked down at my breasts. *Hey,* I was about to shout back, *they're real!* Just in time, the man pointed to the face peering out through my rear windshield. "The dog!" he called. "Boy or girl?"

Dude. As in, what my ex-husband isn't anymore. As in, the sorts of guys I heard one morning on talk radio. The two were taking turns listing the things men hate to hear women say. They saved the best worst statement for last: *I used to be a dude.*

One evening around the dinner table, I told the children a Sephardic (that is, Spanish Jewish) saying: The rich man's rooster lays eggs; the poor man's hens lay none. I asked them what they thought it meant. Having grown up working class, I thought it would be obvious. But despite my financial struggles and our precarious circumstances, my children locate themselves in a different economic stratum from the one I grew up in. Their shoulders are unburdened by class chips. The aphorism's meaning escaped them. What they did come up with was, like their take on many things these days, an interpretation I imagine few other children would think of: The rooster, they suggested, was either a *transsexual* or a *cross-dresser*. Note that transsexuals and cross-dressers are two categories. My children know the difference.

Because he is a transsexual—someone who chooses to change his body and not just his clothes—the ultimate goal of Tracey's alterations of appearance packed a phrase of its own: *gender reassignment*. From the beginning, this term struck me as peculiar beyond all the others. It suggested that gender was not a given at birth but doled out sometime after, assigned arbitrarily, perhaps, like a Social Security number, or else deliberately, like a credit rating or a job, dispensed from a distant source, and subject to distant change. It placed the transgendered person in an oddly passive role, awaiting reassignment from a mysterious entity that might or might not grant it, like an enlisted person petitioning for relocation from Fort Dix to Fort Bliss. To my ears it rang too polite for what Tracey was about. *Voluntary prick removal* seemed more on target.

Unspeakable words; words we can't bring ourselves to say. Out of grief or fear. I offer two. One, mine and real. The other, my children's, invented.

Mascara: a word that I temporarily couldn't make myself utter. It happened a few days after Tracey's initial announcement that his gender was about to become the center of our lives. We took off for a previously arranged weekend trip to celebrate Father's Day (another painful phrase, an occasion

that has since become a sore spot in the year for my children). Upon arriving at our hotel, I discovered that I'd neglected to pack mascara in my luggage. "I need to stop at a
drugstore," I told Tracey. "I forgot a cosmetic."

"Which cosmetic?" he wanted to know.

"Just a cosmetic," I said.

"Yeah, which one?"

We went back and forth for a while. Eventually he gave
up asking. He had to, because I couldn't get the word off my
tongue. Mascara. From *maschera*, Italian for "mask," appropriate enough when talking about the doffing or donning of
disguises entailed in cross-dressing or gendering, mascara
was suddenly too dangerous or too intimate to speak. I mentally clutched my little cosmetics bag as if he wanted in
(which he did) and by holding inside all the words of its con-
tents, I could keep him out (which I couldn't).

Thwunga: a nonsense word Tracey and the children had
made up long before for the game of being playfully tossed
onto a bed. One night Adam, in his nascent role as dad stand-
in, wanted to comfort Bibi. He took to tossing her onto her
bed, something she loved. She was enjoying it until he
shouted happily, *"Thwunga!"*

Laughing and crying at the same time, Bibi told him,
"You can't call it that! You have to come up with a new
name!"

This little moment seemed to encapsulate it all. Our ability to help and support one another and survive and go on
and enjoy things. The good stuff we could pull from the past
into the future. The way even something trivial had the
power to make the sadness brim. The need for new names.
There is a Jewish folk custom of taking a different name
when gravely ill, in the hope of confusing, and thus evading,

the Angel of Death. My girls and boy still want to have fun. They just hope that by calling their fun something new, they can escape the notice of the hovering angels of hurt.

In *A Grief Observed,* C. S. Lewis wrote that "in grief nothing 'stays put.'" He said—I could claim I intend no pun by quoting an amputation metaphor, but it would be a lie:

> How often will the vast emptiness astonish me like a complete novelty and make me say, "I never realized my loss till this moment"? The same leg is cut off time after time. The first plunge of the knife into the flesh is felt again and again.

Grief. There it is. No need to fear it. That, after all, is the scary word all these other words have the power to conjure. The deep well of which they may haphazardly tap. And make it all new again.

NO-FAULT DIVORCE

For most of my life, I regarded divorce like head lice. It happened in other families. Not to people who were dirty, or inferior, or who deserved it. Just to people who weren't me. The well-run home simply did not include it.

The home I grew up in was not run well, but immigrant cultural ethos kept divorce (mostly) from its door. In my extended family, I can think of only one divorce in my parents' generation, one in mine. Among my close friends now, two have divorces in their pasts, a few are married to men who had previous marriages, but I know all these people in their current, remarried states. I haven't seen their relationships fall apart. On the other hand, I've repeatedly had the experience in recent years of learning that some couple I know only slightly, but who gave every appearance of being as happily, solidly wed as I once thought I was, had parted ways. Each time I was dumbfounded. As if the people involved were inventing divorce. When Tracey and I took our marriage vows in San Francisco's City Hall, the judge said, "This is the first marriage for both of you—let it be the last." I smiled, twenty-two and smugly certain it could never be otherwise. I was still smug—at least certain—when, not long before my life went to pieces, my middle child begged for a promise that we would never divorce, and Tracey and I both obliged her without hesitation. But we know from the oft quoted statistics that divorce is the endgame in half of all marriages. Why *not* me?

The story of the second year of our split is a report from the killing fields of divorce, in which the once happy couple complete the process of mutation into bitter, vindictive enemies. I had thought that it was only in Shakespeare's comedies that characters did nothing more than cross-dress to become unrecognizable to people who knew them well. Only in his tragedies that one person took against another for no reason. That wasn't real life. Right?

How did we get here?

No matter how trite, how obvious, it must be said: Divorce is hell. A breakup involving no legal proceedings is bad. Divorce is worse. If you have ever gone through a divorce, chances are you know what I mean when I say divorce is ghastly. Staggeringly, unspeakably bad. Unspeakable not in the sense that nothing can be said about it—I obviously have a good deal to say, and I'm far from the first—but in the sense that no words can quite encompass the dreadfulness. If you have never been divorced, think of the worst breakup you have experienced and imagine playing it out on a public battlefield, in a series of skirmishes spanning months, in which you are attacked by a mercenary (your ex's attorney) who doesn't know you but who craves your blood. Whose weapons are information taken from your life or made up out of whole cloth. Details like the figures in your checkbook, the words you spoke in your most anguished fights and intimate moments. Imagine paying thousands of dollars to hold still and let the bullets whiz past your ears—or tear through your flesh. And say nothing. The second or third time Tracey and I were in court together, I stood up at the end of the day's session and turned to leave the small room, only to find myself confronted by the curious stares of a handful of strangers seated three feet behind me: the next case up. They had been very quiet, as one generally is in the presence of a judge who holds one's children and financial future in her hands. I hadn't realized anyone not connected to our divorce was in the room. We'd had an audience. It was like sitting up at the end of a gynecological examination to find the next patient perched fully clothed beside the stirrups. (Why didn't they wait their turn in the corridor, as we did? Perhaps their attorneys felt that listening to our problems would give them a greater appreciation of their own.)

My marriage died a slow, agonizing death through the courts as well as out of them. It took me the better part of the year after Tracey moved out to retain a lawyer, for the simple reason that one *retains* legal representation by paying a *retainer*. I had no money. I knew no lawyers. During that year, friends suggested divorce mediation, a much less pricey alternative. I tried to talk to Tracey. He seemed to want to work things out. We had been talking to each other, working things out between us, for years. Why couldn't we do it now? During several months of talking, I began to believe that Tracey and I might reach a legal agreement. Might actually end up civil co-parents, possibly even friends. Then Tracey changed his mind about everything we had come to terms on. Everything was once again up in the air. What had become the theme of our last two years of cohabitation now became the theme of our split. He wouldn't stand by his word. I couldn't trust him. I had no choice but to find a lawyer and a way to pay him or her.

I asked people I knew for the names of local attorneys. I was offered names unasked. A woman who had recently gone through not only divorce but post-divorce legal wrangling over the terms of custody of her child recommended the two attorneys she had worked with. (The thought that there could be *more* court and *more* attorneys after the divorce was horrifying then, when I didn't yet know what I was in for, and even more so now that I do.) Friends sought recommendations on my behalf. In desperation I asked some well-connected friends if they knew an attorney who might take me on pro bono or cheap. They didn't, but the next day they sent me a check in the amount of the going retainer rate in my neck of the woods. This was an incredibly generous loan, recognizing as they did that it would likely fall to my descendants to repay theirs. It's a gesture I would have refused in the past—I would have thanked them profusely and mailed the check back. I would have found another way or done without. Now there was no other way. There was no doing without. Even so, I nearly returned the check, the sight of which made me feel acutely uncomfortable and acutely grateful. In the end, I gave it to a lawyer.

My attorney came well recommended—by chance, two people I respect mentioned her name to me in the same week, and I later heard that she was the attorney Tracey and his friends would have wanted for him if I hadn't gotten to her first. Finally, though, my choice rested on a factor that strikes even me as odd: God. I wanted someone who would understand and respect the importance of religion in my life. Someone religiously Jewish would be the best fit, I thought, but a

serious believer of any other faith would run a close second. I
decided L was it. She was Catholic, and I'd gotten the impression that her religion mattered to her. I have no idea if this
impression was correct. Did she say something that led me to
this conclusion? Or, given the thicket of personal information
in which I live, did someone else tell me that about her? In
any case, I was looking for someone with whom I would have
a time-limited business arrangement, not a best friend. Why
did faith matter so much? Why did it matter at all?

Religious values came into play at serendipitous moments
during the divorce. Tracey obviously told his lawyer that I
had deep spiritual discomfort with alterations of the body,
because she felt the need to address this point in her initial
written statements to the court. My attorney didn't make a
point of my religious values in court, nor did I wish her to.
But one day, sitting side by side in the corridor outside the
courtroom, she said something to me that left a deep impression. She was scribbling furiously on yellow legal pads (yes!
that's what they're really for!), responding to accusations
and demands from the Other Side. She broke off, pen in the
air, and turned to me.

"You know," she said, apropos of nothing, "you've got to
consider that God made him this way."

"Yes! Yes!" I cried. "That's what I've told him! God made
him a man for a reason!"

"No." She shook her head. "No, I mean, God made him a
transsexual." She turned back to her pad. The conversation
went no further. There was nowhere to go with it. It wasn't
an excuse for his choices, his behavior. Still—God made
Tracey a transsexual. No arguing with that.

Even having retained an attorney, I held off on filing for divorce. According to my attorney, there was a nice way to sue for divorce (warn the soon-to-be ex to expect a polite letter) and a nasty way (no warning, contentious letter). I wanted to do it the kindest, gentlest way possible, knowing it would be received as a kinder, gentler declaration of war. I longed to dissolve my marriage. It felt increasingly, peculiarly excruciating to still be married to a person I had come to think of as at best a stranger and at worst my enemy. But I also feared the legal process—chiefly that decisions about my children would land in someone else's hands. Secondarily, the financial ramifications of single motherhood were not pretty. I thought I should try to get on better, at least negotiable terms with Tracey before the process started. In the end this proved impossible.

Tracey was increasingly volatile, his behavior erratic and unpredictable. His relationships with all three children, Bibi especially, were rocky. There were frequent blowups during visits, and I came to expect hysterical phone calls from Bibi whenever the kids were with him. During the months Tracey and I tried to negotiate the terms of our divorce in long telephone calls and a few face-to-face sessions, I believed that he—and his relationship with the children—was becoming more stable as the tensions quieted between us. I've never been able to understand why our détente didn't last. When things went bad again, I accepted that I needed a custody agreement to put some controls on the children's visits with him.

An aspect of Tracey's instability was that he was often asked to leave the places he rented. (Reason unknown. Whatever the problem, it wasn't trans bias, since he vetted potential landlords for their attitudes before renting.) Where

Tracey lived in the beginning of our separation, before the kids or I had seen him "dressed," before many of the people we knew were even aware of what he was up to, was no small matter for us. I didn't want my children's first glimpse of their father as a woman to happen by chance. We also needed some space if we were to have a chance to reclaim our lives. Reveling in the new life that, in his words, was unfolding for him, Tracey had new friends, traveled often. He saw the kids when he was in town and available. Keen to start over, he was strangely unsympathetic to my needs, the kids' needs, for some unfolding of our own.

His first two living situations were in towns about a half hour's drive from our home. This felt too close for our comfort. But in the spring of that first year, about ten months after moving out and at the same time I was retaining a lawyer, Tracey told the kids that his current landlady had gone nuts, taken against him, and asked him to leave. Coincidentally, the landlady's daughter, who didn't live there, had also gone nuts, taken against him, and asked him to leave. He told the children that he planned to move very close to us, five minutes down the hill from our home. The kids asked him not to. He ignored them, they said. Frustrated, they tried several times to talk to Tracey about their worries. "Whenever we try to talk to him about it, he just starts saying how much we're going to like his new place and tunes us out," Adam and Bibi complained. This meant we would all be walking the same streets, shopping at the same stores, frequenting the same public library. Summer was coming and he was moving into a house abutting the free swim hole that was one of the very few pleasures I could offer my children.

One Sunday morning after this announcement, Tracey arrived to pick up the kids. With the kids in the house, I met

Tracey outside and tried to talk to him about the move. We quickly started fighting. Tracey, enraged, pushed past me into the house and slammed the door, shutting me out. I opened the door and went in. I found Tracey in my daughters' room with the door closed, squeezed into the lower half of their bunk beds with both girls, whispering and giggling.

"Please step outside," I asked him calmly.

Tracey paid no attention.

"Please come outside with me."

He went on whispering to my daughters, who were unsure what game was being played.

I asked Tracey several times to come outside with me. Then I said, "If you won't step out, I'm going to have to call the police and have them ask you to leave."

I said this quite calmly, not as if making a hysterical threat. Tracey acted as if I weren't there. He went on giggling and whispering. I'd never seen him behave this way before. Was he trying to goad me into phoning the police? I made the call. I think I appeared to be taking sedate, measured steps. In reality, I was frightened. Tracey wasn't thinking about the children. He didn't even seem to be thinking about his own interests.

Still ignoring me, Tracey went into Adam's room, where the DVD player was kept, and started to watch a movie with all three kids. I didn't want to involve the children any more than was strictly necessary. I had to warn Adam, so I took him aside and told him that everything was fine (sure), that some police officers would be coming by, and that he could keep watching the movie with his sisters while they were at our house. Used to hearing weird news from his parents, Adam had no particular reaction. It was a little different when they actually arrived. Adam was in the throes of police admiration at this point in his young life. The squad cars knocked him out.

Then I waited. I paced. I had rather a lot of time to pace while the police in my tiny town drove around lost, looking for my address. I checked on Tracey and the kids, looked out the window for the cops, ran to answer the telephone each time they called for directions, to ask, again, why it was they were coming and to ask, again, whether Tracey was armed. I gave directions, explained what was happening, assured them no weapons were involved. "How about if I wait outside and wave to you when you drive by?" I finally suggested. They gratefully accepted my offer. Standing next to the roadside red flag that clearly marked my house number, I waved them in.

The police response made up in bulk what it lacked in speed. No fewer than three squad cars and at least six officers converged in my driveway. They came with me into the house and I showed them to Adam's bedroom. They asked Tracey to step out of the bedroom, with greater success than I'd had.

As soon as we were all in the kitchen together, they frisked him.

"I said it wasn't like that!" I exclaimed, horrified.

"We can't know for sure if someone's armed unless we check for ourselves," one officer very reasonably explained.

Throughout this procedure and the conversation that followed, Tracey rolled his eyes, chuckled, and shook his head as if he were playing along with a child's game of cops and robbers. He was above it all; the whole thing had nothing to do with him. Still, the officers were more effective at getting him to agree to leave the house than I had been and to promise that he wouldn't barge in again against my wishes.

"You can file a temporary restraining order against your

husband," they told me. "That means he has to stay away from you until tomorrow morning, when you'll all have to appear in court."

Adam, who had joined the party at some point, begged me not to. The next day was his birthday (his fourteenth— look how far we've all come since his bar mitzvah a year ago!). He and his sisters were supposed to be enjoying a birthday outing with Tracey at that very moment and to celebrate with me tomorrow. To both the police and me, Tracey seemed at that moment, unlikely to do anything risky after what had transpired. I had been warned by my attorney and others to be very careful about requesting a re-straining order, to do it only if absolutely necessary and cer-tain to be granted. Requesting one that was denied, I had been told, would make me look bad and ultimately weaken my chances of gaining custody. In the end I declined. Possi-bly a mistake, since Tracey later taunted me that this was proof that I had no real concerns about his behavior.

What came out of that day was that I saw that I had to file for divorce. Now. That week, my attorney had Tracey served with divorce papers. Tracey was shocked, *shocked,* to discover that marital sundering was taking place on our premises. I was finally taking the first step to end our mar-riage, three years after it had ended.

This was one of the points at which Tracey threatened to cut off financial support. He didn't make good on his threats (clearly he was advised that to do so could mar the image he wanted to project of a deeply concerned father . . . er, par-ent), but I was in a constant state of insecurity. Juggling the full-time care of three children and our home, working as a freelance writer and editor and also a substitute teacher in the public school system, I spent my days careening franti-

cally between our house in one town, the three different
schools my children attended in three other towns, and a
string of one-day jobs in a half-dozen other schools that I
never knew about more than an hour before I was supposed
to report to them, often less. With the divorce in progress, I
would sometimes have to take a day off from all forms of
employment to appear in court. On such a morning I would
rise at four, just like any other day, get my children up,
dressed, fed, and washed, and drive them to their schools. I
would arrive in court, where I would pay several hundred
dollars an hour to hear that I was a lazy, useless loser who
refused to do any form of work in preference to freeloading
off Tracey—who at this point had spent two of the preceding
three years off from his job at full pay and was tentatively
returning to part-time fully paid employment, and who had
no parenting responsibilities beyond visiting with his children at will. While listening to these descriptions of myself, I
would keep one anxious eye on the clock—I had to get out in
time to make the afternoon rounds of my children's schools
to collect them. Assuming there were no after-school activities or appointments that day, we'd return home via the supermarket and I'd begin an evening of laundry, dinner
making, serving and washing up, lunch making for the next
day, homework, baths, bill paying, housecleaning, social calendar management for three children, bedtime reading, cuddling and emotional support, and hopefully, if no one was
having a meltdown that night, logging in a few hours at my
computer and then falling into bed early enough to rise again
at four and do it all over again, with the addition of a substitute teaching job should one turn up.

The first time we went to court, I dressed all in black. It seemed appropriate. When I told this to my one divorced female friend, it turned out she had done the same. Her ex, however, hadn't made the same clothing choices as mine.

That warm June morning, the elevator doors slid open on the second floor of the county family court and I stepped out. Before me sat my husband of twenty-some years in a long skirt and blazer. Probably makeup; I wasn't capable of noticing the finer details. My very first glimpse of Tracey dressed as a woman. I stared at him and he stared back. I'd long seen him with grown-out hair, plucked brows, and shaved face. In women's jeans and on one or two occasions in women's shoes. Why was this so utterly weird and different? It was, though. He wasn't Tracey. He wasn't a woman. He was Tracey-dressed-as-a-woman. A version of his features transposed onto a person he was not. The moment was three years in the making, three years in the dreading, but it was as if it were all happening in this instant. It was as if I had gone to bed one night with my husband and woken to this morning. This recognizable stranger.

I can't remember if we said hi. I think we nodded, but maybe nothing at all passed between us. Then the world started up again. I walked down the hall.

I had expected it. In one of the long, ranting e-mails that were common at this juncture, Tracey had written something vaguely menacing about no longer concerning himself with my comfort. Never mind that from my point of view the past three years hadn't been much about my comfort. I'd understood him to be telling me that he would show up in court in women's clothes. Since I'd never seen him "dressed" before, it seemed the idea was that I'd be freaked (the otherwise lovely occasion would be spoiled!) and he would gain some kind of edge. I kept cool. Mostly I just didn't look at him. He sat with his attorney (his *first* attorney; this was before she was suspended from practicing law for financial misdeeds) at one end of the corridor outside the courtroom, a busy narrow space in which lawyers glad-hand each other all day long and a lot of legal business seems to get done. I sat at the other end with my attorney, who kept my wandering gaze off Tracey with periodic instructions of "Look at me! Look at me!" and my friend Dawn, who came to lend moral support. Dawn and my attorney would periodically look over at Tracey with bemused frowns and laugh. Dawn hadn't seen Tracey since our split. They had never been friends. That night, he left a chatty, girl-friendly message on her answering machine telling her how good it had been to see her that day and asking her to call. As if they'd had tea.

I thought we would be at the courthouse for an hour or two that morning. We were there the entire day. We spent most of it in the corridor, the attorneys fighting each other on our behalf, bookended by two appearances before the judge. At one point I wanted to go out and put more coins in my parking meter. "Get a ticket," my attorney snapped. "You can't leave." What was accomplished that day was that our divorce was officially set in motion. I don't know why this took all day. I would be hard-pressed to say precisely why and how (aside from Tracey's outfit) it was all so hellish. I didn't eat anything before court to guard against untoward tummy reactions to Tracey's getup, and we took no breaks. Early in the evening after feeding my children, I sat in my backyard and drank a glass of cheap white wine. The first nourishment I'd had all day.

For the next year we continued to fight about everything that had to be settled in order for our divorce to happen. We fought over legal custody of the children (basically who had the right to make important decisions about them) and physical custody (whom they would live with). I wanted sole custody of both kinds. Tracey wanted shared custody of both kinds, even though he didn't intend to have the children live with him.

"You won't get sole legal." My attorney shook her head. "It's granted only in very extreme situations. But you'll get physical custody. They live with you full-time now and he doesn't want them to live with him. You're sure to get sole physical."

Tracey's attorney must have told him something similar. In the end I agreed to share legal custody; he agreed not to fight for shared physical. We said we would more or less continue the visiting schedule already in place. I make this sound simple and speedy. It was anything but. For months we talked about the children as if nothing else existed. I forgot anything else existed. When there was nothing left to say about them, we remembered money.

The big problem about money was, we had none. To be more precise, we had little. Too little for an intact family of five, way short of what was needed for two households. I felt no desire to get back at Tracey financially. I was also in no position to take care of my children without a significant financial commitment from him. We went around (and around and around) on the details of child support, alimony, and above all, what would happen to the house. The fight over the house went on for months, with me desperate to remain in it with the children, Tracey eager to collect his share of the proceeds, which he said he needed for expensive gender

reassignment surgery, if he could force me to sell. My kids'
very vocal attachment to their home, their one source of stability through the years of change, was the key factor in us
hanging on to it. While we were going through personal turmoil, nationally and internationally the mortgage crisis hit,
financial markets nosedived, jobs dried up, and I feared the
homelessness and penury that I heard and read about daily.
While we attempted to sort out our finances—that is, to
magically turn not enough into more—Tracey's attorney
urged us to see a financial counselor who worked with divorcing couples. I was dubious. What could this woman tell
us that we didn't already know? The attorney (this was still
his first attorney) insisted that the money spent on the counselor would be more than made up for in money saved. My
attorney agreed. Tracey really wanted to see her and said
he'd pay. Sure it was a waste of time and Tracey's money, I
ended up agreeing to go along to demonstrate my coopera-
tive spirit.

We e-mailed the counselor, Frieda, the numbers (income,
expenditures) and made a late Sunday afternoon appointment to see her at her home, an hour's distance away in a
town I didn't even know the whereabouts of. We decided to
drive there together, which meant spending more time in
each other's presence than we had since Tracey had moved
out over two years before. When we arrived Frieda opened
the door for us and I walked in. She smiled tensely and studied my face for a moment without speaking. Tracey walked
in and Frieda studied his face. She turned back to me and
said, "Hello, Christine." Turned to Tracey and said, "Hello,
Tracey." It was nice that it had taken her only a cursory
glance to figure out which of us was the genetic female. However, we already knew who was who. Her recognition didn't

add anything. This turned out to be representative of the session.

Frieda had a sign up in her office that read: A MAN IS NOT A FINANCIAL PLAN. How true! It might as aptly have pointed out: A MAN MAY NOT EVEN BE A MAN. Seated beneath this sign, Frieda offered us her wisdom: "You need more money." Her insight into our situation was that we were of limited means. She had no idea what people of limited means did to stay alive. Even when it came to questions we had about things like tax laws, she couldn't help us.

For her advice, we owed Frieda two hundred dollars. Tracey, so eager to see her, had agreed to be solely responsible for the fee. Apparently he'd expected to be billed later. "I don't have my checkbook," he told her. He looked so depressed that I couldn't stand the thought of him receiving her invoice in the mail. I took out my checkbook and paid her myself.

The meeting with Frieda took place at the end of the summer, the summer a year after I filed for divorce, which was a year after Tracey moved out, which was two years after our marriage ended. Yes, this was getting old. I wasn't out to get Tracey, my attorney was not out to get Tracey, and at this point, in contrast with other points in time, I didn't think Tracey was out to get me. With everyone making conciliatory noises, we had more or less completed the really difficult financial negotiations and it looked as if the whole thing could finally end, without a lot more pain and bitterness. Perhaps it would have. But it was at this moment that Tracey's first attorney got herself suspended from the practice of law. Promising to hire an attorney who would understand that we were ready to cut to the chase, Tracey went out and did the exact opposite. He hired a large, loud, and abrasive woman who evidently started foaming at the mouth the moment Tracey first uttered my name. My attorney knew her well as a noxious presence in our neck of family law but told me afterward that she had never seen her behave so viciously before, had never witnessed *any* divorce as vicious as the one ours now became. While I had experienced his first attorney as bizarrely hostile (whereas my attorney went out of her way to be polite, respectful, and even helpful to Tracey), the second made her look like my fairy godmother.

In their first lawyer-to-lawyer phone conversation, Tracey's number two started off by yelling at my attorney and threatening me. This turned out to be the highest point of civility in her behavior to both of us. In negotiating sessions and in court that fall, she attacked me while Tracey sat gazing at her and chuckling appreciatively. "It's as if," my attorney commented, "he's awestruck." Everything we had decided, every hard-won agreement, had to be revisited. At one meeting, at a combined attorney fee rate of around six hundred dollars per hour, Tracey and both lawyers fought at length over ten dollars. No one listening in on our proceedings would have guessed that this was a no-fault divorce. They would have guessed it was a whole lotta fault divorce and that the fault was mine. Sometimes I forgot myself the actual reason we were divorcing, as I listened to Tracey's lawyer tell the story of how a devoted husband and father— the one sitting on the left in the long floral dress—had single-handedly raised three children in one state while single-handedly working to support them in another, and been paid back by a wife who cruelly dumped him without provocation. My attorney continually played defense. Since his never did, she wasn't required to reconcile the image of an impoverished superdad with the reality of a man who had always lived apart from his children at least half the week while pursuing his career and who for the past two years had had brief visits with them while traveling often in the United States and abroad.

On the morning of our final court appearance, all I wanted was to *get divorced.* The very worst outcome of that day realistically possible was that we would leave court still married. The idea was unbearable. To avoid that fate, we had to present the judge with a complete settlement. Otherwise we faced a lengthy and very expensive trial, and who knew exactly how or when it would all end? We spent hours outside the courtroom, still fighting about everything, my attorney running back and forth between Tracey and his attorney and me dutifully relaying their demands and the insults his lawyer lobbed my way.

Even when we went before the judge, agreement signed, his attorney couldn't resist jumping to her feet and continuing to rail against me. While this went on, I stared at the frondy green plants in the recessed courtroom window and thought that I would remember them forever. I will. I said nothing, my attorney said little. "Can you both really live with these terms?" the judge asked us. "I don't want to accept a settlement that brings these two people back to court somewhere down the line," she told our attorneys.

I didn't know how I was going to live with our agreement. All I knew was that I had to. There was what felt like a protracted and terrifying segment of time, probably actually minutes, in which I feared that I wasn't going to leave the courtroom a single woman. Then it ended. The judge, clearly worried, announced her verdict: "I accept this agreement."

An odd little ritual concluded the day and my marriage. Just before we'd entered the courtroom, my attorney had warned me that as the petitioner for divorce, I would be told to stand, state my name and my children's names and ages, and answer two questions.

"Is there any possibility that husband and wife might be reconciled?" the judge asked.

"No, Your Honor."

"Why did the marriage break down?"

"My husband began to live as a woman."

Whenever the judge looked at Tracey or at me, distress creased her brow. At this moment, perhaps mirroring me, she looked especially pained. "I grant the divorce," she said. "Good luck."

It was over.

As I had planned, I went directly from the courthouse to a hole-in-the-wall espresso bar with the best coffee in town. I ordered my favorite indulgence, a skinny mocha. While the barista made it, I mentioned (it somehow came up!) that I had just been divorced.

"What do you mean by 'just'?"

"I mean I walked here from the courthouse," I told her.

She said, "If you've just gotten divorced, you must be out a lot of money. The coffee's on the house."

I thanked her and walked down the street to a bench overlooking a pond with a little man-made waterfall. I sat down with my coffee. It was a beautiful November day, warm enough to sit outside without cringing. I was doing exactly what I had promised myself I would do with my first post-divorce moments. Unlike so many plans, so many promises, this one worked out perfectly. A couple of weeks later, I would throw myself a girlfriend brunch during which my friends and I would drink Bloody Marys and Bellinis and walk down my road singing Gloria Gaynor's "I Will Survive" en masse. Just now I wasn't ready to talk. I wanted to savor my newly official solitude. But everyone was waiting to hear, and I owed my friends the news. I sent out a group e-mail from my cell phone. For the subject line I typed: **I AM DIVORCED**. There was no message.

Part Three

PEOPLE SAY THE DARNEDEST THINGS!

We all have moments of finding ourselves, while bleeding, in the presence of a vampire.

Late on a Friday afternoon, I was rushing through some last minute pre-Sabbath shopping in the congested aisles of my local Trader Joe's. Between the bins of grapefruit and oranges, I spied a woman I know slightly whom I had not seen for several years. When she noticed me her face underwent a profound alteration. She looked *very* upset and *very* happy to see me. Okay. I know what that means.

"Hi!" I waved a friendly wave and tried to keep going—I was in a hurry, she was already talking to someone else, we had never been friends to start with.

There was no chance she was letting me get away so easily. This woman, who is very tall and physically imposing, with severely cut spiky gray hair, is not, in my experience, given to cuddling. She had never touched me when we met in the past. Now she lunged. I don't mean she gave me a polite hug, took my hand, touched my shoulder. I mean she threw herself at me.

"I guess this means you know how my life has changed," I said cheerfully.

"Yes," she fairly wailed. She was close to ecstasy. She told me what she knew and how she knew it. She told me how sorry she was.

"Thank you."

"It's so *terrible* for you."

"Yes, well, it's hard on the children, but I've moved on," I told her.

A shadow of disappointment crossed her face as what I'd said threatened to sink in. She brushed it off. She smiled. "It's *dreadful* for you," she insisted. She clung to my arm.

Eventually I extricated myself and dashed through the rest of my errand. As I headed to my car, my first thought was that I was glad my children hadn't been with me. My second thought was that they easily might have been and that sooner or later—sooner, as it turned out—they were going to have to field prying questions from quasi strangers, and they needed to know that these kinds of chance encounters were out there waiting for them.

That night I told them the story. I acted it out, using a dinner guest as a stand-in for me. I draped my smarmy sympathy and my arms over our guest's shoulders and poured on the gleeful insistent grief. We howled with laughter. Catharsis.

In fairness, I have to admit that several times in the first year after Tracey moved out I had the more or less opposite experience. I ran into someone I knew slightly in some public place and found myself starting to cry in response to the barest, least concerned, least personal of greetings.

What I'm going to say here runs the risk of sounding like damned-if-you-do-damned-if-you-don't griping about people who said nothing to me about the breakup of my marriage and those who said the wrong things. It isn't, but that's what it might sound like. So I want to state at the outset: I don't blame those who panic when they run into me at a social event. I don't resent the breathtaking chill with which some responded to my regrettable tears in the cereal aisle. (Well. Not much.) It's difficult to say the right thing to someone who has suffered a loss. It's difficult to say anything at all. Offering condolences after a death can feel like an awkward and uncertain burden. (I've heard the traditional Jewish phrase *May you be comforted among the mourners of Zion,* spoken only by a rabbi standing before a congregation.) It's hard to know what to say to someone you don't know well who is going through a separation or divorce. How was anyone going to come up with the right words for a woman in my situation? What were they supposed to say—I'm so sorry to hear that your husband has traded you and your children for a pair of pink panties?

Nevertheless. One of the ways I chart the panoply of experiences my children and I have had is through the public reaction to the breakup of our family. By that I mean comments, questions, and stares, in some cases a weird strained silence, from people we know slightly or really not at all. I suspect we field a larger and more diverse array of remarks than most unfamous divorcing families. Tracey and I were once a tight couple and well-known as such in our community. The nature of our breakup called into question everything that had come before. It invited—so I gather—a level of intrusive curiosity beyond what is generated by less sensational splits. Tracey's metamorphosis managed to generate a few articles in newspapers and magazines, and I dodged a very short rash of interest from local television stations. Mostly I've endured scrutiny in face-to-face encounters. As a private person, a person who couldn't talk about her marriage even with her closest friends, much less write a book about it, going through something as extremely personal as a breakup under communal gaze has certainly been new.

People are fascinated by Tracey, and I am fascinated by their fascination.

When I began my public life as a transwidow, I knew who knew by the curious or pitying stares we got. Occasionally, as in the incident at Trader Joe's, by the hugs from people who normally wouldn't touch me. Some seemed genuinely sympathetic. Many acquaintances who didn't know me well enough to make it natural to say something direct said something indirect or nothing at all. Then there were the others. People I've known socially, whose restraint and discretion I've appreciated, turn out simply not to have known. Even several years after Tracey moved out of our home and began strolling the streets of our small town in skirts, I found myself stumbling unwittingly into painfully intrusive interrogations from people I didn't know intimately but who knew something intimate about me—they knew about my ex-husband. I have changed a lot since my marriage ended, and I now find it easy and pleasurable to be friendly—to enter into conversation with people I know by sight, with complete strangers at the café table next to mine. But friendliness has its risks. People who are desperate to talk about Tracey find encouragement in anything. They think they've got me at hello.

A pair of experiences broke new ground in our trans-warped lives. Both took place at the Jewish day school that my middle child (the only one of my kids who was elementary school age at the time) attended when Tracey was launching his coming-out venture. The first experience was Bibi's. One day in third grade, a classmate socked her with the announcement "My parents say your dad has become a girl." The child was not a friend. She didn't make her statement as if it were a nice thing to say. A rabbi's daughter, she was well connected in the social hierarchy of the school, an insider. Bibi had already experienced her as something of a bully. At this moment, in the middle of her school day, Bibi was just hoping to forget her home life for a few hours, hoping no one at school knew about it or would comment on it if they did. Need I say it? She had no idea how to respond.

The second experience was mine. Attending a school assembly, I randomly sat behind another mother, a therapist, who had always responded to my casual hellos grudgingly when she responded at all. At some point during the performance she realized I was there, turned around, smiled, and greeted me warmly. "How old is your little one now?" she asked about Lilly, who was with me. The conversation would have been normal except that it was not. She fired questions as fast as I could answer them. I knew something was up, but it stupidly took me a minute to understand the nature of my new popularity. She reached the point of her interrogation a moment after I guessed where she was heading. "Has your husband had surgery yet?" Uttered in exactly the same tone as she had asked, "Where does your little one go to preschool?"

"You'd have to ask him," I told her.

The eager, wide-eyed smile vanished. "I'm sorry!" She whipped her head back around to face our children onstage.

I still see her from time to time. She's never spoken to me again.

Yes, in the end Bibi and I decided the Jewish day school was not the best place for her or our family (duh), but really these experiences could have happened almost anywhere. And did. We had to get used to being blindsided.

When my marriage ended, I often thought of moving away. There's nothing original in wanting to start over with a clean slate after a notorious split, particularly when you live in a small town. If we had moved away before Tracey went public, we would never have had experiences like the ones at school or at Trader Joe's. Would have hated to miss those. Or to miss everyday cheery encounters such as the one at the Gulf station the other day, when a very nice man I know slightly but haven't had a conversation with in years called out "Hi!" across the space of two islands of pumps and two rows of cars from where he was fueling his tank to where I was fueling mine. "Hi!" he yelled. "I've been meaning to call you! A friend of mine was a transsexual!"

There are so many reasons I didn't leave town when my marriage ended and why I haven't left since. One is the law. Tracey was unlikely to go along with any plan that involved us making a fresh start in a new place. If he tried to stop us, I would need permission from a judge to move away, and my lawyer thought I was unlikely to win that permission unless I could demonstrate a compelling reason (for example, relocating to live with family) to move to a particular place. In fact I had no particular place to go and no particular means of going there. It's tough to be a single mother in an area I know well and where I have a home to live in and friends to call in an emergency, much harder to imagine pulling it off in a town where I was starting from zero and knew no one. I

didn't want to leave my friends, and my children didn't want
to leave theirs. Moving away would have cost money I didn't
have. It would have cost some things I did have, the small
elements that now make up the life I've managed to con-
struct. The community I've managed to build. Still. My failure to leave—this is the way I tend to think of it—is a thing
I second-guess. Not a day goes by that I don't ponder not
whether I should move away, but when. Also where and how.

Very occasionally, what's striking is not what someone says.
It's what someone doesn't say. Once in a while I've been
greeted with chilly reluctance when I would have expected
something warmer. Of course, I can't know why exactly. If I
lived somewhere else, I might think I was being avoided for
my association with a transgendered person. Living as I do in
the Valley of the Politically Correct, I'm more likely to be cut
because I chose not to stay married to a transgendered person.
Or because the acquaintance in question has heard Tracey's
version of our breakup from him or from one of his camp.

An entirely different kind of *not* saying occurs with people
who are adamant that they will show no emotion upon hearing that one's husband is living as a woman. It is as if they
have been training all their lives for this moment, the moment
when you will tell them, "My husband has decided he's a
woman," to have *no reaction whatsoever.* Have they practiced
not reacting to anything? Or just to this particular situation?
No Reaction Whatsoever (NRW) training must certainly be
required of the personnel of elementary and secondary schools,
libraries, medical practices, and personal care salons, among
other professions, in the Valley of the Politically Correct.

I had a gratifying experience telling one would-be mistress

of facial control my news. "My marriage is over," I announced over dinner. A couple of friends who already knew were present. I was informing one who didn't. "It's been over for two years. I've been lying to almost everyone."

"I'm sorry," she said in a voice modulated to express polite noncommittal sympathy.

"Now tell her why!" another friend insisted.

"Tracey is living as a woman."

My friend nodded without a trace of surprise. But perhaps her NRW training had been interrupted before she'd earned her certificate. After a moment of nonreaction had passed, she spoke. She said only two words, but they were the right two and she said them repeatedly and with just the right note of stupefaction. "Oh shit," she said. "Oh *shit*."

I've heard that people can still remember where they were and what they were doing when they learned of the assassination of John Kennedy. After the World Series Earthquake in San Francisco in 1989, people became obsessive about telling one another their stories of the moment the quake hit. Residents who had been out of town at 5:04 P.M. on October 17 (for the record, I was at home in the Haight-Ashbury and I can barely resist telling you my memories now) found themselves alienated from what briefly became the defining experience of Bay Area belonging. The narrative urge was so prevalent, one particular phrase began to circulate: "Thank you for not sharing your earthquake experience."

Similarly, people love to tell me how and where and when they first saw Tracey. If they haven't seen him, they tell me how they heard about him. Sometimes they speculate about whether they have seen him. "Maybe I've seen him and not

known him," people say. "Would I know him?" they ask me.
"Would I?"

"Well, things have *changed,* haven't they?" says a neigh-
bor with whom I have never exchanged a personal word.
She's accompanied her daughter to my door on a Girl Scouts
cookie-selling mission; we haven't seen them since the same
errand brought them a year earlier. When I fail to respond,
she repeats herself, "Things have *changed,*" in case I didn't
catch her meaning. I am practiced enough by now that I can
read her excited, eager smile. She has a story she is dying to
spill, and if I give her the teensiest opening, she will spill it.
Likewise, in the coatroom of my synagogue I run into a man
who was once a fellow student in a class on Jewish texts,
back in the horribly oppressive but notoriety-free days when
my marriage was over but nobody knew my marriage was
over. "Seems like there have been some *changes* since then,"
he says. (These people lack only the mobile Groucho Marx
eyebrows to make the performance complete.)

"Changes?" I say as I speedily exit the coatroom. "What
changes?"

At another event, I fall into easy conversation with a
woman with whom I have had the odd cup of coffee or dinner
in the past but have recently fallen out of touch. When we
last saw each other, she knew that my marriage had ended
and asked no intrusive questions, made no comments, indulged in no innuendos. I'd thought she was singularly re-
freshing. I was wrong. When we last saw each other, she
didn't *know.* Now she knows. She needs to tell me how she
knows. She needs to discuss pronouns, and the politically
correct use thereof. I stop talking. I visibly withdraw. She
talks faster.

I don't believe any of these people are thinking about

whether I want their stories. They are titillated—perhaps *captivated* is a better word—by Tracey and by their own response to Tracey. They want attention for that response—for Tracey's effect on them. When they see me they think, Who better?

To this group I can only say, "Thank you for not sharing your Tracey experience."

A catalog of odd reactions from near strangers would not be complete without a discussion of the L-word.

Do real lesbians get asked if they are lesbians? Do random strangers, gay or straight, not hostile, approach lesbians they don't know and make pleasant remarks about their sexual orientation as if they were noting the weather? If the answer is no (please tell me it is no), I can only assume that some people, upon discovering that an acquaintance is the former wife of a transsexual, feel the need to say, "This means you are really a lesbian. That's okay with me!" Or, when speaking to the trans ex-husband, to give the greatest gift of flattery possible by saying, "As far as I'm concerned, you're a woman!" I've had a number of odd lesbian Encounters of the Third Kind during the past several years. The first—again, the one that alerted me that such encounters were out there waiting for me—actually happened not to me but to Tracey.

Tracey generally plays little role in the children's school, social, or religious lives. But one day he picked up Bibi from a rehearsal for a play she was acting in. The mother of another child, a woman whose name I don't even know, approached Tracey and exclaimed, "I didn't know Christine had a female partner!"

Tracey corrected her—sorta. He told her, "Actually,

we've broken up." What he didn't say was, *I am a man, actually, and we have broken up.*

I know this story because Tracey, likely delighted by the incident, told Bibi, who dutifully recounted it to me. I think of this incident as my coming out as a lesbian. I wasn't even there for it. Bibi, who of course could have lived without knowing about it if only Tracey had let her, was distressed by it. At first. As time went by, I got her to see this kind of thing as my shadow life, the alternate existence to my conventional heterosexuality. Now when these things happen she laughs and tells me, "You're the least gay person I know!" She enjoys the irony. We both enjoy the irony. If being a lesbian gives me an unearned PC patina in some crowds, it can't be helped. I can live with it. The alternative would be to go around in a T-shirt that reads, I LIKE LESBIANS, I JUST DON'T HAPPEN TO BE ONE.

There is personal curiosity on the one hand and political grandstanding on the other. And some people have two hands. To his admiring fans Tracey is a martyr, a patron saint, Our Lady of Gender Variance. In the Valley of the Politically Correct, he expected approval—and he got it. Bigtime. But sometimes that vestigial ticking organ lodges within the rib cage of even the PC of this earth. One afternoon a woman I know only slightly came up to me when I was waiting for my daughters to get out of school. She took my hand. "I've just recently heard the reason your marriage broke up," she told me. "I work with transgendered clients a lot in my work. But that has nothing to do with you. For you," she said, "this must be very difficult." That was all she said. She let go of my hand when she was done speaking. She didn't ask for confidences. She had no Tracey story to tell. She was simple and she was sincere. She left me feeling that if you are going to go up to someone you don't really know, who has lost her husband in the way that I have, and say *something*—this, surely, was about as good as it could possibly get.

Will it ever end? Can we ever make our way through the Valley of the Politically Correct as anything other than the former wife and the children of a transsexual? Will there ever come a day when our lives are entirely free of Tracey watchers? I never imagined that public titillation would last this long. Maybe it's just something in the air. Maybe trans is the flavor of the moment. Maybe *no one* anywhere thinks of anything else. As the year 2010 drew to a close, *The New York Times* suggested that it would be remembered as the year of the transsexual. The prediction apparently stemmed from several instances of men (some trans, some not) appearing in fashion spreads sporting women's clothes. No doubt the *Times* saw itself as merely reporting on a trend. But the tenor of the piece was undeniably celebratory: the inclusion of men (literally!) in women's threads is a good thing if it is anything. Perhaps it is. For my children and me, many of the years beginning with 2005 will be remembered as the years of the transsexual. For future years, we have higher hopes.

CUT IT OFF!
I DON'T NEED IT!

It was autumn, roughly five months into my life as a separated woman. One day, for no evident reason, a finger of my left hand went red and painful and swelled into a fat little balloon. Some days went by during which I expected the problem to take itself away. It didn't.

"You have to get it looked at by a doctor," friends insisted.

I am doctor-averse by nature, and seeing someone meant a co-pay I couldn't afford. But the thing dragged on and finally I made an appointment with a nurse practitioner in town.

Like me, the nurse couldn't find any sort of wound. "There must be a tiny pinprick somewhere on the surface of the finger that allowed bacteria to enter," she explained. She prescribed antibiotics and told me to come back if it didn't get better right away.

In the next couple of days it got much worse. Darker. Fatter. More painful. The pain began to be distracting. Still, I didn't take it very seriously. I would have lived with it a good while longer before shelling out another co-pay. But friends, alarmed, kept phoning to ask about the finger, urging action. "Go back today! Don't wait!"

I returned to the nurse. This time she looked at the finger and called a doctor in her practice to join us. The doctor, a tiny woman with a generic European accent, studied my hand.

"I would hate to see you lose the finger," she said pleasantly.

I watched her hold my hand and listened to the echo of her words. Their meaning wafted slowly toward me. She was contemplating the amputation of my finger. Not doing it herself, presumably. Surgeons do that sort of thing. Right? Not family practitioners in downscale offices? She didn't speak of *loss* as if it were a bizarre and unthinkable outcome of my situation. She said it as if it were a distinct possibility. If it happened, we would all share mild regrets. Two things occurred to me. One, the obvious funny-ironic but also funny ha-ha metaphoric value in being threatened with something castration-like. (I mean—what would Freud say?) And two, the obvious funny-ironic but also funny ha-ha metaphoric value of my *ring* finger heading for the chopping block. Because that was what it was. How could I have failed to notice before now? Before being faced with its extinction, at least as a current part of my body? This fat, red, naked finger was the very one around which I had worn a small white-gold diamond ring and a small engraved white-gold band for nearly all my adult life. What a relief. This was a finger for which I no longer had a need. The loss of my finger would be no great loss.

Nonetheless. I thought that I would like to try to keep it.

I left the doctor's office with a prescription for a different antibiotic. I took to soaking the finger. Gradually the redness and the pain went away. The swelling stayed. It stayed until my friend Nina, a massage therapist, took the finger in her strong hands and squeezed. Hard. The skin burst. The poison was released, the swelling went away. She had healed me. The finger never bothered me again, but the incident left me changed. By the time the burst skin had mended without a trace, my body had changed, profoundly. My life, equally so.

First: The antibiotics upset my stomach so that I couldn't eat, not just for the week I took them, but for a week or two after as well. I lost weight. I *shed those pounds!* as the diet ads say, the pounds I still carried from my third pregnancy and more recently from a single-mother lifestyle of snacking on the run. I lost just a few pounds to the antibiotics, but it was enough to shift the utter hopelessness with which I regarded my body. I changed my diet. I adjusted my clothing size down several notches. When the ladies I'd grown up among were widowed, they put on shapeless black and never took it off again. Transwidowed, I went to a thrift store in town where I could find T-shirts and jeans for single-digit-dollar sums. I put away and eventually gave away the nice loose middle-agey clothing in which I had hidden for years. I began to walk. Not for exercise. For anxiety. That fall, winter, spring was an anxious time (ha ha). In my anxiety, I became addicted to walking. I'd get jumpy and head for the road. During months when I was in the habit of hibernation, I walked and walked, several times a day some days. When summer came, I set off on a walk I take only in good weather, a lovely uphill hike that wends past a big beaver dam and a small horse farm, a walk that makes me sweaty and breathless, a walk that is work. This time I was stunned to discover that, lost in thought, I had reached the top of the hill in minutes, not sweaty, not breathless. The most unlikely thing had happened. Inadvertently I'd become healthy.

Second: Epsom salts. I mentioned that along with the antibiotics I soaked my finger. The doctor recommended soaking in Epsom salts. I didn't have any. I said I'd get some, but of course I didn't. Late in the evening of the day the doctor had spoken of my losing the finger, one of the friends who had been checking up on me, somehow guessing—we weren't all that well acquainted—that I was not the sort to run out and buy Epsom salts for myself, unexpectedly turned up at my door. Holding out a box of Epsom salts. A red, white, and black box shaped like a half-gallon milk carton. I looked at the box and a phrase that I'd been working very hard to keep from coming into existence took shape in my mind. Ooh, I thought. I'm in love. The box of Epsom salts. I have it now. It is the most romantic gift I have ever received.

There is the story I've been telling, and then there is this story, the Epsom salts story, that runs parallel to the other. Well, not entirely parallel. Sometimes intersecting, interweaving. Okay, not sometimes. Often. Constantly. It's my life, so I know that through some of the story I've been telling there has been this other story that I have not been telling. Yet I forget it, writing this one. It feels like the separate trajectory of a separate life. It's easier to leave it out. It complicates. It changes my understanding of what *is* my story. That is, changes it once again. My story was about marrying young, gradually creating a family, a life, a Jewish life. Then my story was about the destruction of that story. The third story is not so much about a different man as about a different me. It offers the ludicrous, offensive, delicious suggestion that everything happened as it did so that I could discover the person I am.

Let's go back a few months before my finger swelled. Late summer of our first months as a single-parent family. The children and I kept busy, went swimming, visited with friends. The school year cranked to a start. We were out a lot. Sometimes when we arrived home we'd find paper sacks of vegetables and apples propped against our kitchen door. Small, elegant handwriting on scraps of paper, on the backs of old envelopes, told me which bag of apples I could feed directly to the children, which were for baking only. No explanations for the potatoes. Because he kept missing me, the man who had grown these things made an appointment to come and see me when my children were at school.

He arrived midmorning, roaring up my driveway in a big blue pickup truck, a vehicle I'd never seen him drive, and walked into my house in jeans and a tattered, faded blue work shirt, not the clothes I usually saw him in. He put more fruit from his orchard, half a sponge cake, on my dining room table. He hugged me. I remember the hug. I remember the faded shirt, his chest at my eye level. I thought at the time: This is *like* having a man come to see me. An attractive, exciting man rearranging the atoms in my atmosphere. Bringing maleness into my home. Bringing tenderness. Danger. It was like that, but it wasn't that. I knew this was a charitable visit. I knew he wasn't for me.

Sam (not his name) and I had been part of the same Jewish community for years. For the past two, which were also my two years of post-marriage cohabitation with Tracey, we'd both been members of the *havurah*, the small group I've already described that met informally in members' homes for monthly Shabbat dinners and seasonal holidays. Sam and his wife had been invited to join the group at my suggestion. They were serious, interesting people who I thought would be a good addition. But despite knowing them in a communal religious context, despite being guests any number of times in their home, I had never exchanged personal words with them. Sam and his wife seemed to me the sort of people one could know for a lifetime and never get close to. When we announced to the *havurah* that Tracey was vacating our home and our marriage to begin a new life as a woman, the group, including Sam's wife, made an almost unanimous decision to back Tracey. Because I didn't know Sam very well, I couldn't imagine that he would be the lone holdout who would offer his support to my children and to me. Because I didn't know his marriage, I couldn't imagine that there was nothing unusual about him and his wife going separate ways.

That morning in early fall, it was still just barely warm enough to sit outside in my backyard at the cheap green plastic table so ancient that the discount store it came from hasn't existed in years. I drank coffee and Sam drank tea. "I want to tell you about myself," he began. He had come with this express purpose, to tell me about himself, his marriages, his family. His ups and downs and reversals.

Later he would tell me, "I had seen your love for Tracey. I could imagine how devastated you were." The night I'd told the *havurah* that our marriage was over, he had been unable to sleep, imagining my desolation and the children's.

Knowing him to be as PC as the rest of the group, I asked him what made him break ranks. "Why did you choose us over Tracey?"

"Because I thought you were getting a raw deal."

His was a mission of *tzedekah*, an act of loving-kindness

through which Jews believe we repair the vessel of our broken world. Put another way, I think he'd decided to be my friend. He wouldn't have expressed it in such religious or intimate terms to himself. Sam just thought knowing him might help me. He had no idea.

Sam and his wife had both been married to other people when they'd met in their late twenties. They'd divorced those people to be together. His first, brief marriage had produced two children, hers one. They'd had a child together. Creating a united family had been tricky, one of several significant sources of stress throughout their marriage. One child had gone through rocky times, but all, now adults, were doing well. Neither Sam nor his wife had been interested in a monogamous marriage, and both had had many affairs. At one point, Sam's wife had divorced him for another man. When her lover unexpectedly died, she'd asked Sam to take her back. No longer in love but lonely, he'd had no faith that he would meet anyone he could feel closer to. They'd gotten back together, and a few years after, when Sam was facing surgery, they'd remarried, first in a civil service, then in a Jewish one. That's the very short, skeletal version of what Sam told me.

But let's go back still further. Years before that autumn morning, roughly fifteen. Tracey and I joined the synagogue in our new town and regularly attended services there, first alone, then with our baby, Adam. From time to time we saw a couple about twenty years our senior with a lovely young daughter. We didn't speak with them, but they somehow made a good impression. When we arrived one week to discover that the service would include the bat mitzvah of the daughter, we expected it to be a meaningful ritual, not the circus these events could sometimes be. It was.

Another Saturday I overheard the man in this family telling his wife and daughter that his coat was missing from the closet after service. "Is it a black wool coat?" I asked him, taking my own black wool coat from the closet.

"Yes."

"I might know where it is."

I led him to a coat that had been left on a sofa in the social hall. It was his.

"I wonder how it got here?" he mused. "Thank you."

I didn't tell him that I had accidentally taken his coat, believing it was mine.

A few years later, I was phoned by a woman who wanted me to conduct a healing service for her husband, who was about to undergo surgery. The services, which I led regularly at the time, were for the purposes of gathering communal support, coming together as members of the synagogue to pray for someone in crisis. I had no idea who the woman was, but both she and the rabbi assured me I would recognize her and her husband when I saw them. As I did. The brief healing service took place after Kabbalat Shabbat, regular Friday evening worship. I recall speaking to Sam only once. "What is your Hebrew name, Sam?" I needed this name for the prayers I would lead. Sam looked into my eyes and softly said his name.

In the spring of that year, leaving a Saturday morning service at the same time, Sam and I paused in the sanctuary doorway and exchanged a few words. Apropos of something, Sam told me that he and his wife were not actually married. "You didn't know that we were living in sin," he joked. "We're divorced."

At these words I felt a fleeting, incomprehensible joy.

Then, without mentioning that they were in fact already

legally remarried, Sam said, "We're getting remarried. We're having a Jewish wedding next week."

No, I thought at him. Standing there talking to a stranger, in love with my own husband, and with our second baby, Bibi, in my arms, I had the bizarre and intrusive thought that this man was meant for me and me alone. I smiled and nodded and said nothing inappropriate aloud. That was our first conversation. It must have lasted approximately three minutes.

During my marriage, I always felt I couldn't allow myself even to think about other men. I locked away those very odd thoughts about Sam. When events caused me to recall the moment some ten years later, my therapist resorted to highly technical language to describe it. She said, "You were having a woo-woo moment."

I continued to see Sam sometimes at synagogue. I remained vaguely aware of him in a difficult-to-define way that I ignored. That summer, Adam attended the synagogue's day camp, and his adored counselor was Sam's daughter. The following winter, Sam called our home. I remember answering the phone, hearing his voice. He told me that his wife was away and his daughter was home from college for the weekend. "We thought it would be nice if your family came to Shabbat lunch."

One of the peculiarities of my memories of Sam is that I can often recall the precise words he said, his face as he said them. I can generally recall what he was wearing. At this lunch, he sat at the head of his table in a tie-dyed T-shirt. The table was laid with an array of cold salads, prepared before the start of the Sabbath. At the end of the meal, without asking myself how I knew it would annoy him, without asking myself why I should wish to annoy a host I barely knew,

I deliberately complimented Sam's daughter on preparing the whole lunch by herself.

"You're making sexist assumptions," Sam scolded, clearly annoyed.

We stared at each other for a moment, and then I rose from the table. Silent. Now that I had Sam's attention, I suddenly understood that I wasn't thinking about lunch. That if I said another word, I was going to risk sounding as if I were flirting.

One spring, Sam invited us to a Passover seder. This time his wife, whom we knew even less well than Sam, was present, along with some of their extended family and friends. In the next couple of years, there were a few more of these occasions. During one there was a moment in Sam's kitchen when he was busy at the stove. I looked at his body and wondered idly what he looked like inside his clothes. Horrified, I swiftly suppressed the thought and kept it from happening again. I *think* I kept it from happening again. When the *havurah* was formed, I saw to it that Sam and his wife were included. They rarely came to group events together. Both were academics with international careers. They traveled constantly, and it was rare to find them in town at the same time. They were wealthy, successful people with places to go. They were high achievers with the material spoils to show for it, but travel in particular seemed to define them. The way culture or religion or ties to a particular place sometimes defines a family.

No one knew that I found Sam a very attractive man. Even I didn't know, outside the moments when I experienced and quickly banished the attraction. Sam certainly never guessed. When he came to see me that first morning and took to dropping in from time to time thereafter, he thought I didn't like him. "Whenever I hugged you," he told me later, "you never hugged back. When I came to see you I never called first because I thought if I gave you a chance to tell me not to come, you would take it."

"Yet you came." I laughed.

"Yes, I came."

When the winter months brought the offerings from his garden to an end, he showed up with books for the children. I invited him to join us for a Shabbat dinner one Friday when his wife was away. That night when Sam walked in from the cold, I lit a fire in our woodstove and the five us gathered around it. The children, reeling in the wake of Tracey's desertion, and the *havurah*'s as well, loved Sam's visits. They laughed hysterically when Sam said he could enliven our fledgling fire by blowing into it with a hair dryer and succeeded only in scattering ashes all over the room. We all thought Sam was having us on about the hair dryer. Doing something uncharacteristically silly to make us laugh. He wasn't. He really thought the hair dryer technique would work. That, of course, only made him all the sweeter.

Sitting before the tepid fire, he remarked, "I have a circulatory condition that makes my hands stay cold."

"I do, too," I told him. "Let me see." I took his hand to test the temperature of his fingers. This, for me, was about as daring as it could possibly get. Tantamount to tearing off clothes and lap dancing for another woman. Nearly fainting, I held his hand for a few seconds and then dropped it. I had the impression that Sam liked me holding his hand. That he didn't like me dropping it. That didn't stop me from continuing to believe he was in love with his wife and making duty calls on me and my children. My holding his hand didn't stop Sam from believing that I couldn't possibly return the feelings that were beginning to trouble him.

A couple of weeks later, his wife again away for the weekend, Sam invited us to dinner at his house. It was a Saturday night. An advance copy of his new book had just arrived from the publisher. He handed it to me. "You're the first to see it," he said, adding teasingly, "I can't imagine anyone I'd rather show it to."

I stood in the center of his kitchen and examined the book. I hoped I would be able to say intelligent things about it. I hoped I looked sexy. Sam moved around me, preparing food with a little smile. His multicourse dinner included, by chance, some of my favorite dishes. Also one vegetable, Brussels sprouts, that was not a favorite but that I cheerfully chewed and swallowed in an effort to be congenial.

That dinner marked a turning point. When I described it to a friend, her eyes widened. She said, "It sounds like he's courting you."

I began to wonder, Does Sam *like* me? My friends were urging me to start seeing men. "Find another husband," some urged. "Just get sex for the time being, and worry about relationships later," advised several others.

I told them about the various single men on my horizon. I told about the visits from Sam. "Forget the married one," they advised. I tried. It wasn't easy. At first. Then it became impossible. What did I think I was doing with Sam? A married man was off-limits in my book, even one in what used to be called an open marriage. Other men got closer, but all I could think about was Sam. I went on a date with an attractive and interesting single man and spent the evening comparing him with Sam. Wondering when I could next see Sam.

One Sunday morning, I went to Sam's house to help him

brainstorm ideas for promoting his book. His wife was once again away for the weekend. I dressed with care, then was so nervous when I arrived that I refused to take off my coat. "I'm too cold," I told Sam. "I'll keep it on." As if coat removal were a provocative act. We sat on either side of a table, drinking coffee. Me in my coat. Sam talked and I tried to focus on his words. I worried that he would realize I had no idea what he saying. I was distracted. I had decided that I definitely would not let anything happen between us. I was afraid that Sam would make some gesture, indicate an interest that I could not return. And I was wondering, Will we ever go to bed?

Sam's wife left soon after on yet another trip, this time not for a weekend but for two months. Sam took her to the airport and arrived at my door with a huge bouquet of flowers. The children and I were on our way out to visit friends, so he didn't stay. What did the flowers mean? I wondered. Remember: I had never had a single adult life, never had an affair. I hadn't even seriously flirted with anyone since I was a college freshman. (Did I ever seriously flirt as a college freshman?) To my limited secondhand knowledge, a man gave a woman flowers after they slept together for the first time. Not before. Was Sam trying to tell me we would never sleep together? (Sam had never heard that one. I checked. Later.)

The following week I told N, my therapist, about Sam. She was surprised. Understandably. As the person to whom I told everything, she thought it was kinda funny that I had never even mentioned the existence of this friend. Much less that I thought we might be on the brink of an affair.

N, never one to pull punches, told me exactly what I had to do. "The next time you and Sam get together you're going to clear the air. You're going to tell him that you feel there's some tension between you. That maybe you're both starting to have feelings that neither one of you expected. You're going to tell him that *if* anything is ever to happen between you—*if,* not when—it will be far off in the distant future. You're going to tell him that you would first have to spend a long time talking about what you're both feeling, and what any kind of involvement might mean for both of you. In particular what it might mean for someone in the highly vulnerable state that you're in."

From N's office I drove directly to Sam's house. He took my coat at the door and I walked into his arms. We had begun.

RED CADILLAC

Could the libido released in such instances be the same libido that had been bound up with the lost loved one and which is now set free? . . . To free herself from him, she has first to free herself from herself. Which means discarding her own image, her own body, by lending it to another man. Mourning here involves a molting of oneself. . . . We could interpret her making love with a man as an act of giving herself, in the specific sense of giving up her image. After this sacrifice, she attains a new freedom.

—Darian Leader, *The New Black:
Mourning, Melancholia, and Depression*

For a long time, I didn't feel that I'd be happy again. Worse, I thought I didn't want to be. I didn't imagine I'd ever fall in love again. I thought I might be with someone. I assumed that I probably would. I had last fallen in love at the age of eighteen. Without articulating it to myself, I vaguely imagined that when people over forty hooked up, they bypassed the heady in love stuff and went directly into the placid partnership phase, if they were lucky enough to tolerate each other at all. I understood how people long together stayed together when passions no longer burned. But with nothing more compelling than a general absence of dislike, how did they come together in the first place?

When I imagined the very best midlife love could offer, I saw this picture: a man and a woman in a large house with a big stone fireplace and lots of old windows made up of many small panes of glass. They smiled identical complacent smiles, gazing through some of these panes of glass at their clipped lawn, their trees, the shiny cars parked in front of their beautiful house. It was perpetually autumn. Early, colorful autumn. They were solid, attractive people with expensively cut gray hair, dressed in tasteful bulky wool sweaters in subtle earth tones. They were well padded, well and thickly clothed. They were not naked because they were not having sex very often. Their relationship was not about sex; rather, it was one in which both partners accepted that in order to be married and normal and reasonably happy, they had to sometimes have sex. In short, they were a couple out of a Hollywood film about solid, attractive people soon to have the shit kicked out of their lives. But they didn't know it, and because this was a still image, they never would. They were deeply, albeit wryly, satisfied with themselves, their (second or third) marriage, their children and each other's children, their investment portfolios. They would always pour the right wine into the right glasses.

How could I imagine that this could be me? That I could even aim for it? I could never pull it off. I don't look good in bulky sweaters. I can't stare calmly through windows. I am not calm. In truth, I am never more than a heartbeat from hysteria. My children fill me with a passionate pride far too infused with terror to ever settle into complacency. My small,

cheap house is a mess, and though autumn does look beautiful from its windows, it is only one season in a year with four.
I would find this man and this woman, my own images of
success, dull. I would find them insufferable. How could this
have ever been my image of love?

What I did not imagine was being bowled over by a love
so acute, so intense, so erotic, it would make me gasp for
breath. A love that would make me realize all that I'd been
missing the whole of my adult life, that would suddenly,
shockingly, clarify everything that had ever made me uncomfortable in romantic books and movies and rock songs.
Everything I'd failed to understand firsthand. The longing
to touch a man, to have his hands on me, his tongue in my
mouth, to have my mouth filled with the bitter-salty elemental taste of life itself that is his taste. That is him. To have
him on top of me, crushing me, to slide on top of him from
his feet all the way up, to feel a heat that radiates outward
from the places we come together. Not just to want these
things, but to long for them, to need them, to—

"You and Sam need to get to know each other out of bed,"
N, my therapist, advised at one point. "Why don't you take
walks?"

"We fool around on walks," I blurted out.

"Ah."

On walks, in the woods, under bridges. In cars, the way
teenagers used to or maybe still do. When we say we won't,
okay, when I say we won't, when we thought five minutes
before that neither of us could possibly want to. It is the best
it has ever been, the best possible, over and over and over.
Yes—sex has changed. It has changed *for* me. It has changed
me. (Sam, too, but that's another story, his.) It is daring, unpredictable, endlessly surprising. Creative. Desire awakened

and reawakened. Feeling good in my body to an unprece-
dented degree. Feeling *in* my body as I've never imagined.
Thinking of him, of long, slow days in bed, I notice strangers
look into my face and double take, finding something unexpected there. Sometimes men look at me and I think, They
can smell it. Sex. A woman brought to life. Friends give this
level of intense erotic connection three months, six months, a
year. Then two. Hedging bets, one skeptic grouses, "It's
bound to mellow after four years." Sex between us is such
that we look for ways to explain it. As if it is something that
needs explanation, as if it is not a gift to be received and
cherished and marveled at and accepted. Side by side in synagogue one Saturday morning, we hear a service leader say
something about getting to the soul through the body. Sam
takes my hand. We don't look at each other. Later, it may be
days later, he says: "The body is the path to the soul."

Or is the body just the path to going nutsy-cuckoo? I'm
wacky with love, sure enough. I love it all. The sound of his
footsteps, the sight of his hands, his scent, his profile, his
smile, his smile in profile. I love the thing I call the edge, the
edge on which we meet. The male edginess of him that makes
our connection, our attraction, so sexy. For the first time in
my life, I am deeply in sync with a man. For the first time
in my life, I am in sync with myself.

What the hell am I doing?

Having this affair while my life in all other areas lies in
ruins is like driving a borrowed mint condition '66 red Cadil-
lac Fleetwood Eldorado. Hair whips face. The top-down
convertible doesn't keep off the rain. On good days it's just
downright ecstasy to drive, to think, Hey, isn't it pretty
great that an indigent single mother of three gets to drive a
hot rod she doesn't even own? On bad days it strikes me dif-

ferently. More like, What the hell is this indigent single mother of three doing, driving a hot rod she doesn't even own? Beautiful. Exhilarating. Highly impractical. And someday, I'm going to have to give it back.

GOOD COMMUNITY,
BAD COMMUNITY,
JEWISH COMMUNITY

"Of course I ruined the lives of my wife and children—but that's another story."

One Saturday morning not too long ago, Tracey was the featured speaker at my synagogue. He told a hero's tale. Described the arc of a brave and epic journey. In other words, he talked about himself. At only one point in his narrative did he refer to the casualties inevitable in such a saga, tossing off humorously and in passing the remark that his self-realization *of course ruined the lives of my wife and children—but that's another story.*

At the conclusion of his talk, the congregation surrounded him. Showered congratulations. No questions were asked. No exceptions were taken to his portrait of courage. He was a hero.

I was told about Tracey's talk by Sam, the man who had made Tracey's children French toast that morning for breakfast, driven Tracey's son to his martial arts class on his way to synagogue, and would hurry away at the conclusion of the service to pick him up at class and drive him home. It was by chance that I wasn't with Sam that morning. It was the day of the annual winter fund-raiser at my daughters' school. It feels bad to do things like that on the Sabbath, but public schools don't organize their schedules around the needs of religious minorities, and we are also members of this school community. So that's where my girls and I were spending the day, with me working at one of the craft-making stations just like all the other parents. Well, most of the parents.

In the course of my marriage, my religious life and Jewish community—the actual communities I was part of at different points along the way and the community I longed for but never quite found—grew increasingly central to who I was, how I wanted to live and raise my children. *Jewish* is a group identity. When we were abandoned by our *havurah,* the small group that we worshipped with, and by our then rabbi, when our larger synagogue community wasn't there for us, there were inevitable scars. Scars I try to forget. I know that I am blessed. I have never for an instant experienced disillusionment with Judaism. We weren't abandoned by God.

When Tracey and I split up, he left the synagogue we'd attended as a family to the children and to me. I wanted to start over with a new synagogue, but the two available were too far away, and in any case, Tracey began attending both of them. With great difficulty I decided I had no choice but to make an uneasy peace with my own congregation. At first I went by myself once in a while. My children, Adam most vociferously, refused to go with me. The kids knew—Tracey told them—that he had many friends at our synagogue. They didn't know that when I turned to the rabbi for support, he had nothing to offer.

I first tried to talk with the rabbi during the months leading up to Adam's bar mitzvah and our separation. I explained what was happening behind the scenes in our family. The rabbi was my age but relatively new at being a rabbi. He had no children, no experience to draw on faced with someone in my situation. The pastoral care class in rabbinical school probably didn't cover this one. What do you say to the congregant who tells you her children are traumatized and falling apart in consequence of losing their father in this unique way? He was hopelessly out of his depth. "This isn't *The Blessing of a Skinned Knee*," he brought out finally. That may not have been one of his finer moments. It also wasn't his worst. When one of my children was diagnosed with a heart condition shortly after Tracey moved out, I knew better than to look to him for support. But we ran into each other one day, and when he asked how we were I told him. He stared at me in silence for a minute, looked appalled, then changed the subject.

My kids didn't know about these things. But they were aware that neither the rabbi nor anyone else from the congregation was reaching out to us. They concluded that no one in their Jewish community cared.

"Why doesn't F love us, as well as Daddy?" Bibi asked about a member of our erstwhile *havurah* and synagogue.

I didn't know what to tell her.

But in this absence of love, I found an unexpected freedom: the freedom to cry during services. Crying, at the time, was the only way I could attend a service. I decided if the congregation didn't care about me, I—the woman who would once have died rather than let anyone know her life wasn't perfect!—wouldn't care what they thought of my tears. Allowing myself to cry meant I got to pray with other Jews. To hear the words and the melodies that I love. Usually nothing happened to disrupt my sense that I was ignored there. But very occasionally something did. There were small, isolated, meaningful gestures of compassion. Long in coming, but sweet when they arrived.

Once a man came up to me after service. "For a long time I've been feeling the absence of *kavanah* in the community," he told me, using a Hebrew word that expresses the spirit, or intention, behind prayer. "Then this morning when I walked into the sanctuary I felt such a powerful sense of *kavanah*. When I looked around, I realized it was you."

From time to time, less dramatic, no less appreciated, someone would say she or he was glad to see me back. I received a couple of notes from congregants who barely knew me but wanted to offer some form of support. Eventually I got over having to cry. I didn't feel at home in the congregation, but I was reconciled. At this point Tracey informed me that he would once again be attending services at the synagogue. Distraught, I asked him to stay away. The children asked him to stay away.

"You promised not to come back," I pointed out. "I've gone through a lot to reconcile myself to this congregation because I thought it was my place, my only place, to worship."

"There's no problem," Tracey insisted blithely. "I said the synagogue was yours—*then*. This is now. We can both be there at the same time. It won't bother *me*."

"We don't live in the same house anymore," I tried to explain. "We can't worship in the same house of prayer. It doesn't work for me."

After a while, I heard that the rabbi had declined to go through the process of contract renewal and was leaving. As his final act, he initiated a campaign to have the synagogue's bylaws changed to declare the welcome inclusion of transsexuals. Transsexuals were already welcome, visible, and included. It simply wasn't stated so in the bylaws. The gesture felt like the rabbi's personal legacy to my family.

I've already described my experiences with the small group, or *havurah*, that my family had celebrated Shabbat and holidays with. When the group so painfully deserted the children and me following Tracey's feminine debut, I shared my anguish with friends outside the Jewish community.

"This is a *religious* group?" my friends questioned, incredulous.

I couldn't explain to people who were giving me so much support why the Jewish community had no warmth to spare my children or me. I didn't, I don't, know. Much worse, I didn't know what to tell my children. So many adults recall experiences with religious communities during childhood that poisoned their relationship to faith for life. I didn't want that for my children. I decided I had to try to offset the bad memories by creating good ones.

Our first post-Tracey Passover gave me the opportunity to lead our family seder solo for the first time. In the Jewish year, Passover is a profound experience of release from bondage, renewal, regeneration, re-creation. That's what this particular Passover was for me. The occasion carried traces of sadness for all that we had lost. I didn't pretend to myself that these feelings weren't present. What's more, I didn't have to engage in pretense with anyone else. From my place at the head of my dining room table, I led the seder with self-confidence and joy and, sweetest of all, with my children's help. When I looked at our assembled guests, unaffiliated

Jews and gentiles who might not have celebrated this holiday at all if not for my invitation to join us, I marveled to think that everyone there knew what the children and I had been through. The fact of their knowing didn't leave me vulnerable or exposed. It made me stronger. It felt good.

That Passover was a coming-of-age milestone event for me. We've had many other wonderful Jewish occasions since, often in our own home. On one Rosh Hashanah, the Jewish New Year, Sam and I grew tired of synagogue hopping in pursuit of a place where I could feel comfortable. We decided to stay home and study the part of the Torah, the Bible, that is read in synagogue on that day. With Lilly curled up against Sam on the living room sofa, Adam, Bibi, Sam, and I had a richly spiritual and wide-ranging conversation as four equal searchers. It was a conversation that inside sanctuary walls probably wouldn't have taken place at all and would never have included children. That Rosh Hashanah day we also inaugurated a private practice of doing Tashlich together. In this New Year's ritual, Jews toss bread crumbs, representing sins or other things they wish to rid themselves of from the past year, into moving water. While a group from the synagogue performed Tashlich at a local river, we found quiet meaning at the edge of a stream near my home, casting our crumbs with one another—and with the dog who dived into the water after them. My children and I, now sometimes joined by Sam, share many such Jewish experiences on our own.

Yet I still long for community. For me and for my children.

Recently I mentioned our community's embrace of Tracey, and its desertion of my children and me, to a rabbi I didn't know at the time Tracey went public. While I spoke, the rabbi nodded and smiled as if anticipating everything he heard. I felt confused. Had he somehow known what I was going to say?

"I'm familiar with everything you're describing," he explained. "Over twenty years ago my father came out as a gay man. Saying you were gay in the late eighties was like saying you're transgendered now. My family felt the way yours did. Our congregation treated him like a hero and we felt abandoned. I remember my mother saying exactly the things you're saying now."

Can the rabbi's story help my children? Would it make them feel better or worse to hear that religious communities commonly turn away at the very moments when, in Bibi's words, you need to feel love? Maybe for children—or anyone?—the assurance that God loves you when you don't feel loved by your fellow worshippers just isn't real. Just isn't enough.

Once during our first year as a single-parent family, Bibi told me, "With all these changes I need something to hold on to!"

"How about *Hashem* [God]?" I suggested.

"Mama . . ." She sighed patiently. "It's hard for me to be religious when I'm eight."

STILL OKAY. STILL WEIRD.

Sometimes Bibi tells me it's too hard to talk with people who haven't lived our story.

"She wasn't *there*," Bibi said of a sympathetic therapist. "She doesn't *know*."

She feels that I'm the only adult capable of understanding her. I know what she's getting at. I've had similar thoughts myself. Sometimes I marvel that no matter how close any of us may be to any other person, this odd encompassing history is something we four have shared and no one has shared it with us. But though the children and I have lost their father, my husband, these were not identical losses. I had my loss and they had theirs. The three of them are intensely united by what has happened to them. But each carries his or her unique, nuanced pain. Each has lost something distinct. It is not one heartbreak, but four. It didn't happen once. It isn't over. It happens anew every day.

I want to say the kids are all right. The truth is they are and they aren't. Some days they are. Some days one or two of them are. It changes from day to day who is and who isn't. Well-meaners often tell me, "Kids are resilient!" How true, I think. That's why we adults are twisted and bent around the childhood scars that have malformed us.

As time went on, Adam began doing better in school and in some other aspects of his life; in other ways he's continued to struggle. In his relationship with Tracey he seems frozen in time, the twelve-year-old boy he was when Tracey stopped being his father. The presents Tracey gives him are toys age-appropriate for that twelve-year-old. When they spend time together, they play computer games and watch television. Homework doesn't exist, and there are no parental pep talks about learning to drive or how to avoid falling off a cliff after high school. Instead of having cut short Adam's childhood, it's as though Tracey carried it with him to his apartment, where it goes on and on forever.

In very rare moments, Adam admits that he sometimes feels sad. Once he said something that sounded as though he blamed himself for what had happened in our family, as children do sometimes magically believe they were the agents of their parents' divorce and had the ability to prevent it. I strenuously assured him that he was not responsible. But even as I spoke, I knew that against magical thinking my words would likely have no power at all.

"I try not to feel angry," Adam tells me from time to time. "Anger is destructive."

Try as he might, he's still mad as hell. I don't see Adam's anger so much as hear about it, mostly from Bibi, sometimes from Adam himself. Walks with Menachim Bagel, our large, mostly sweet-tempered, but occasionally aggressive dog, seem to inspire confidences. During one such walk, my large, mostly sweet-tempered, but occasionally aggressive son spoke about anger. "I still consider myself a gentle person," Adam announced. "But I know that now I'm also a very angry person."

"What's made you an angry person?" I asked him.

"Daddy."

We discussed the relative anger-relief benefits of the workouts and martial arts he's done. Then he said he thought he'd hit on a way to channel rage that knocked out all the others: he might want to be a lawyer.

He reminisced about the earlier days when he would blow up during visits to Tracey. He'd storm out of Tracey's apartment and take off on foot in the direction of town, miles away. Coatless, without cell phone or money. Bibi would take off after him, wailing hysterically, "I thought you would never leave me!" To Adam, this kind of scene illustrates the destructive power of his anger. He lost control, and it was devastating for his sister.

"As much as Bibi loves her big brother," I told him, "the 'he' she thought would never leave her isn't really you."

"Oh," he breathed, relief dawning in his eyes. "Yeah."

Sometimes Adam says he's "fed up" with Tracey. He startled me recently by declaring, "I want nothing to do with Daddy after I graduate from high school." The remark seemed to come out of nowhere, as his rare statements about Tracey tend to. Another day he said, "Daddy refuses to acknowledge anything other than that he has some biological relation to us."

"What does that mean, honey?"

"He won't take responsibility for leaving his family. His children."

Though Tracey has long since gone full-fledged femme with the children, Adam still presses him into shooting baskets, throwing a football back and forth, swinging a softball bat with him. On rare occasions Adam gets to hang out with another boy and his dad. He spends time in a support group of teenage boys and the men generously willing to mentor them. He comes home from these occasions romping with enthusiasm. He tells me what a relief it is to be with men. Boy Interrupted, he still longs to be a regular kid with a regular dad. He can't quite let go of what he once thought he had.

"Daddy still looks like a man," he insisted recently.

"Tracey may never look like a woman to us," I told him gently, "but to people who didn't know him before, he probably does."

Adam looked skeptical. Then he told me, clearly pleased with himself, that he makes Tracey's girlfriend refer to Tracey as "he" or "your father" when she talks to Adam and his sisters, even though this is not to her liking.

"Denial," Adam admitted cheerfully, "is a great coping mechanism."

For Bibi, a little denial would be a good thing. Unlike her brother, my older daughter lacks access to this survival tool. She sees, thinks, feels, understands—way too much.

For several years she was plagued by nightmares. She has them now, much less often. She, too, struggles with anger and, more openly than Adam, with sadness.

Once she asked Tracey why he had to live as a woman if it meant leaving his family. "He told me," Bibi confided, "that if he hadn't, he would have committed suicide." Shaken, Bibi spoke of this for a long time after. Perhaps coincidentally, perhaps not, when she got upset at a minor frustration during a fifth-grade recess, she threatened to kill herself. The episode freaked Bibi's entire cohort of girls and occasioned a series of meetings with the school counselor.

Not long after, we were shopping for sandals together while a young man near us tried on high heels. Bibi watched him furtively. I watched Bibi. The excitement of shoe shopping abandoned her. Her back rounded and she sank into her chair.

Children look to adults to stay the same. Mine have watched their father change his personality, his appearance, his lifestyle, his address, and his name. They've changed, too, but they would have anyway and it's anybody's guess who they *would have* been. Bibi is in the thick of the preadolescence that Tracey tried to hustle her into at seven. Maybe she would wrestle with body image and eating disorders in any case. Maybe every clothing purchase would be an occasion for agonized self-examination even if the dress-up games had never occurred. I can't know.

I do know that all three kids can be inventive and sometimes surprising observers of the process of becoming themselves and the effects of family history on that process.

"Sometimes I feel enraged with Daddy, and then I get so depressed I feel overwhelmed," Bibi told me one day. "I feel like I'm sad even when I'm happy." Sometimes her attitude toward Tracey is protective. He is often ill, mysteriously so, and has made Bibi his confidante. She tends to keep her fears about his health to herself, then, in little bursts, to share them with me. She shares the burden she feels. "I worry about him. I like feel I have to worry about him because Adam and Lilly don't."

Childlike and old beyond her years, Bibi added, "I wish I wasn't so mature."

Shabbat dinner on Friday nights is a special time to talk about the previous week's highs and lows. "Let's tell goods and bads," one of the children is likely to say when we're all seated. During the last such conversation, Lilly said, "This week I told Daddy how much it upsets me when people call him a woman. Daddies," she asserted, "aren't women." At eight she has become self-conscious about having a transgendered father for the first time and has asked Tracey to stay away from her school. "I'm afraid kids won't like me if they know my dad's a girl," she said sadly.

Despite her fears, or because of them, she is still given to coming out with her zinger at unexpected and, er, awkward moments. "I have to tell you a secret," I've heard her stage-whisper on first playdates or while driving another child home in our car. "My dad's a girl!" As if this fact were a towering and precarious load that she was forced to carry everywhere and she just had to dump it sometimes. Recently she told me that Tracey had said to her what he once said to Bibi, that he chose life as a woman as an alternative to suicide. Lilly was having nightmares about it. "Will you tell him I don't want him to talk with me about that?" she asked me. It isn't hard to guess at Tracey's motivation here: now when Lilly experiences grief or anger at him for choosing his new life over his family—over her—she will understand that such feelings are tantamount to wishing him dead. Guilt and fear for his life will smother normal emotion.

"Lilly's just going through it now," Bibi commented sagely about her younger sister. "She's only just realizing that Daddy left the family and why, and she's angry at him all the time. She has to go through it alone," Bibi explained, "because Adam and I are over it."

"Over it?"

Oh, honey, I thought.

Carefully, not in these words, I suggested that, like acid reflux, what happened in our family would likely back up on her and her siblings at different stages of their lives, and the burn would have to be coped with all over again.

But if all this makes it sound as though my children walk around in black crepe, clutching damp hankies, they don't. We don't. We are a loud, loquacious bunch and we make one another laugh.

One day, watching a television show in which a male character rhapsodized about the feel of a kimono he had worn for his wedding, Bibi commented archly, "This man likes to wear dresses."

"Yes," I replied without thinking. "Don't marry someone who likes to wear dresses." Realizing what I'd said, I hastened to qualify. "Oh!" I spluttered. "If you're a lesbian, it's fine to marry someone who likes dresses!"

Bibi just laughed.

Darian Leader, author of *The New Black: Mourning, Melancholia, and Depression* writes:

How a parent has represented a loss is crucial for the mourning process: as we see again and again clinically, when a loss is not symbolized in a family history, it so often returns to haunt the next generation.

How will my children symbolize their loss? How do I represent it for them? There are many answers to these questions. One that I'd like to mention is the American Girl doll.

Though my daughters are not collectors of the high-end period dolls that come prepackaged with names, ethnicities, and personal histories, Bibi, at least, takes an interest. She's seen the dolls, read some of the books. She likes the backstories. One night she read me descriptions of some of the doll characters from an American Girl catalog. Each doll had her own historical challenges—for example, the Civil War or the white man's decimation of Native American culture—to cope with. It seemed a fair guess that each would triumph in the end. Bibi was gratified that a Jewish doll had been added to the line. However remote the Jewish character's biography was from Bibi's, it was clear that my daughter saw herself reflected, recognized, in the fact of a Jewish Girl doll.

That got me thinking. Following a family pattern frowned upon by some critics, mouth quickly followed thought. The next moment I was bubbling over about American Girl: The Transsexual.

My first idea, inspired by the descriptions Bibi was reading to me, was not a transgirl but a girl whose big challenge was that her father was trans. I could see the catalog copy: "At the county fair, everyone compliments Katie's new gingham dress. Katie wonders what they'll say about her father's!"

Bibi, I have to say, wasn't laughing. She rolled her eyes in a how-can-you-joke-about-this snit. But her imagination was snagged. She had to jump in—she couldn't help herself. "The doll itself can be transgendered," she suggested. "But how would you do it? If it's a boy doll in girls' clothes, he's just going to look like a girl doll."

True!

We put our heads together. We came up with a boy with a name along the lines of Butch, short boy-hair, and a frilly wardrobe. Alternately there was Sue, long hair stuffed under a newsie's cap, britches, and a longing to be male. We agreed that the characters' historical eras would determine other details. Sue, for example, would probably have just been considered a tomboy in a past in which gender identity distinctions had yet to be invented. Now she'd be on her way to therapy, hormone treatments, and sexual reassignment surgery. My daughter's imagination was up and running. Disapproval or not, she was with the project. For a moment, Bibi hadn't lost a father. She'd gained a marketing idea.

When he was small, Adam and I shared an interest in architecture. Together we read books, looked at buildings, went to exhibits. We talked about the structures he would like to build when he grew up. He talked about the house he would like to build for me. Sometime during the year after Tracey and I bought the house my children and I still live in, which was also the year before Tracey told me our family life was at an end, Adam asked me, "How would you describe your dream house?"

I thought for a moment and then told Adam the truth: "This is my dream house, the house we live in." I had never before owned a home. My parents had never owned a home, nor had my grandparents. As far back into my childhood as I can reach, I experienced the longing to own a home of my own. Now I did. "My dream house," I told Adam, "is the house, any house, that's mine." Our small, modest, unfinished house in which everything from the well pump to the roof had been done uniquely, comically wrong, was the fulfillment of my dream.

The family I made with Tracey was also a home. Now I understand that this family was the fulfillment of my dream. Not his. Not ours. It was what *I* wanted. Nonetheless, we did make this family. It was unfinished and everything in it was uniquely, comically, beautifully done, built upon a foundation with one hidden, fatal flaw. We lived in it together for a time. *We* were not happy in it, perhaps, but I was. I can't go back and rewrite that history even if I wished to. I was happy, the children were happy. It was a beautiful family. My children are keenly aware of their pain, their losses. But do they remember, really remember, what it is they have lost?

When Lilly was in first grade, each child was given a week to introduce the class to their families. At Lilly's request, Bibi and I and Menachim Bagel, our dog, visited with Jewish holiday foods and activities. Lilly and I decorated a display table and bulletin board with books, objects, and photographs we selected together. The photos were of Lilly and people important to her: her brother and sister and me, her grandmother, her best friends, our family's closest friends. I didn't know what to do about Tracey. I couldn't just pin up old photos in my possession that included Tracey as Daddy and leave it to Lilly to explain who that man was now. As she isn't shy about discussing our family makeup with me, I waited for Lilly to bring up Tracey. She never did. It was as if she didn't notice Tracey's absence. In Lilly's family collage, Tracey didn't exist.

On the other hand, Lilly went through a phase in which she took to saying almost daily that she wanted her life back. She explained that by this she meant she wanted to return to a time when her father was a man and her parents were married and she lived with both of them. Not yet two years old when Tracey changed the course of our lives, she has, of course, no memory of any of this. She imaginatively creates what she can't remember ever having had. One day she drew two figures with the caption "My Mom and Dad realize they really love each other."

My older children remember, but not as much as I'd like. Adam told me recently that he dug up an old photograph of his father—a "before" shot—and was startled. Like a child whose father has died, he has begun to forget what he looked like. To lose the memories of an intact family that included a father. Bibi has largely lost them already. Lilly had none to start with. Without photographs, it would be as though that family never existed.

A peculiar pain ensnares old family images. Ensnares the carrying out of family-focused projects for school that involve going through old or maybe not so old family photographs. We experience the disconnect between who we are now and who we were in the pictures of just a few years ago. The disconnect between the simple pleasure it was once to look at these photos together and what it means to look at them now. Still pleasure, but pleasure mixed with shock. Grief, sometimes. The photographs insist that there was a family, a life, in progress. Then it stopped. Something else began, and we have the new photographs to prove that, too.

When my children and I look at the old photos, we don't know what to think. I don't know what to think. How can they? One day I was sifting through snapshots to meet some specific school project demand for one of the children. Bibi came upon me and picked up a shot I had uncovered of our family of four when she was a baby. She started to cry. She said she wanted to keep looking at it. She said she wanted to take the photograph inside her. She said she wanted to be inside the photograph again.

Bibi has a way of growing distant and edgy, throwing up a barbed-wire fence between us, when she is unhappy. A barrier

I can't penetrate. She threw it up once during what would otherwise have been a pleasant occasion, a rare dinner out for just her, Adam, and me. I pressed her to tell me what was wrong; she deflected. I didn't back down. Finally her anguish exploded. "I already can't remember good times together as a family of five!" she cried. This moment was exquisitely painful. I couldn't smooth it over. I didn't try. Sitting on stools around a high table in the sandwich shop they had chosen to be taken out to, the three of us talked. We had lovely time after all.

Adam's and Bibi's vanishing memories make me sad. I want my children to remember the father they had, our family as it was. Why? Why, if it might cause them to yearn for something they can never get back? Isn't it a selfish wish, isn't it for me and not for them? Because it was so important a part of my life? Because I don't want to be the only one who remembers it? Because I don't like to think that someday no one will remember it? It is for me, but it isn't only for me. It's for them, too. In some way, I feel that if they have the memory of this family, they'll have something of it, as opposed to nothing. Like a dormant memory of speaking another language or riding a bicycle, it will lodge there inside them, an ability to be accessed. Proof that this thing, a happy family, is possible. Possible for them.

THEREFORE CHOOSE LIFE

I call heaven and earth to witness against you this day: I have put before you life and death, blessing and curse. Therefore choose life that you may live, you and your seed.

—Deuteronomy 30:19

What does God want of me?

That was the question. From the night of Tracey's game-changing announcement through the years of anguish, separation, and divorce that followed, I didn't wonder why things were turning out as they were. Instead, I was preoccupied with what God wanted me to do about it. This question played over in my mind, agonized and somewhat muddied while I still located myself inside my marriage, far sharper and more urgent as I moved outside it, as I left behind a sense that I was a victim of Tracey's decisions and saw myself as an active agent in my own life.

Along with becoming an emotional open book to my friends, I opened the book on religion. Throwing caution to the winds, I began to talk about God with friends whose spiritual lives I knew little or nothing about. It didn't become a conversational refrain—I just referred sometimes to my thoughts and questions. To my amazement, identifying a deep spiritual value, even using the G-word, did nothing to harm my reputation. No one's face froze into a here-comes-the-religious-nut smile. No one avoided my company. My friends didn't reject me for bringing my spiritual preoccupations into the conversation any more than they had rejected me for opening up my drama-filled intimate life. Turned out many had spiritual preoccupations of their own.

What does God want of me? I lived with this question during the long dark months when I began to understand that my marriage and my husband were at an end but still could not accept these things as facts. Asking this question eventually led me to offer Tracey his freedom, as I've described, the freedom to go away and start life over. He didn't go away. He did start his life over. I should have been calm and supportive and given up the outward illusion of our marriage a whole lot sooner. In other words, I should have stopped loving Tracey when he made his intentions clear. Because I think that's what would have been necessary. Then I could have let go. Let the vessel fall, with a minimum of *Sturm und Drang*, the vessel that was Tracey's body, his male form. The vessel that turned out also to be the life that held us together and held me, private and captive, inside it. If I had it to do over, I'd do it differently. In fact, if I had it to do over, I wouldn't do it. I'd let someone else do it for me. Someone capable of doing it with equanimity—a Buddhist, let's say.

What does God want of me?

I fell in love with a married man. The fact that this man was in a marriage in which the couple spent a great deal of time apart leading separate lives, in which affairs were the norm, in which his wife had left him for another man and returned to him only when her lover died, maybe made it all right for him. It didn't make it all right for me, but it allowed me to do it, as I would never have entered into a relationship with a man who was part of the kind of marriage that I understood. Among all the ways I have changed, the uncharacteristic things I have done, this, surely, is the most uncharacteristic of all. Yet I made this choice. I took this step. A step off the roof of a skyscraper.

At the best of times, I'm unsuited by temperament and deep conviction to conduct an affair. This was not the best of times. I was traumatized by recent events—at the point I got involved with Sam, two and a half years of them. Wound up so tight that the first time Sam's fingertips touched my skin, I had the sense that he was breaking through ice to reach me. The last time I had fallen in love, I'd been a college freshman. Now I was a newly single mother in emotional, economic, and social free-fall. The survival of three shattered children depended on me and me alone. I had an ugly divorce to get through, a home to hang on to, a self to salvage, a life to re-create. The very last thing I could do was enter into a torrid affair. I'd found out the hard way that being alone was manageable. Light, uncomplicated companionship would probably do me just fine for this stage of my life. A steady, supportive relationship would be best of all. A long, agonized, draining affair filled with exceedingly high highs and exceedingly low lows? Count me out. I simply could not enter into such a relationship. Could not and would not. And did.

What does God want of me?

For a long time I asked this question and listened to God's silence. God, it seemed, had nothing to say to me. I was not asking my question when, one beautiful sunlit morning driving home after delivering my children to school, a line from the Torah appeared in my thoughts. *Therefore choose life.* Judaism recognizes that life is a choice; there is another possibility. I understood immediately and with excitement that this was the answer I'd been waiting for. Cryptic. Entirely dependent upon interpretation. But at last I had something to work with.

Therefore choose life.

Therefore.

As in, a summation. As if I'd presented my case. Described life as I had known it. Detailed my thoughts and needs. My anguish, fears, and desires. And the answer was, Okay. Taking all that into account. Given everything. Holding everything in mind and heart at once. What you must do is:

Choose.

Choice is conscious and it's deliberate. It's a commitment, short-term or long-, to a particular path. Tracey had made choices, was making new choices all the time. I was pushed and pulled, boxed in and shut out, by them. Buffeted about. Now it was time to start making some of my own. Not just wait to see where the next wind blew me. Choose. To be specific, choose:

Life.

Choose life. Well, that's clear, isn't it? Only, what's life? What *exactly*?

Sam felt like life. Sam *was* life, life as I had never known it and never thought to know it. And if he had brought me to life, his experience was that I had done the same for him. He had made peace, or believed he had, with a marriage of barriers and partitions, limitations and distances. His greatest ambition in his marriage was to achieve an absence of do-

mestic strife. He had lost interest in having affairs, hadn't
been planning to ever have one again. He hadn't imagined
that he was happy, but he'd been certain he was resigned.
Even after he realized he was falling in love, he wasn't thinking about altering his life. Much less rocking it to the core.

We began as friends, then friends who were also lovers.
We thought we could stay friends and contain our love. It
overflowed its tight boundaries. Love, like life, can be difficult to keep in check. I heard a story about Elizabeth Tay-
lor. It was said that when she and Richard Burton were
criticized for becoming publicly entangled while both were
married to other people, she told the press: We are very sorry
if we hurt anyone, but we can't pretend we're not in love.
Whether or not it really happened, the story struck a chord.
We didn't want to hurt anyone. We couldn't pretend not to
be in love.

The power of our physical connection was a revelation in
itself and so much more. It helped me to feel present in my
body, and happy to be there, as I don't recall having felt even
as a child. Being with a man connected to his land, his garden, his fruit trees, and his animals offered me new ways to
develop parts of myself I had discovered when I moved to
New England. A lifelong city girl, I was once intensely uneasy in any location in which I could not phone for pizza or
receive *The New York Times* home delivery. (In truth, I still
like these things. But I no longer gasp for air if I find myself
outside their sphere. In fact, I live outside their sphere.) Once,
on a weekend visit to a friend's cabin in the Sierra foothills, a
few hours' drive from my San Francisco home, I had experienced heart-thudding panic standing in a clearing at night
with my host and fellow guests. I think we were supposed to
be savoring the absence of man-made light and sound, maybe

listening for the rustle of trees or a hoot owl. Maybe looking at stars. We were supposed to be enjoying ourselves. The others were enjoying themselves. I thought they were insane. I was not anxious. I was terrified. My fears were a mix of nonspecific elemental dread of the pitch dark wilderness, which made me feel not expansive but exposed, and a conviction that the locals would take this opportunity to rid themselves of unwanted urban weekenders and shoot us all dead. Now I am one of those locals. With firsthand experience of the satisfactions of community connections, no guns, and town pride when tourists visit from the city. Living surrounded by woods, some of them my own, I am at ease outside civilization's sight to a degree that the me of the Sierra weekend wouldn't even have found desirable, much less realistic. I take deep, anxiety-free pleasure in solitary walks between the trees. Still an urban creature, I find that my awe in the presence of the wild is permanently unjaded. I listen for the cries of coyotes in the night, brake for turkey flocks, bears, small red foxes, a mama moose with her two calves, all residents of these hills alongside us. Sam offered new experiences. The care and feeding of horses. Walks to the orchard to pick apples or sour cherries for a pie, to the garden to dig the evening's menu out of the ground at dusk. He offered these things to my children and so much more. I watched Adam proudly drive an old tractor. I watched Bibi flip pancakes the *only*—that is, the Sam—way to do it. I watched Lilly hurl herself into Sam's arms and beg him to sing her to sleep in his buttered-gravel baritone. I realized that healing was possible. Not just for me.

But it wasn't simple. It didn't take me long to admit to myself that this was not a friends-with-benefits situation. (Though we are friends. And there are benefits.) To admit the absurdity of my ever having imagined that I would be capable of that kind of arrangement. I was swept up into the sort of romantic drama I had spent my life avoiding. To Sam's wife, this was just another affair. Their marriage(s) had survived many. It would survive this one. For Sam, it was uncharted terrain. In his earlier adventures, he hadn't fallen in love. He didn't know what to do. The process of figuring it out would be painful and slow. At times I felt as if I were at the bottom of a hollow pit. At others as if I *were* a hollow pit. If our relationship made me feel this way, how could choosing Sam mean choosing life? Didn't I owe it to myself and even more to my children—*Therefore choose life that you may live, you and your seed*—to withdraw from this affair and find a new path to love and wholeness? Yet my heart was committed. I loved the highs. Even the agonies of tormented love were preferable to the agonies of transwidow-hood, which they effectively replaced. And though I met other attractive men, they somehow never became real for me. I had no sharp regrets about keeping them at arm's length. Feeling as I did about Sam, I couldn't do otherwise.

I had taken my friends into my confidence with the failure of my marriage. In my first months with Sam, I could have locked them out again, all too easily. For a moment I imagined this future for my friendships: I wouldn't tell anyone about Sam. As the sole remnant of my communal Jewish life, he crossed paths with no one else important to me. If my friends detected suffering, I could always feed them the distresses of Tracey to keep them satisfied—it's not as though I would have to make something up. If they detected happiness, I could feed them the joys of new freedom. As time went on and Sam became a bigger part of my emotional life, there would be more and more to keep mum about. Eventually the real me would be a stranger, with an unknown life. My friends might not even guess that there was anything hidden. Just the way it used to be.

Nah-uh. I'd made a choice to leave that way of operating behind. I wasn't going to return to it.

"Does she know about me?" Sam asked, startled, when I said something about a friend of mine in the early days of our association. It was one thing to have a marriage that quietly allowed for outside relationships, quite another to openly conduct such relationships in a small town.

"She does," I told him. "My friends know me now. I can't go back to not being known."

He accepted it.

Accepting it eventually unleashed my motley crew into Sam's life. It introduced him into theirs. More important, it brought what would otherwise have been an isolated and isolating relationship into my village. While Sam and his wife separated and eventually divorced, my friends offered support and astounding patience with a moral and emotional dilemma entirely of my own making. They didn't judge. Those who didn't share my compunctions worked hard to understand me. They refrained from eye rolling. From pointing out that a woman with deep spiritual reservations about a relationship might resist entering into it. My friend Dawn, who has an active Christian life of her own, helped me to recognize that my connection with Sam was sacred to me and that I needed our relationship to be conducted with a corresponding integrity. When I described my can't-live-with-him-can't-live-without-him turmoil to Michael, a friend from whom I didn't expect a religious response, I received advice that astonished me. "Don't choose," Michael suggested. "Pray. Pray for things like strength. And if that kind of petitionary prayer doesn't work for you, make your prayer a statement. Say, 'Whatever I do, I do with You.' "

What does God want of me?

Therefore choose life.

Whatever that enigmatic answer meant when applied to Sam, it surely means these friendships.

Before I got involved with Sam, I abstractly imagined the reserves of time and energy necessary to launch a new relationship. How was I, working mother of three, to tap such reserves at this point in my life? I was seriously daunted. And right to be. This is *work*. The everyday, the intertwining of two long-established lives, can be hell. Sam and I both come with baggage. Loads and loads of it. If our relationship is an early-twentieth-century ship (please don't think *Titanic*), mine maxes out the baggage allotment in steerage. His even weightier load consists of the Louis Vuitton steamer trunks and hatboxes from all the staterooms on deck. Hefting all this weight (no porters allowed!), we attempt to dance as a couple. One step forward, two steps back. No surprise we often seem to lack elegance. Such agility as we can lay claim to springs from the intensity of our love, our still mysterious certainty that in some way, for some unknown period of time, we were meant to come together. My friend Indira once answered a routine "How are you?" e-mail with the breathtaking sentence "I am floating with God's grace." Our pas de deux may be jerky, but when Sam and I give up trying to stick to solid earth, we discover and rediscover an amazing ability to float. By God's grace, we float. There is no other way to understand it.

Speaking of grace.

Okay. Maybe there have been times when my life has

looked like a train wreck. But when I review the past years—as I write, six since the night of Tracey's momentous announcement—and when I gaze around me now, train wreck is not how it strikes me. Blessing and grace is what I see.

More than in any other way, I have experienced God's grace in my life in the forgiveness of those I have wronged. By this measure, there are no more graceful people on earth than my three children, to whom I give the opportunity to forgive me daily.

I give them this opportunity by getting tired and impatient and sometimes overwhelmed. My fears and anxieties over them—their well-being now! their wondrous, terrifying futures!—spike, and I manifest the spikes by reacting to messy rooms and missed school deadlines as if these were stashes of drugs and weapons discovered beneath their pillows. They forgive me for wanting to save them from themselves and everything else. They forgive me for not being able to. For being irrational in my love for them. For not giving them the father I thought I was giving them. For not giving them the mother I thought I was giving them. For not giving them the intact secure home that was their birthright.

Therefore choose life that you may live, you and your seed.

Every day I vow to make each moment with my children the very best that it can be. Many days contain moments of achieving this goal. Every day contains moments of failure. They forgive.

Forgiveness is a gift exceptional to receive and a bitch to give. Especially when the person who has wronged us isn't asking for it. Each year the Jewish calendar designates a period of time around and between the most sacred days of

Rosh Hashanah, the Jewish New Year, and Yom Kippur, the Day of Atonement, when we are to ask forgiveness of one another and of God.

A couple of years after our marriage ended, I told Tracey during a telephone call, "I feel like I can't even ask for forgiveness for not being a better support to you in your process."

"I've forgiven you long ago," he replied.

At some point before then, he had written in an e-mail that he was sorry for the pain he had caused me. He has never asked my children and me to forgive him for the things I find it hardest to forgive, the many individual choices he's made about how to go about changing his life that I have found most damaging, particularly for the kids. To ask for that forgiveness, he would have to acknowledge the things he's done. He would have to acknowledge that he could have behaved differently. And he would have to acknowledge the terrible effects of his behavior, again, particularly on the children. These are three things he has never acknowledged. They don't fit into his narrative trajectory from oppressed victim to courageous hero, and for this reason, I don't imagine he will ever admit them, even to himself.

For his choice to stop being my husband and our children's father and to start his life over as a woman—for this, which might seem the hardest thing to forgive—I do forgive him. It was by making this choice, and this choice alone, that Tracey felt he could be true to himself. To his deepest self. At the end of the day, who can be blamed for that? Because he believed that he was doing what he had to do, it is easier, ironically, for me to forgive Tracey than the community who supported him and abandoned my children and me. A territory lies between active anger and the peace of forgiveness. With regard to this group, I locate myself in that territory. I don't feel angry, but I blame them. I wish I didn't feel this way, but I do. By these people, many of them women, many of them Jewish, many of them feminists, my children and I were betrayed. In the Valley of the Politically Correct, their choice wasn't difficult or brave. It required them to be deeply true to nothing and no one. It was cowardice, pure and simple.

Do my children forgive Tracey? There is no easy answer. Some days, in some ways, yes. Some days, in some ways, no. My story is far from over. Theirs has barely begun. We are on an amazing ride, very much in motion, and we don't know where the next blind curve will take us. Wherever it does, I feel no hesitation about saying: The things that have happened to my children should not have happened. So far they've survived, but childhood shouldn't be an adversity to overcome. No caring parent could wish that for her children. No caring parent could justify it.

"Their suffering will turn out to be good for them in the end."

Some onlookers have dared to make this suggestion. For my children, I utterly reject it. For myself—that's a different story.

That suffering has had a purpose is something we can never determine about someone else. It's a thing we can decide only for ourselves. Years ago, I heard a woman who lived with a chronic illness admit that being sick had made her a deeper person. "But," she added, "I would rather be healthy and shallow." I sympathize. I admire her candor. I don't equate illness with an ex-husband in skirts. But mine is a different truth.

I've gone through some changes. Sex changes. My husband "changed sex." He did what he needed to do to achieve wholeness. So did I. My experience of physical love and of the deep physical and emotional connection I can have with a man, of my own sexuality, of myself as a sexual being, has changed profoundly. Sex has changed me. When I look back now, it seems obvious that I spent years afraid of my own sexuality. I spent years afraid of my strength because I thought that if I revealed myself to be a strong, independent woman who could raise her children alone, that's what I would be: alone. With great difficulty I've let go of those fears. I've integrated my sexual nature and my strength into the person I am. More than anything, it shocks me to realize that I have changed so much that I can't wish myself back into the past. While I would never choose any of it for my children, the things that have happened have made me the person I now am. I would rather be me now than me then. This is what I've had to go through to get here.

Recently I took a lovely walk with Sam and our dog, Menachim Bagel. We passed a young family, a mother and a father with a baby in a pack on his back. Watching them together, I was rushed by memories. Tracey and me with one, then two, then three small children, babies in backpacks, walks. My God, we were happy! That's what hit me. As if it were a surprise. In recent years I've absorbed Tracey's revisions, come to believe I was delusional to believe for so long that we were happy. I was not delusional. We were happy. We had a long time together. Now that time is over. We were married and now we're not. My children had a father, now they don't. *Finito.* Closure. But no, I can never have complete closure. The man I was married to, the man I loved, no longer exists. But he didn't die. If his death occurred now, it would be not the death of the man I married, but the death of the person he's become. When I think of him in the present tense—say, for example, when he's on his way over to pick up the children—I unconsciously anticipate the arrival of a person I can more or less recognize. It never happens. When I see him he is a stranger. He's a stranger over and over again. A stranger I will never know. I can't do anything about that. Except cease to let it trouble me.

I began this book with a tale from rabbinic literature about a dying rabbi and a shattered vessel. When I encountered the story, during the beginning of the end of my marriage, I recognized its message to me and I was afraid. The story was about very painfully letting go. It told me I had to let it all fall: the person I was, the life I had built. I tried to find ways not to do it. I delayed. It was the hardest thing that I had ever been called upon to do.

More recently, I found myself preoccupied by another rabbinic tale, this one called "The Forgotten Story." The great rabbi known as the Baal Shem Tov gave each of his followers a job to do after his death. To Yaakov, one member of his inner circle, he said, "You will go out into the world and tell stories of me." Like biblical prophets from Moses to Jonah, Yaakov didn't want this task. He didn't want to be a penniless wanderer. He wanted a family, a livelihood, connections to a place. Still, he went. He traveled and told his master's stories. One day he visited a rich man he'd heard would treat anyone well who brought him stories of the Baal Shem Tov. But when Yaakov tried to tell the rich man a story, he was struck mute. His host, generous and kind, urged him to try again. Repeatedly Yaakov attempted to tell stories. Repeatedly he was unable to speak. Finally he arrived at the story he was meant to tell. Finding his voice, Yaakov told the rich man that once when he was traveling with the Baal Shem Tov, they arrived in a town where an infamously anti-Semitic priest was about to speak and incite the gathered crowds to murder Jews. The Baal Shem Tov summoned the priest, and the priest, astoundingly, came to see him. Yaakov didn't know what passed between them, but the priest disappeared after that meeting and was never seen again. When the rich man heard Yaakov's story, he began to cry. "I was that priest," he told Yaakov. The Baal Shem Tov had instructed him to change his life, and he had done so. But his crimes were great. There was no guarantee that God would ever forgive him. "Someday," the Baal Shem Tov told him, "someone may tell you your own story. If your story comes back to you, you will know you have been forgiven." The rich man had recognized Yaakov as his messenger. When Yaakov couldn't speak, he thought that he would never be forgiven and had fallen into despair. Now he was released from his past. Yaakov, too, was released. He hadn't known he was a messenger. He had wanted to choose life but was given a task that felt like life's antithesis. He needed to deliver this story in order to be set free. The rich man needed to receive it. Yaakov had fulfilled his purpose. The rich man gave him the means to settle down and start a family. His wandering was over.

Why did this story haunt me? Which of these characters was I? When I thought it over, I understood that I was the rich man, trapped in the agony of waiting to feel that life can begin again, needing my story returned to me. And I was Yaakov, the only one who could tell that story. My story couldn't come to me from outside. If I wanted to encounter it in the world, I had to send it into the world myself. My odyssey began with the end of life as I had known it. Only by telling my story could life begin again. For a long while I didn't know if I could tell my story. I didn't know if I could choose life, even if I could understand what choosing life entailed. In truth, I couldn't do these things. Not the person I was. I had to change. Become someone I had never been. I had to become—there's no other way to say this—a woman. The woman I was meant to be.

I want to conclude with a grand gesture, a summation, something that will chart the distance I have come and illuminate all that I have learned. I haven't got it. What I have is an image, a bright hot moving image that I can't get out of my head. It's an August afternoon. We are crowded around an outdoor table at a café created from an old mill, Sam, Adam, Bibi, Lilly, Menachim Bagel, and me. The river that once powered the mill rushes over stones. Lilly, who can never sit still, eats while dancing, holds one end of a long peanut-sauced noodle in her mouth, and before she can suck it in Menachim Bagel grabs the other end in his jaws, and for an instant the tiny spritelike girl and the huge dog race to see who can eat the most the fastest while Sam, Adam, Bibi, and I laugh and laugh.

This isn't a metaphor for anything. It's life. If it isn't life, I don't know what is.

ACKNOWLEDGMENTS

My deepest gratitude to the friends and family members whose support is described throughout these pages; and to Pamela Malpas and Nichole Argyres for their belief in this project and their help and encouragement every step of the way.